B

D0930099

Naturalism
and
Rationality

Frontiers of Philosophy

Peter H. Hare, Series Editor

Advisory Board

Naturalism and Rationality

Edited and with an Introduction by
NEWTON GARVER
AND **PETER H. HARE**

PROMETHEUS BOOKS
BUFFALO, NEW YORK

Published 1986 by Prometheus Books
700 East Amherst Street, Buffalo, New York 14215
Copyright © Department of Philosophy
State University of New York at Buffalo
All Rights Reserved

Library of Congress Cataloging-in-Publication Data

Naturalism and rationality.

   (Frontiers of philosophy)
   "Conference on Naturalism and Rationality"—Introd.
   Bibliography: p.
   Includes index.
   1. Rationalism—Congresses. 2. Naturalism—
Congresses. I. Garver, Newton, 1928-   . II. Hare,
Peter H. III. Conference on Naturalism and Rationality
(1985: SUNY at Buffalo) IV. Series.
B833.N38   1986   146   86-20532
ISBN 0-87975-350-1

Printed in the United States of America

Acknowledgments

This volume could not have appeared without the conference at which the contributions were presented. Our first thanks, therefore, must go to those at the State University of New York at Buffalo who provided the funds that made the conference possible: the Marvin Farber Memorial Fund, the Department of Philosophy, the Conferences in the Disciplines, the deans of the Faculty of Social Sciences and the Faculty of Educational Studies, and the Goodyear Chair in Economics. It gives us satisfaction to be associated with an institution capable of supporting such a significant intellectual event without external assistance.

Next we wish to express appreciation to those participants, in addition to the contributors, who helped make the discussions stimulating and worthwhile: Kenneth Barber, Murray Brown, Joan Bybee, Kah-Kyung Cho, Georges Dicker, Ronald Giere, Mark Kaplan, Jerrold Katz, Henry Kyburg, Kenneth Lucey, William Mishler, David Nyberg, Hugh Petrie, and Michael Radner.

The mechanical arrangements for the affair would have been impossible without yeoman work on the part of Patrick Murphy, without the secretarial assistance of Judith Wagner and Marie Fleischauer, and without the unwavering support of the Department Chair, Jorge J. E. Gracia. In the matter of amenities going beyond the bare necessities, we are particularly grateful to Steven B. Sample, President of the State University of New York at Buffalo, whose generous reception for the Department of Philosophy at the time of the conference provided a touch of style, well beyond the scope of our budget, that is sure to linger in the memory of participants.

Some of the papers were already committed for publication elsewhere at the time of the conference, and we appreciate the assistance of the authors in helping to arrange for their inclusion in the present volume. We thank Basil Blackwell Publishers for permission to include "Optimal Deterrence," first published in *Social Philosophy and Policy;* the editors of *Ethics* for permission to include "Rationality and Human Evolution"; the editors of *Reason Papers* for permission to include parts of "Rationality and Unnecessitated Choice" first published in that journal in 1985; and Harvard University Press for permission to include "Epistemology and the New Connectionism," which is drawn from Goldman's book, *Epistemology and Cognition.*

Contents

Acknowledgments   *v*

Introduction
  Newton Garver and *Peter H. Hare*   11

PART I: THE BROAD PROBLEM

Ambiguities of Rationality
  Max Black   25

Rationality and Unnecessitated Choice
  Antony Flew   41

COMMENTARY: Flew on "Rationality
and Unnecessitated Choice"
  James H. Bunn   53

Self-interest, Rationality, and Equality
  Alistair M. Macleod   59

COMMENTARY: Self-interest and Moral Behavior
  Lansing Pollock   73

PART II: NATURALISTIC EPISTEMOLOGY

Epistemology and the New Connectionism
  Alvin I. Goldman   79

8 Contents

COMMENTARY: Rationality and Anatomy
Christopher Cherniak   99

COMMENTARY: The Limits of Reductionism
Erwin M. Segal   109

Naturalizing Rationality
Hilary Kornblith   115

COMMENTARY: Rationalizing Naturalism
Duncan MacIntosh   135

Naturalizing Epistemic Terms
Robert G. Meyers   141

COMMENTARY: Meyers on "Naturalizing
Epistemic Terms"
John T. Kearns   155

Reliability and Two Kinds of
Epistemic Justification
Murray Clarke   159

COMMENTARY: Clarke on "Reliability and
Two Kinds of Epistemic Justification"
Charles H. Lambros   171

A Naturalistic Approach to
Rational Deliberation
Paul Weirich   177

COMMENTARY: Weirich on "A Naturalistic
Approach to Rational Deliberation"
Marjorie Clay   189

Contingency and Consciousness
in Husserl's Phenomenology
Brice R. Wachterhauser   195

COMMENTARY: Contingency and
the Motives for Phenomenology
Shaun Gallagher   209

Part III: SPECIAL PROBLEMS

Rationality and Human Evolution
Allan Gibbard   217

COMMENTARY: Gibbard on "Rationality
and Human Evolution"
Zeno G. Swijtink   235

Optimal Deterrence
Steven J. Brams and *D. Mark Kilgour*   241

COMMENTARY: Brams and Kilgour
on "Optimal Deterrence"
Paul Diesing   263

COMMENTARY: Brams and Kilgour
on "Optimal Deterrence"
Zeno G. Swijtink   267

Index   275

About the Editors   283

Notes on Contributors   285

Introduction

There are ironies as well as achievements that emerged from the conference on naturalism and rationality, of which we are here presenting the proceedings. One irony is that, although we planned the affair as a research conference to contribute to the "cutting edge" of current philosophical activity, the terms in which we phrased the main topic are well worn with use and not precise enough to cut through the smog of cocktail party conversation. Their elusiveness is a topic of explicit comment in some of the papers. Indeed, the irony exploded out at us in the keynote address by Max Black, with the recommendation (omitted from his published paper) that we abandon the words 'rational' and 'rationality' altogether. The other main irony is that the broad topic is as ancient as philosophy itself. Already in the Stoic definition of man as a rational animal we see clearly the roots of the topic to which the papers in this volume are addressed. In spite of these ironies, however, the participants found the conference to be both stimulating and helpful in connection with the work they are doing at the research edge of contemporary philosophy. It is our hope that the publication of these proceedings may be a source of continued stimulation.

It is our purpose in this Introduction to provide a background and overview to aid readers in capturing the spirit and significance of the conference. It will be well, then, to begin with the broad problem. Although several of the papers could not have been written even two or three years ago, they are all, in one way or another, struggling with problems arising out of the ancient view of humans as half rooted in nature (the animal part) and half (the rational part) transcending the world of facts and causes into the "world" of norms and reasons. All animals belong to the natural order, and to be a particular sort of animal cannot erase this fact. Nonetheless, rationality is normative, for to call a belief or action "rational" connotes approving (or at least condoning) its having been adopted. What is normative seems radically different from what is purely descriptive: it is the difference of the *ought* from the *is*. Suppose, for example, that we look at the definition Brand Blanshard gives, in his recent book *Four Reasonable Men,* of a rational or reasonable person as one who bases beliefs and actions on evidence. On first sight this definition seems straightforwardly descriptive. But stimuli do not come marked as "evidence." We are affected by all sorts of stimuli, which affect our beliefs and actions in all sorts of ways; and the only ones that count as evidence are those that *ought* to determine our beliefs and actions in a certain way. The difference between a stimulus that determines a belief or action because it is intimidating or enticing, and one that determines belief or action because it is evidence, is hard to establish without normative terms. In his trenchant challenge to naturalism, Antony Flew insists that this distinction is fundamental and that it can in no way be overcome. Naturalism, very broadly, is the view that the difficulty can be overcome; that normative appraisals can be derived from descriptive ones.

As a result of the distinction between emotional causes (which prohibit choice) and rational causes (which require choice), we can see that there are at least two senses of 'naturalism'. Rational choices, and indeed all the uncoerced choices Flew discusses, do occur in the natural world around us. They can, furthermore, be described as well as most other things in the world. 'Naturalism' sometimes connotes simply that choices and norms can be described, and that they are part of natural activity in the world we are familiar with. But such a broad conception of naturalism cannot succeed in either evading or resolving the traditional problems: it leaves them focused instead on what will or will not count as "describing" choices. Flew reminds us that they cannot be described deterministically; for that matter, they cannot be indeterministically described either. That is to say, they cannot be described just by means of those terms scientists and philosophers have found indispensable for describing matter and motion. A deterministic or materialistic conception of nature is a narrower one than a conception of nature that leaves open how to describe such things as unnecessitated choices. If one thought that there was only this narrower sort of naturalism, one would think Flew to be challenging the very idea of naturalism itself, rather than just the variety of naturalism in which all causes are mechanistic and all choice is either random or necessitated.

The challenge Flew's paper presents to naturalism is both trenchant and traditional. Part of his argument rests, as mentioned above, on the incongruity of normative and descriptive language. The other line of thought begins with the idea that a naturalistic account must simply describe what happens, that the most reliable and objective description of what happens is one that conforms to the natural sciences, and that the methods of the natural sciences require description in terms of traditional Humean causation. This is a wholly natural way to interpret naturalism. One finds this reading assumed in James H. Bunn's interesting comments on Flew, as well as in Erwin Segal's comments on Alvin Goldman's paper (though it is rejected by naturalists such as Allan Gibbard and Goldman himself). It is apparent that choice, as well as normative evaluation, goes beyond mechanistic description of what has happened. On this reading, therefore, unnecessitated choice and normative evaluation cannot be assimilated to a naturalistic view of human affairs. As Bunn points out, a naturalistic account of the kind that Flew outlines is bound to be a deterministic account, in which we would be like prisoners, rather than like free beings. The contrast between freedom and constraint developed in the papers of Flew and Bunn is an echo of Immanuel Kant's well-known characterization of freedom as transcendent rather than naturalistic—though Flew's other work makes clear that he would be likely to distinguish two varieties of naturalism rather than adopt a transcendental point of view. Whether one agrees with this Kantian perspective or not, Flew's paper is a powerful insistence that the concept of naturalism is as desperately in need of clarification as the concept of rationality.

The challenge Max Black presented in his keynote address

appears in the present volume in substantially revised form. Although he here omits the radical suggestion that we abandon the word, he reviews all the difficulties of elucidating what it means to call a belief or an action or a person "rational." His method is empirical: he makes no claim that rationality *has* to be highly problematical, he simply reports that it is. He first presents a selective survey of alternative definitions found in the literature: the obvious incompatibility of stridently confident alternative definitions of rationality constitutes persuasive evidence that a neutral and objective definition will be very difficult to achieve. One might think that one could overcome the divergence among philosophers—for whom 'rational' may have become a term of art—by turning to its use in common speech. Particularly illuminating in this regard—and particularly discouraging for would-be definers—are the results Black reports from a questionnaire asking respondents to judge twenty actions as rational, irrational, or neither: there was *very* little agreement. So he refers to the concept as "incorrigibly elusive." But he nevertheless presents a paradigm based on playing chess. In terms of this example, we may be able to elucidate the common use of the word, which, after all, we are able to employ without difficulty in a very large number of ordinary contexts.

One of the problems of the concept of rationality might be called the problem of scope. Alistair Macleod refers to this problem when he speaks of different theories of rationality: Type 1, Type 2, and Type 3. Type 1 theories conceive rationality as applying only to beliefs; Type 2 theories add actions to the scope of rationality, as does the definition given by Blanshard; Type 3 theories allow hopes, fears, desires, and so forth, to be characterized as rational or irrational. (One wonders if and when persons can be said to be rational or irrational.) Macleod himself gives Type 3 scope to the concept of rationality, whereas the majority of contributors to this volume consider rationality in the narrowest scope. Questions of rationality, Macleod argues, hang together with the principle of self-interest, which is intelligible only in terms of a Type 3 theory. This is an ingenious and useful argument, throwing light on the larger issues lying behind the conference theme. Nonetheless, as Lansing Pollock points out, there are difficulties about this doctrine, and they need more careful exploration than Macleod has been able to present in this short space.

Another problem about rationality is that of stringency; or, as J. L. Austin might have put it, whether it will be 'rational' or 'irrational' that wears the trousers. On the one hand, something might be considered rational only if it is a belief, action, or attitude required by some principle of rationality, and something will then be considered irrational if it is not rational. On this more stringent conception there will be only one rational answer to any question, only one rational theory in any field, only one rational action in any circumstance, and so forth. On the other hand, as Black suggests, it may be 'irrational' that wears the trousers, and then a belief, action, or attitude may be considered rational if it is not irrational. In this case there may be an indefinite number of rational answers to a question, and an indefinite number of rational actions in a given situation, and so on. It is this less stringent conception of rationality that Gibbard explores in his paper, and it would be a gross misunderstanding of what he proposes if one were to criticize him for not having explicated rationality in the more stringent sense. It is an open question whether anything is ever rational in the stringent sense, and it is very doubtful whether the word 'rational' could be explicated in the stringent sense in all its ordinary uses. Certainly Black's chess paradigm more easily lends itself to the less stringent understanding of rationality, since there are many situations in the game where several alternative moves would all be rational, and would be distinguished from other moves that would be irrational in those same game situations. The evolutionary process described by Gibbard promotes rationality by eliminating irrational answers rather than by insisting that there be only one right answer. One must keep the problem of stringency as well as the problem of scope in mind when reading the papers that follow.

One characteristic of rationality is that it is only in a social context that a belief, action, or attitude is said to be rational or irrational. The social dimensions of rationality are referred to in the papers of Black, Macleod, or Flew, and they receive special prominence in Gibbard's contribution. Indeed, Zeno G. Swijtink comments that the "sociological turn" constitutes a powerful and radical innovation in our conception of rationality, one that generates novel arguments against current popular accounts of rationality in terms of subjective utility or preference. Just as Gibbard uses the broader, less stringent conception of rationality, so he also uses a broader conception of nature: a naturalistic account need not conform to physical science but may conform instead to biological or evolutionary science. The thrust of Gibbard's paper is to show that rationality could be expected to evolve naturally in the course of human development, as a consequence of the benefits and advantages accruing to those who participate co-operatively in society. This idea is a special development of the notion, quite contrary to Thomas Hobbes, that cooperation occurs and develops naturally in a state of nature, without external co-ercion. A recent elaboration of this idea in the context of Game Theory, and with particular reference to the iterated Prisoner's Dilemma, is in Robert Axelrod's book, *The Evolution of Coopera-tion*. Whereas the classical Prisoner's Dilemma seemed to show that a self-interested individual would normally be noncoopera-tive when acting rationally, Axelrod shows that cooperative strat-egies can pay off far better in the long run: that they are robust, stable, and likely to be dominant. Reading Axelrod one realizes that the classical game theorists, like Hobbes, ignored a central fact: social relations have temporal dimensions, and never dis-count the future entirely. Just as Macleod develops the social as-pects of self-interest in his paper, so also Gibbard calls attention to the way in which social aspects of rationality enhance its nat-ural evolutionary development.

The paper by Steven Brams and Mark Kilgour elaborates another aspect of the social dimension of rationality. In his con-tribution to the conference, Brams discusses the Prisoner's Di-lemma, as well as the elaboration of Chicken known as the De-terrence Game. The Prisoner's Dilemma and Chicken are the only two of the many simple two-person game matrices in which there seems to be some threat that rational behavior will lead to dis-aster. Whereas Axelrod brings in the dimension of time to show that disaster need not accompany rational choice in the Prison-er's Dilemma, Brams and Kilgour refer instead to the fact that the outcomes are probable rather than certain. We can see here that the conception of the natural world, or naturalism, that Brams and Kilgour employ is probabilistic rather than deterministic, in line with modern scientific conceptions; and in line, too, with the ancient slogan that "probability is the guide of life." The com-ments of Paul Diesing and Zeno G. Swijtink not only remind us that there is a gap between Game Theory and its practical application, but also raise useful questions about its status as a theory. Swijtink also reminds readers of deep problems with the concept of probability as applied to intentions. In his queries about testability and fine-tuning Swijtink may be assigning to the Deterrence Game a more traditionally descriptive or explanatory role than Brams and Kilgour have intended. But even if some of the questions involve such misunderstanding, answering them should help to clarify just what status the Deterrence Game has as a model of one dynamic of the arms race. In any case, the paper by Brams and Kilgour is an exciting hint of a way in which conceptions of rationality can be reformulated in practical and attractive ways within the context of modern Game Theory.

The bulk of the papers address a more narrow issue within the general topic, namely, the issue of naturalistic epistemology. Current naturalism in epistemology emerged from frustrated attempts in the 1960s and 1970s to repair the traditional definition of 'knowledge' as 'justified, true belief' in the face of counter-examples provided by Edmund Gettier and others. This failure to give a satisfactory account of epistemic justification seemed to imply the impossibility of knowledge. This impossibility seemed implied also by Thomas Kuhn's attacks on scientific knowledge, Wilfrid Sellars's attacks on "the given," and Richard Rorty's attacks on epistemology in general. Unwilling to settle for skepticism or the abandonment of a theory of knowledge, epistemologists cast about for other theories of justification and found them in naturalistic accounts. It happened that W. V. Quine had already sketched an "Epistemology Naturalized." Although it had been largely a naturalistic *metaphysics* that led him and his pragmatist predecessors to adopt a naturalistic theory of knowledge, their epistemological arguments closely paralleled those independently developed by philosophers working on contemporary problems of epistemology. Similarly, Sir Karl Popper's previously developed "evolutionary epistemology" has served to encourage these more recent naturalistic tendencies.

Developments outside professional philosophy have also played an important role. Much excitement has been generated in recent years in the overlapping fields of cognitive psychology, artificial intelligence, computer science, decision theory, game theory, and neurophysiology. Investigators in these burgeoning sciences have been making rapid progress in providing naturalistic accounts of human thought.

In short, philosophers drawn to naturalism by problems in recent epistemology have found their incipient naturalism confirmed and stimulated by both prestigious historical precedents in philosophy and revolutionary work in the sciences.

How is naturalistic epistemology different from traditional theories of knowledge? Traditionally, epistemologists have attempted to find out how we *ought* to arrive at our beliefs. The question of how we *do* arrive at them was considered the province of psychologists and thus philosophically relevant only in clarifying what changes are called for in our practices. In contrast, naturalistic epistemologists think that the question of how we ought to arrive at our beliefs cannot be answered independently of the question of what our actual practices are. The normative question is not, they think, independent of the descriptive question.

How the normative question is conceived to be related to the descriptive question varies from one naturalist to another. Radical naturalists (e.g., Quine) hold that the normative question is best replaced entirely by the descriptive question since the only legitimate questions about evidence and justification of belief are psychological questions. Much more common among naturalistic epistemologists is the view that, while psychology should not replace epistemology, it is necessary in guiding us toward a satisfactory epistemology. The authors in the volume have various conceptions of what form that guidance should take.

Alvin Goldman describes the recent psychological theory known as "New Connectionism." Though he does not attempt here to sketch a complete epistemology, his discussion is an illustration of naturalized epistemology in that he urges us to be guided by psychology in developing our theory of knowledge: "If acceptance mechanisms, or WTA [winner-take-all] mechanisms, are basic, wired-in features of our cognitive architecture, epistemology should be concerned with their optimal utilization" and not bother with procedures that are neurophysiologically impossible. 'Ought' implies 'can'. If a procedure is psychologically impossible, epistemologists have no business insisting that we ought to use it.

Christopher Cherniak, in his commentary on Goldman's paper, extends the empirical inquiry and finds our neurophysiological capacities much more limited than the connectionist model assumes. There is no connectionist "free lunch." In light of neuroanatomical reality, he suggests, we ought not to attempt a completely consistent cognitive system.

In his separate commentary on Goldman's paper, Erwin Segal is disturbed by what he takes to be Goldman's implication that beliefs can be reduced to "basic wired-in features of our cognitive architecture" without reference to the effects of the environment, or other factors. However, it is not clear that Goldman is committed to such reductionism. Another interpretation of Goldman's paper might indicate that he is trying to show only that it is inappropriate for epistemologists to insist that we ought to follow procedures that are physiologically impossible. That is not a reduction to the "architecture" any more than urging a person not to drive a car over a weakened bridge is a reduction of the practice of driving to the architecture of the bridge.

Hilary Kornblith offers another form of naturalized epistemology, one in which psychological inquiry into the processes of belief acquisition guides us to the procedures "an epistemically responsible agent" would use. This inquiry shows that such an agent's beliefs will be regulated only by the desire for truth and, consequently, those beliefs will be acquired "in something of a slapdash manner." Duncan MacIntosh argues in response, however, that regulation by some considerable epistemic competence is required for epistemic responsibility, rather than just a desire for truth.

Robert G. Meyers is another of the many naturalistic epistemologists who make the concept of reliability central to their theory. The reliabilist holds that a belief is epistemically justified if it is the result of what psychological inquiry has revealed to be a reliable process, i.e., a process that usually results in true belief. To Meyers such a theory has the advantage that it makes human knowledge continuous with knowledge found in other animals, and he thinks that, at least as an account of *perceptual* knowledge, it is convincing. However, he doubts that a reliabilist account will work for *inferential* knowledge. Whereas in the case of noninferential knowledge justification is a matter of input-output mechanism, in the case of inferential knowledge it is a matter of an *ability* to provide certain kinds of arguments. Although generally sympathetic with naturalism, Meyers is not certain that the latter sort of knowledge can be adequately explained within a naturalistic framework. The commentator, John T. Kearns, has much more drastic doubts. He expresses the view that Meyers, like other reliabilists, by replacing our ordinary concept of justification with a new concept, avoids but does not begin to solve the problems of epistemology.

Often in discussion of naturalized epistemology a distinction is made between internal and external justification, and each type of justification has its advocates. Murray Clarke suggests that it is helpful (in analogy with justification in ethics) to think of the external type as "objective" epistemic justification and the internal type as "subjective" epistemic justification. Roughly, a belief is *objectively* justified when it is formed by a reliable process; a belief is *subjectively* justified when it is formed by a process that the believer *has reason to believe* is reliable. Both kinds of justification, Clarke argues, are needed in the analysis of epistemic justification, and, furthermore, they are compatible. Consequently, he hopes to make peace between the externalists and the internalists. Though it voices an interest in securing peace between these epistemological factions, Charles Lambros's commentary suggests that conciliation between *unmodified* externalism and internalism is impossible. However, the different approaches can, he thinks, be made compatible by asking some compromise of both parties to the dispute.

The reliabilist/externalist account of justification found in naturalized epistemology, Paul Weirich suggests, can be used effectively in the analysis of rationality outside epistemology in a naturalized account of deliberation. We can judge a decision-making procedure in terms of its successes as we judge a belief-forming process in terms of the reliability of its results. Accordingly, he maintains, we must engage in empirical inquiry into "the evolution of attention-focusing processes, their probabilities of success, and the means of improving the quality of attention-focusing processes." However, in her commentary, Marjorie Clay argues that Weirich's analogy between belief-formation and decision-making simply imports the problems of naturalized epistemology into the analysis of deliberation, since both naturalisms erroneously assume that 'rational' is a context-neutral concept with sharp boundaries.

In the history of philosophy there have been, of course, many critics of naturalistic accounts of rationality in general and epistemic rationality in particular. Brice K. Wachterhauser considers one such critic. Edmund Husserl, he argues, failed to come to terms with the natural reality of rational consciousness in that he "failed to come to terms with the very contingency of consciousness itself," that is to say, with "the fact that we just happen to have the type of consciousness that we do." Husserl proposed instead a transcendental account in which all consciousness is intentional and supposed that "we cannot give a coherent account of such immanent features of rational activity as the application of normative standards of reason like clarity, simplicity, consistency, etc., while assuming that these standards are determined by causal factors like biology, history, and psychology."

Shaun Gallagher's commentary suggests that Wachterhauser is not entirely fair to Husserl, since the latter does not, he believes, reject all forms of naturalism, but only those that deny the possibility of transcendence. Here we see again the centrality of the issues raised by Flew. We might add that Husserl's is not the only philosophy where it is difficult to determine the extent to which naturalistic accounts of rationality are accepted or rejected. The same problem of historical interpretation arises with many important figures in the history of philosophy, and this is a problem that has yet to be addressed by current naturalists.

Naturalistic epistemology is only part of a contemporary intellectual movement that is much broader than professional philosophy. As we see, for example, in the paper by political scientists Brams and Kilgour, there is today a renewed confidence in the power of rigorous description to answer the most serious questions faced by humankind. This confidence is not a materialistic positivism that dismisses troublesome questions as cognitively meaningless and attempts to give mechanistic answers to the questions that remain. It is rather a conviction that the perennial questions are cognitively meaningful and that the resources can be found in descriptive, nonmechanistic science to make genuine progress in answering them. We present these conference papers in the hope that they will help readers decide how far that conviction is justified.

Newton Garver

Peter H. Hare

Part One

The Broad Problem

Max Black

Ambiguities of Rationality

> *What is the answer?* [and after a
> pause] *but what is the question?*
>
> —Gertrude Stein's last words

THE FUNDAMENTAL QUESTION

In the Platonic dialogue *Phaedrus,* Socrates is made to say, at the
outset of a discussion about love:

> [I]f anyone wants to deliberate successfully about anything, there is
> one thing he must do at the outset: he must know what he is de-
> liberating about; otherwise he is bound to go utterly astray. Now
> most people fail to realize that they don't know what this or that
> really is; consequently, when they start discussing something, they
> dispense with an agreed definition, assuming that they know the
> thing; later on they naturally find, to their cost, that they agree
> neither with each other nor with themselves. (*Phaedrus,* Hackforth
> translation, Cambridge, 1972, 237, b-d).

I take Socrates to be asking for an initial definition of love. Accepting his sensible admonition at least provisionally, I propose
that we try to agree on a preliminary definition of rationality; but
this will prove harder than might be initially expected. For one

25

might hope that a preliminary definition would omit any question-begging *doctrine* about the definiendum and this proves to be a difficult task.

Socrates' own account of "what he is deliberating about" illustrates the difficulty of excluding premature doctrine. He says that we "all see that love is an irrational desire which overcomes the tendency of opinion towards right, and is led away to the enjoyment of beauty and especially personal beauty" (Jowett, *The Works of Plato,* New York, Dial Press, p. 393). Is this an account of what we *mean* by love—or is it a debatable doctrine about love? Is it absurd to say that Socrates' friends loved an ugly man? I think that Socrates was not providing a definition of "love," but was rather offering a mistaken account of the nature of love.

MOORE'S PROCEDURE

My quotation from the *Phaedrus* might well remind us of the famous opening sentence of G. E. Moore's *Principia Ethica.* Moore starts by saying that differences and disagreements in ethics *"as in all philosophical studies* (my italics) are mainly due to a very simple cause: namely to the attempt to answer questions without first discovering precisely *what* question you desire to answer." This implies that we should start by defining the target of the philosophical inquiry. But Moore's subsequent discussion leads him in fact no further than distinguishing the quality of goodness from a determination of the extension of that quality (i.e., to a determination of the things that *are* good).

If we were to use Moore's famous technique of the "open question" in our present search for a definition of rationality, we might well end with the unilluminating and somewhat embarrassing conclusion that rationality is just rationality "and no other thing"—and thus be led to conclude that rationality is indefinable. But the open question argument has been sufficiently discredited by subsequent criticism.[1] Whatever we think of Moore's view that goodness is indefinable because it is a simple quality, it is surely evident that rationality, at any rate, is complex, and hence amenable in principle to the kind of analytic definition that Moore sought.

Philosophers, economists, social scientists, and many other scholars have indeed been lavish in supplying, often with striking assurance, mutually conflicting definitions of rationality. It seems that those who have most earnestly meditated on the nature of rationality cannot even agree at the outset about "what we are deliberating about" under the elusive label of 'rationality'.

RUSSELL'S DEFINITION

Bertrand Russell once said, with customary dogmatism:

> 'Reason' has a perfectly clear and precise meaning. It signifies the choice of the right means for the end that you wish to achieve. It has nothing whatever to do with the choice of ends (preface to *Human Society in Ethics and Politics* [London, 1954]).

(I shall not distinguish for the present between 'Reason' and 'rationality'.)

This conception, which is often called one of *instrumental rationality,* continues to be extraordinarily influential. It is, for instance, an important assumption of widely accepted models of Bayesian choice theory.[2]

No matter what Russell says, we can and should deliberate rationally about "ends." This is so, even when the ends in question are desires (traditionally, one of the limits for the applicability of rational considerations). Consider the kind of case discussed by J. D. Mabbott in "Reason and Desire" (in R. F. Dearden et al., eds., *Education and the Development of Reason* [London, 1972, pp. 320-331]). I have two desires, say to go swimming and to continue to work on this paper. Reflection that I can swim only if I go now may properly lead to the postponement of gratification of the second desire, *even if that desire is the stronger* (i.e., if I would rather write than swim if I were forced to choose between them). This important type of *management of desires,* as it might be called, demands and can receive rational deliberation. (In such cases, as Mabbott says, Reason can no longer be plausibly regarded as the mere "slave of the passions.")

OAKESHOTT'S DEFINITION

In an essay entitled "Rational Conduct" *(The Cambridge Journal,* vol. 4, 1950), Michael Oakeshott, in sharp opposition to Russell, vigorously objects to any kind of recommended conduct "in which an independently premeditated end is pursued and which is determined solely by that end" (p. 5). His own substitute for the instrumental conception runs as follows:

> [T]he only significant way of using the word 'rational' [a charming counter-echo of Russell's dogmatism about the meaning of 'Reason'] is when we mean to indicate . . . *faithfulness to the knowledge of how to conduct the activity we are engaged in."* (p. 20, italics in the original text)

More succinctly, "practical human conduct may be counted 'rational' in respect to its faithfulness to a knowledge of how to behave well" (p. 26). A conception surely too vague and broad to be useful.

HUMAN BEINGS AS PREEMINENTLY RATIONAL

Many of the available and mutually conflicting conceptions of Reason are motivated by the ancient and still influential notion that, as Locke puts it, "the word *reason* . . . stands for a faculty in man, that faculty whereby man is supposed to be distinguished from beasts, and wherein it is evident that he much surpasses them" *(Essay concerning Human Understanding,* ed. A. C. Fraser, Oxford 1894, vol. 2, p. 386).[3] Darwin said that "of all the faculties of the human mind, it will be admitted that Reason stands at the summit" *(Descent of Man,* London, 1871, vol. 1, p. 46).

This may well be doubted, however. The Earl of Rochester, for one, called Reason "an *ignis fatuus* of the mind" *(A Satire Against Mankind,* p. 12), and said he would "rather be a dog, a monkey, or a bear, Or anything but that vain animal who is so proud of being rational" (p. 5).

Gilbert Ryle identified the rationality involved in the ancient view that man is essentially a rational animal with our power of exercising "Thought." He found Thought "in the most hospitable sense of the word" involved in such distinctively human activities as playing games, seeing jokes, striking bargains—and even feeling impatience or irritation (see "A Rational Animal," reprinted in Ryle's *Collected Papers* [London, 1971, vol. II, p. 419]).

In a similar vein, Richard Robinson has claimed that "the word reason is our name for the ideal of thinking" *(An Atheist's Values,* Oxford, 1964, p. 105). Nothing in Ryle and Robinson's conceptions excludes the possibility, *pace* Russell, of using reason to think about the choice of *ends.*

Such examples of rampant disagreement could easily be multiplied. It would not be unfair to conclude that the above cited dicta show their authors to be using the key word in different, if possibly related, senses.

In actual usage by philosophers and other scholars, 'Rationality' is a concertina word, sometimes swelling, in a "hospitable spirit," to extravagant extension, but at other times contracting to implausibly narrowed stipulations. The concept of rationality, one might say, is *incorrigibly elusive.*

WHY SO MUCH DISAGREEMENT?

We cannot afford to be complacent about such radical disagreements in analytical definitions of rationality. The targets of the incorrigibly elusive concepts of rationality and its semantic associates are important. Even if we resorted to the drastic remedy of a temporary or permanent ban on the use of the label, we would still need to discuss the benefits and limitations of what we applaud as "rational" or stigmatize as "irrational." But before discussing what might be done to improve the relevant philosophical investigations, it might be helpful to diagnose some of the main reasons for modern and ancient disagreements about "what we are talking about." I would like to suggest the following explanations.

1. 'Rationalty' and its associate 'Reason' (with a capital R) refer to highly complex matters. It is suggestive to recall that Aristotle and other Attic thinkers had no single word or phrase equivalent to our 'rational' or 'rationality'. Thus Aristotle frequently uses the three words, *nous, logos,* and *dianoia* in dis-

cussing rationality. (Apparently Cicero introduced the comprehensive label *ratio* much later.) We might profitably follow Aristotle's practice, by separately identifying related but distinguishable aspects of what is involved in approvably "rational" choice, belief, and attitude.

2. 'Reason' and 'reason' suffer from belonging to the untechnical vocabulary of nonprofessionals. But men or women "in the street" would find it very hard to say what they mean by 'reason'. The would-be precise and technical label of 'rationality', contaminated by its origin in common usage, tends accordingly to be ill-defined. Because insufficiently technical in actual use, 'rational' and 'rationality' are prone to unnoticed distortion, a hazard that does not arise in such well-defined scientific terms as, say, 'entropy' or such patently technical philosophical terms as 'opaque reference'.

3. Since 'rational', in both common and philosophical usage, is and is usually intended to be a *laudatory* epithet (although there are striking exceptions even to this), there is a standing temptation to incorporate the investigator's normative ideals in its meaning. But questions about whether rationality is (always? sometimes?) a good thing ought surely not to be begged by definitions embodying the analyst's unargued value judgments.

4. Ancient and modern conceptions of the nature of rationality and the role of Reason tend to be distressingly inadequate to the roles of intelligent thought and deliberation in "rational" choices between available alternatives. For the classical conception of Reason as a special "faculty" that controls the otherwise unbridled forces of "passions" (or, in Hume's famous *volte face*, acts as the "slave" of such irrational influences) clearly will not do. I would suppose it sufficiently obvious that application of active intelligence should itself be regarded as motivated by a "passion"; and the mythology of independent "faculties" has long ago been abandoned by professional psychologists. In the absence of agreed and thoroughly tested views about how our minds work in making choices or in arriving at beliefs, philosophical views about the nature of rationality are apt to remain unsatisfyingly primitive.

5. The theory of definition implicit in the views of most scholars who have discussed the "nature of rationality" usually conforms to the Aristotelian or Linnean scheme of definition by classification and division *(per genus et differentiam)*. But even the first step, of determining "what kind of a thing" rationality is, presents formidable difficulties, as anybody who tries to answer that question will be able to confirm.

STARTING FROM EXAMPLES

In trying to articulate such complex, though familiar, concepts as 'cause' or 'knowledge' or the other concepts that continue to engage the best efforts of philosophers, I have often found it helpful to start from "paradigm cases" of the correct use of the concept-label.[4] For instance: in searching for a paradigm case of the application of, say, '(logically) valid', I would start by considering an exemplary argument that would generally be agreed to be unquestionably valid, "if anything is." Then, if all goes well, one can proceed to look for the criteria that we actually use in recognizing the paradigm instance as an unquestionable case of correct application of the concept in question.

However, I have found it surprisingly hard to find a paradigm case of rational choice. On the other hand, it is somewhat easier to find a case of *irrational* choice. (Consider, for instance, the case of a child who eats some spinach "because I *hate* the taste of it." Even that episode, however, might be explained as an attempt to annoy a parent or a perverse desire for self-mortification!) I am tempted to think that, in J. L. Austin's phrase, it is 'irrational' rather than 'rational' "that wears the trousers." But surely there is more to rationality than the absence of irrationality. Given the difficulty of finding unproblematic paradigm cases of rational conduct, I have therefore preferred, in the present inquiry, to report some selected judgments of rationality by educated respondents.

A PRELIMINARY SURVEY OF USAGE

Some years ago, while helping to conduct a seminar on rationality and related topics for graduate students at Oxford, I distributed a questionnaire. (It is reproduced as an appendix to this paper.) Some philosophical friends who had heard of my experiment obtained permission to distribute the same questionnaire at the University of Durham (circulated among faculty members) and at York University, Toronto (in a large introductory course in government).

The reader will notice that those answering the questionnaire were offered two ways of evading the application of "rational," "irrational," or "neither" (see the instructions for saying "can't answer" [option C] or "undecided how to answer" [option U]. The participants were also invited to comment on the questions and were urged to work on the questionnaire at leisure.

On examining the results, my first surprise was to find that very few of the respondents used the evasive responses (though one humorist did write "C" for each of the twenty items!).

In summarizing the results, I treated the responses to a given item as if they constituted an election of one of the most appropriate answers. Thus, at Oxford, with eighteen respondents, I regarded the most favored answer (e.g., "R") as *"electing"* that verdict if ten or more chose "R."

At Oxford, only 7 items were thus "elected," the other 13 showing no overall majority. Even so, the "majorities" were usually slender: 6 of the 7 "elected" items received "votes" of only from 10 to 12 out of a possible maximum of 18. At Durham, with 10 dons participating, 8 items were elected. But when the results for Oxford and Durham were pooled, only 4 items showed majorities. When the Toronto results (with over 100 undergraduates participating) were combined in the same way, still less agreement resulted. Only items 1 and 14 evoked substantial agreement from the entire group of participants ("rational" for items 1 and 14).

It might be objected that the lack of agreement in application revealed by my admittedly somewhat amateurish survey of usage resulted from the controversial nature of some of the examples used rather than from variations in the meanings attached to the rationality labels. I feel the force of this criticism, though I do not accept it. I would be much interested in the results of better investigations by some of my readers. But I am rather confident that further experiments will confirm my present conviction that 'rational' and 'irrational' are now used by laymen and professionals with striking lack of consensus.

A LINGUISTIC APPROACH

I would not wish to leave the impression that I consider further investigation into rationality a hopeless task, in view of the extreme variations in available answers to the "fundamental question." On the contrary, I wish to recommend what might be called a "linguistic approach," having at least the advantage of relative novelty.

My proposal is to start, as none of the scholars to whom I have referred seem to think worthwhile, with an examination of how the *word* 'rational' and its cognates are actually used by ordinary persons, uncommitted to any theories about "the nature of rationality."

I hope it unnecessary to defend myself against the common and scornful objections of philosophers who use "Ordinary Language Philosophy" as a term of abuse. I do not wish to be a lexicographer and am rather interested in what the word 'rational' and its cognates *mean* (to use a simplistic and possibly misleading formula), i.e., in the notion or *concept* of rationality.

In so doing, I shall be agreeing with Peter Geach, in his *Mental Acts* (London, 1967). But I shall not follow him in taking "having a concept" in a "subjective sense"—as "standing for a mental capacity belonging to a particular person" (p. 13), wishing rather to use 'concept' as we do when we say that two persons "have the *same* concept" (cf. Frege's *Begriff*). I am interested in the standard uses of the word in question, not in individual and possibly idiosyncratic deviations from such uses. This is an empirical program, normally requiring no field-work, since as competent users of English we can rely on "what we would say" and in which circumstances.

One of the many important lessons that linguists have learned from Ferdinand De Saussure has been to think of a language as a structured system—"an organized totality . . . in which the various elements are interdependent and derive their significance from the system as a whole" (S. Ullmann, *The Principles of Semantics,* New York, 1957, p. 8). A special case of this is that words "belonging to the same sphere" signify partly by way of opposition or contrast (so that 'red', for instance, implies *not* blue, green, and so on). Hence there arises the important but still somewhat neglected notion of a *semantic field:* "closely-knit sectors of the vocabulary, in which a particular sphere is divided up, classified and organized in such a way that each element helps to delimit its neighbors and is delimited by them" (according to Jost Trier, as reported in Ullmann, p. 245).

In the present context, we should need to use the related notion of a *conceptual field,* in which words belonging to "the same sphere" can be linked not only by opposition, but also by subordination and superordination and other syntactic, semantic, and pragmatic relations.

APPLICATION TO THE CASE OF RATIONALITY

In trying to delineate the conceptual field to which 'rational' and its cognates belong, we would be faced with a series of subtasks, such as the following:

First: which other concepts are logically and conceptually linked with rationality? The list should probably include, in addition of course to 'rational' and 'irrational', also 'reason', 'choice', 'action', 'decision', 'belief', 'attitude', 'feeling', 'risk', 'uncertainty', 'probability', 'worth', 'value', (and such modal notions as) 'shall', 'should', 'must' and so on. (I am aiming here only at illustrations, not at completeness, if that idea even makes sense.) Even this partial list is formidable, already recalling something of the richness and complexity of the conceptual field to which our key words belong. We should also wish to explore the effects of metonymy, i.e., the admissible fillers for the context, 'rational such-and-such'.

An important part of the task of delineating the relevant conceptual field would be to consider the relation of 'rational' to such semi-normative words as 'intelligent', 'sensible', 'thoughtful', 'well-considered', 'praiseworthy', and so on, and a corresponding list of terms and phrases of dispraise (e.g., 'hasty', 'biased', 'prejudiced', and many more).

Nor should we neglect such broader questions as "what roles do uses of 'rational', 'rationality', and their semantic allies and enemies play?" We need to understand the roles that the targeted words play in our language, thought, and actions and to consider what losses, if any, would result from banishing the examined concepts from our language and thought.

It would be foolish to predict the outcomes of such a program of research, here only incompletely sketched. But I shall venture to guess at the kinds of results to be expected.

HOW TO BE RATIONAL: THE CASE OF THE CHESS PLAYER[5]

I propose now to consider some features of what may be the best available extended example of practical rationality—the familiar and instructive one of a good chess player's behavior. For surely what good chess players do is as close to any ideal of attainable if imperfect rationality that we can reasonably entertain: compared with decisions made in the course of a chess match, the decisions made in private life, the market place, or a law court are bound to appear as necessarily fumbling and unsatisfactory.

The relative determinateness of the chessplayer's task of playing rationally by finding the "best move" arises, clearly, from the arbitrary and precise constraints imposed by the "rules of play," that generate sequences of "legal moves," normally too complex to permit exhaustive analysis. It is easy, however, to prove the surprising result that there must always be a "best" way to play, even though it is beyond human power to know what the optimal strategy is.[6] Thus the invariable outcome of any chess game with "best moves" on both sides must follow from the rules: a faultless encounter must always end in a win for White, a win for Black, or a draw—whichever of these is always the right answer.

But to know that this theoretical "solution" exists is of no help to an actual player, faced with a bewildering multiplicity of legal moves, beyond the powers of even a chess genius like Bobby Fischer to analyze exhaustively. If we assume no more than 10 reasonable possibilities for each move (i.e., roughly 3 moves to be considered by White, each of them leading to 3 reasonable replies) the number of possible games lasting 40 moves will be of the order of 10^{40} (one followed by 40 zeroes). It has been estimated that a billion machines examining a billion such games each second and in constant operation since the solar system came into existence would by now have achieved only one ten-millionth part of the task of scrutiny![7] This mechanical mode of evaluation is clearly too preposterously difficult to be worth considering.

In the light of such considerations, one might reasonably conclude that chess is too difficult a game to be played rationally. Yet vast numbers of human beings, of moderate intellectual capacity, do manage to play the game with steady and *deserved* success. How, then, does a skillful player manage to perform this seemingly impossible task?

In answering the question, we can rely upon introspective evidence or, better still, upon the instructive "protocols" assembled and analyzed in Adrian D. de Groot's pioneering book.[8] I have already said that a reasonably good player does not consider all the legal moves available to him and does not engage in extended sequential calculations of consequences except in especially "critical" junctures. Such essential simplification of the problematic situation requires what may be called a patterned or Gestalt-like perception of a given position: unless one is a mere beginner who "can't begin to imagine what should be done," one sees the relatively few "candidate-moves"[9] as salient possibilities against a highly structured background. The skilled player does not perceive a mere aggregate of squares occupied by pieces, but rather features describable in the distinctive (partly qualitative, partly quantitative) language of chess strategy and tactics: "a weak King," a "strong center," "batteries of pieces," "open files," and so on. Such a patterned grasp of the situation, reinforced by memories of parallel situations and their outcomes, distinguishes a few moves as alone worth consideration and rejects others as being, at least initially, unworthy of consideration.

Of course, a skillful player will proceed to calculate the likely consequences of each of the limited number of "candidate-moves" that are initially judged to be worth taking seriously. But in an actual game (by contrast with the protracted sessions in which masters aim at exhaustive analysis of "adjourned games") such analysis of anticipated consequences is necessarily truncated and incomplete. It is worth making the further point, familiar to any good player, that such analysis may well modify or radically transform one's view of the given position: attempts to solve the perceived problem are apt to change one's conception of the nature of the problem. The process of rational choice is dynamic—to use a word that has perhaps been overworked in the literature.

The dynamic process of finding a rational solution to a problem of decision in playing chess does not and cannot occur in an intellectual vacuum: a chess player with a *tabula rasa,* wiped clean of all preconceptions and preformed convictions, would almost almost certainly succumb in short order to a "Fool's Mate" or some comparably ignominious fiasco. Any moderately instructed player is strongly guided by memories of his own previous successes and failures and, still more importantly, by the sifted experience of whole generations of masters. The accessible tradition supplies defeasible general maxims, standardized routines for accomplishing particular subtasks, detailed models for the initial deployment of pieces (the "opening"), and much else. Such deliverances of a rich tradition can function as premises of the requisite "practical reasoning" and usually need not be questioned, but any of them *can* be questioned and perhaps rejected in special cases. (Here, we are far from the unquestioned premises of Russell's model.)

Such reliance upon traditional deliverances, used in a not uncritical situation, surely supplies the good chess player with "good reasons," however inconclusive, for his choice: it would be eminently unreasonable to ignore the available experience of past players, however fallible and defeasible the lessons to be drawn from them may be.

The necessary reliance in such concrete exemplifications of practical reasoning on what might be called "indubita"—premises stronger than mere presuppositions of working assumptions— seems to be quite characteristic and typical of available instances of extended rational choice.[10]

ENVOI

Any reader who might expect me to end with a concise answer to the "fundamental question" will have to be disappointed. I believe it is fair to say that in philosophical discussions of rationality, there is a sense in which we do *not* "know what we are talking about" and can never do so, if what is demanded is a concise definition. To provide one would be as difficult and as pointless as demanding an initial or terminal definition of playing chess well (or understanding poetry, or behaving morally, or leading the good life). But there is a less stringent sense in which we do initially understand, however sketchily, what we mean by playing chess well—and the same applies, *mutatis mutandis,* to the still more complex notion of rationality, whether in private or in public contexts. I would be sorry to be taken as opposing further analytic investigation of the role of rationality in appropriate contexts. On the contrary, I believe that much remains to be learned about this important if elusive notion.

Appendix

RATIONALITY AND IRRATIONALITY: A QUESTIONNAIRE

The purpose of this questionnaire is to get some empirical evidence about how people apply the words 'rational' and 'irrational'. Each of the following 20 items identifies something *you* might do. In each case, you are asked to say whether you consider doing so would be rational or irrational. Please answer by writing a capital letter to the left of the item number, according to the following code: R = 'rational'; I = 'irrational'; N = 'neither'; C = 'can't answer'; U = 'undecided how to answer'.

Please answer all the questions. Comments, which will be welcome, may be written on the back of the sheet. Especially helpful would be (i) explanations of answers; (ii) comments on choice and formulation of items; (iii) suggestions for improving the questionnaire.

_____ 1. To presume that a stranger of whom you have asked directions is answering truthfully.
_____ 2. To envy somebody else for his/her good looks.
_____ 3. To be satisfied with a good outcome of a task when you might expect a better result at little cost.

—— 4. To pay \$30 for a one-in-a-thousand chance of winning \$50,000.

—— 5. To think that an argument with false premises will have a false conclusion.

—— 6. To let somebody die in a fire rather than risk burning your hands in trying to save him.

—— 7. To resent injury done to you.

—— 8. To enjoy music played as loudly as possible.

—— 9. To think that life exists elsewhere in the universe.

—— 10. After an ordinary coin has been tossed and has come down heads 5 times in succession, to expect it to do the same the next time.

—— 11. To be afraid of spiders.

—— 12. To prefer X to Y, Y to Z and Z to X.

—— 13. To think that somebody else is happier than you.

—— 14. To bet on a horse winning and also, at the same odds, on its losing.

—— 15. To like someone for no assignable reason.

—— 16. To refuse to argue about whether friendship is a good thing in itself (regardless of its contributions to other things).

—— 17. To refuse to bet on a certainty.

—— 18. To regret a past action that cannot be undone.

—— 19. To try to construct a perpetual motion machine.

—— 20. To answer this questionnaire.

NOTES

1. See Arthur N. Prior, *Logic and the Basis of Ethics* (Oxford: Oxford University Press, 1949) and the important earlier work by W. K. Frankena, "The Naturalistic Fallacy," *Mind* (1939), pp. 472 ff.

2. See my discussion and criticism of the Bayesian model in "Making Intelligent Choices: How Useful Is Decision Theory?" *Dialectica*, 39 (1985):19–34.

3. Locke says that "The word *reason* in the English language

has many different significations" and his editor, Fraser, comments that *Reason* is "among the most ambiguous of philosophical terms." He takes Locke to be using it as "synonymous with *reasoning*" (p. 384).

4. For some appeals to paradigm cases, see for instance, my "Making Something Happen," in *Models and Metaphors* (Ithaca, N.Y.: Cornell University Press, 1962) or "Reasonableness," in *The Prevalence of Humbug* (Ithaca, N.Y.: Cornell University Press, 1983).

5. This section is excerpted, by permission, from my paper "Some Remarks About Rationality," in *Philosophic Exchange* 2 (1977).

6. Let a "strategy" for White (in game-theoretical style) denote a complete policy for playing the game, taking into account all possible replies by Black at every juncture. If there exists an optimal strategy for White (leading invariably to a win or a draw), he commits himself to that strategy and plays accordingly. If not, then for every first move by White, Black can adopt a strategy that defeats him. Thus with "best play" on both sides, there must be a single predetermined result (win for one player or a draw), the same in each case. For another indirect argument, see Morton D. Davis, *Game Theory* (New York: Basic Books, 1970), pp. 16–18.

7. Based on a discussion in C. H. O'D. Alexander, *A Book of Chess* (New York, 1973), p. 23.

8. Adriaan D. de Groot, *Thought and Choice in Chess* (The Hague: Mouton, 1965). The author persuaded a number of chess players, including masters, of varying degrees of skill, to "think aloud" while examining a number of selected situations and chess positions. The records thus obtained were the "protocols" (supplemented by subsequent discussion with their producers).

9. I take this expression from a later book by a grandmaster, which interestingly supplements de Groot: Alexander Kotov, *Think Like a Grandmaster* (London: David and Charles, 1971).

10. Current efforts to simulate chess playing skill in computer programs sensibly ignore cost-benefit analysis, trying instead to incorporate the requisite knowledge of tactics and strategy to which I have alluded. Such programs try, although with only moderate success so far, to take account of the "patterned perception" and reliance upon maxims of play that I have emphasized.

Antony Flew

Rationality and Unnecessitated Choice

My text is taken from Peter Geach's dissertation on *The Virtues* (Cambridge: Cambridge University Press, 1977):

> When we hear of some new attempt to explain reasoning or language or choice naturalistically, we ought to react as if we were told someone had squared the circle or proved $\sqrt{2}$ to be rational: only the mildest curiosity is in order—how well has the fallacy been concealed? (p. 52)

In meditating upon this text the first points to seize are: that every explanation is an answer to a question; and hence that, whenever more than one question can properly be asked, there must be room for more than one answering explanation. Such alternative explanations, therefore, will not necessarily be rivals for the same logical space.

The primary contention that explanations are answers to questions can be somewhat frivolously enforced, yet enforced nonetheless effectively, by reference to a recent "Andy Capp" comic strip. The tried and suffering Flo is shown protesting: "There was twelve light ales in the pantry this mornin'—now there's only ONE! 'ow d'yer explain THAT?" To which her incorrigible husband responds, with deadly predictability: "It was that dark in there I didn't see it."

The corollary of that primary contention—which is that ex-

Some paragraphs in this paper have appeared in print previously, in a much longer paper published in *Reason Papers* (Santa Barbara, California) in 1985, and they appear here by the kind permission of the editors of that journal.

planations or, for that matter, justifications directed at different questions do not have to be, of necessity, competitors—had better be explicated in a less lighthearted and more abstract way. So consider next the speech act of asserting the familiar, colorless proposition p. There are at least three kinds of question that can be asked about this pedestrian performance. One, in requesting an explanation why the performer believes that p, asks for a statement of the performer's warrant for so believing. It asks, that is to say, for evidencing reasons for harboring the belief that p; for the rational justification for so doing. Another, in requesting an explanation why the same person chose this particular occasion to express the belief that p, asks what was the point and purpose of this particular speech act. It asks, that is to say, for the performer's motivating reasons for so acting.[1] The answers given are always in the first instance offered as explanations, though in these two cases they may also constitute attempts at justification. The third kind of question treats the speech act as consisting in physiological ongoings, and asks about their causes.[2]

The moral to draw here is that Geach's naturalistic opponents refute themselves, *if, but only if,* they present their naturalistic explanations as necessarily precluding additional explanations or justifications in terms of evidencing or warranting reasons. They refute themselves, that is, *if, but only if,* they insist, as in fact so many have insisted and do insist, that full and satisfactory answers to questions of the second and third kinds must leave no room for equally satisfactory answers to questions of the first kind.[3] For, in so insisting, these naturalistic scientists are in effect maintaining that they have discovered, and now know, that no one ever either has sufficient evidencing reasons for believing that p or is otherwise in a position to know it. And against this it is, surely, absolutely right "to react as if we were told someone had squared the circle or proved $\sqrt{2}$ to be rational."

But now, nothing said so far even begins to establish, either that the same applies to all attempts to show that there is no such thing as choice, or that there can be no question of discovering causally sufficient conditions of all the physiological ongoings that are in fact involved when someone is truly said to have expressed their knowledge that p. Consider one throw-away statement from James Q. Wilson's *Thinking about Crime* (New York: Random House, 1977):

Stated another way, if causal theories explain why a criminal acts as he does, they also explain why he *must* act as he does, and therefore they make any reliance on deterrence seem futile or irrelevant. (p. 58, italics in original)

This, in what is here the appropriate sense of 'cause,' is false. It is as essential as it is uncommon to distinguish two fundamentally different senses of the word 'cause'. In one of these, the sense in which we speak both of the causes of astronomical phenomena and of ourslevs as agents causing movements of inanimate objects, causes truly do—*pace* Hume and the whole Humean tradition—bring about, and thus factually necessitate, their effects.[4] Given the total cause, that is, nothing except a miraculous exercise of supernatural power can prevent the occurrence of whatever is in fact the due effect. In this first, physical or necessitating interpretation, complete causal theories do indeed explain why what does happen *must* happen.

Yet it is only in a second, quite different, personal or inclining sense that we can talk of the causes of human action, whether criminal or otherwise. If I give you good cause to celebrate, perhaps by sympathetically informing you of some massive misfortune afflicting your most detested enemy, then I provide you with a possible motivating reason for celebration. But I do not thereby necessitate the occurrence of appropriate celebrations. You yourself remain not merely an agent but, as far as this goes, an altogether free agent.

Certain criminologists, seeking the supposed concealed, necessitating causes of crime, once asked a convicted multiple bankrobber: "Why did you rob banks?" He replied, with the shattering directness of an Andy Capp: "Because that was where the money was." Not yet corrupted by any supposedly rehabilitative Open University courses in sociology, he did not pretend that his criminal actions had been anything but his actions. As an agent he was not, and could not have been, inexorably necessitated. This has to be true since, from the mere fact that persons were in some respect agents, it follows necessarily that they were in that respect, and in a fundamental sense soon to be further explicated, able to do other than they did.

Once this basic distinction between the two causes is mastered it becomes obvious that we need a parallel distinction between two determinisms. Certainly, to say that some outcome is fully determined by physical causes does carry rigorous necessitarian implications. But, equally certainly, to say that someone's actions are completely determined by causes of the other sort— earlier called motivating reasons—is, if anything, to presuppose the contrary. The "psychic determinism" to which Sigmund Freud appealed in psychology is thus not the local application of a universal determinism of the first, necessitating sort. Instead, the two determinisms appear to be flatly incompatible.[5] It is, therefore, diametrically wrong to try to conscript what historians and other social scientists offer as explanations of human actions *qua* actions to serve as support for a necessitarian determinism.[6] On the other hand, if a naturalistic explanation is to be construed as one that provides a complete account in terms of necessitating physical causes, then Geach must be dead right to dismiss the possibility of any such explanation for the phenomenon of choice.

The conclusions previously drawn still leave room for both a question and an objection. The question is: What is the link between choice, in this libertarian understanding, and rationality? The objection is that, if this is what choice implies, then there neither is nor could be any such thing. A suggestion in answer to the former comes from the second volume of the *Postscript* to Sir Karl Popper's *The Logic of Scientific Discovery*. In this *Concluding Scientific Postscript,* actually entitled *The Open Universe: An Argument for Indeterminism* (London: Hutchinson; Totowa, N.J.: Rowman and Littlefield, 1982), Popper argues that

> if "scientific" determinism is true, we cannot, in a rational manner, know that it is true; we believe it, or disbelieve it, but not because we freely judge the *arguments or reasons* in its favor to be sound, but because we happen to be so determined (so brainwashed) as to believe it, or even to believe that we judge it, and accept it, rationally. (pp. 92-93)

Suppose that we could not by any means have believed other than we did; then we cannot take credit for having, as rational beings, judged that these particular beliefs, and not others, are true. We cannot, therefore, truly claim to know. Popper proceeds to add an important, equally correct comment:

This somewhat strange argument does not, of course, refute the doctrine of "scientific" determinism. Even if it is accepted as valid, the world may still be as described by "scientific" determinism. But . . . pointing out that, if "scientific" determinism is true, we cannot know it or rationally discuss it . . . has given a refutation of the idea from which "scientific" determinism springs.

This seminal idea is, we must assume, part of what Geach would call naturalism; and it is in fact self-refuted inasmuch as such a naturalist can be taken, as surely he must be, to claim nothing more or less than to know that his scientifically grounded naturalism is true.

If, however, Popper's argument is to go through, then it has to be allowed that no computer or other device, the ongoings in which are completely determined by necessitating causes, can correctly be said to know that any of its operations are valid or that any of its output is true. I myself gladly accept and affirm this essential limitation upon the potentialities of all such artifacts. Yet to Popper it might seem uncomfortably like a finding of 'linguistic philosophy'.

Before plunging headlong—albeit, as Gilbert Ryle loved to say, not very shamefacedly—"into the morass of language philosophy" *(Ibid., p. xxi)* we must in passing notice both that much if not all belief is immediately necessitated, and that this fact can be used to bring out one particular corollary of the previous contention. This is a corollary that cannot but be agreeable to anyone who has ever been to school with Popper.

That at least some beliefs are immediately inescapable is best seen by recalling Hume's doctrine of what Norman Kemp-Smith christened "natural beliefs"—the belief, for instance, that in perception we are directly aware of some mind-independent reality.[7] The congenial corollary is that, the more beliefs we find to be, in certain circumstances, immediately inescapable, the more vital it becomes to try to withdraw from such possibly deceiving situations; and, in a cool hour and a quiet place, to expose ourselves and both these and other beliefs to the full force of all rational objections—that is, to criticism.

Such constant willingness to expose ourselves to well-girded and truth-concerned criticism is, beyond doubt, always, if not always quite immediately, within our power. It is also, as recently

I have been arguing in many different places, the "one most certain test" of the sincerity of our professed personal commitments to the theoretical search for truth; as well as being, as I have also argued on the same occasions, the most telling touchstone of the authenticity of our professed dedication to the stated objectives of whatever practical policies we may choose to favor.[8]

At the beginning of *The Open Universe* Popper announces his intention to present his "reasons for being an indeterminist." At once he adds: "I shall not include among these reasons the intuitive idea of free will: as a rational argument in favor of indeterminism it is useless" (p. 1). His warrant for saying that any such direct appeal to experience is useless, a reason which he formulates in a fashion too misleading to quote here, is that he may be mistaken even about the nature of what the behaviorist would call one of his own behaviors. Insofar as this is a token of a Cartesian argument type—in any area where we may conceivably be mistaken, we can never truly know—its validity, if it were valid, would have to be recognized as putting an insuperable obstacle in the way of any fallible being achieving any knowledge whatsoever.[9]

Even Popper's original disclaimer, referring as it does to "the intuitive idea of free will," is importantly misleading. For the crucial question is not whether we ever act of our own free will, but whether we ever act at all. When we say of someone that they acted not of their own free will but under compulsion, still they did act. The case of the businessman who received from the Godfather "an offer which he could not refuse," is thus vitally different from that of the errant mafioso who was gunned down from behind without warning.

We may both colloquially and truly say of the former, offered the urgent choice of having either his signature or his brains on a document within thirty seconds, that he had no choice, and hence that he could not have done other than he did.

But of course these everyday idioms must not be misconstrued, as so often they are. In more fundamental senses, the businessman who acted under compulsion did have a choice, and could have acted other than he did, however understandably intolerable the only alternative remaining open to him. In these same more fundamental senses, to have a choice, to be able to do otherwise, is essential to what it is to be an agent. In these same more fundamental senses, again, the errant mafioso literally did not have a choice. Because he did not *do* anything, he could not have *done* otherwise, for in that moment of unexpected and sudden death, he ceased both to do and to be.

What I propose to do now is to sketch—and it can be no more than sketch—an argument for saying that the two mutually exclusive notions of physical necessity and of being able to do otherwise only are understood, and only can be, by people who have had, and who throughout their lives continue to enjoy, experiences of both realities. They—which is to say we—have enjoyed and are continuing to enjoy experiences both of unalterable necessity and of effective agency. It is therefore, just not correct to maintain that the entire universe is subject at every point to ineluctable necessity. Were this claim true we should not be able even to understand it, much less to know it to be true.

By far the best place from which to start to establish our last contention is the splendid chapter "Of Power" in John Locke's *Essay Concerning Human Understanding*. This is a chapter the message of which was missed by Hume—as Popper says here, "one of the very greatest philosophers of all time" (p. xix). He missed it because—in this, like Kant later—he could not entertain any fully legitimate idea of necessity other than the logical, and because he had to defend his insight that causal propositions could not compass any necessity of that logical kind. Locke starts with a statement of what he proposes to prove:

> Every one, I think, finds in himself a power to begin or forbear, continue or put an end to several actions in himself. From the consideration of the extent of this power . . . which every one finds in himself, arise the ideas of liberty and necessity. (II [xxi] 7)

Locke's technique for enforcing this point about our familiarity with our agent powers—our experience of them—is to contrast with these what we do know or may know about what we cannot do. Unfortunately, Locke, like Popper, wrongly assumes that the sixty-four-thousand-dollar question is not whether we are and can know that we are agents choosing this alternative when we could have chosen that, but whether we are and can know that we are free agents choosing between alteratives, at least two of which we find tolerable. This fault we have simply to discount, making the necessary mental transposition as we go along:

We have instances enough, and often more than enough, in our own bodies. A man's heart beats, and the blood circulates, which 'tis not in his power by any thought or volition to stop; and therefore in respect of these motions, where rest depends not on his choice, nor would follow the determination of his mind, if it should prefer it, he is not a free agent. Convulsive motions agitate his legs, so that though he will it never so much, he cannot by any power of his mind stop their motion (as in that odd disease called *Chorea Sancti Viti),* but he is perpetually dancing. He is . . . in this . . . under as much necessity as moving, as a stone that falls, or a tennis ball struck with a racket. On the other side, a palsy or the stocks hinder his legs from obeying the determination of his mind, if it would thereby transfer his body to another place. (II [xxi] 11)

What truly there is want of here, we must repeat, is not *freedom* but *agency;* not the lack of any tolerable and uncoerced alternatives, but the lack of any alternatives at all. Against this straightforward appeal to experience, Popper would argue that it is always conceivable that we are mistaken about what is or is not in fact subject to our wills: that some of us in the past have been afflicted by sudden paralyses, or that any of us may now have suddenly acquired unprecedented powers. Certainly all this is conceivable: we are none of us either infallible or all-knowing. But the great mistake is to assume that knowledge presupposes infallibility; that where we may conceivably be mistaken, there it is impossible for us ever to know. The truth is that, to know, we need only to be in a position to know, and to be claiming to know something that is in fact true.

Locke also suggests, albeit in a less satisfactory terminology, that necessity reigns where action is not; the human behaviors that are not actions must be necessary. Thus he writes:

Wherever thought is wholly wanting, or the power to act or forbear according to the direction of thought, there necessity takes place. [II (xii) 13.]

And, a page or two earlier, we read:

A tennis ball, whether in motion by a stroke of a racket, or lying still at rest, is not by anyone taken to be a free agent . . . because we conceive not a tennis ball to think, and consequently not to have any volition, or preference of motion to rest, or *vice versa;* and therefore . . . is not a free agent; but all its both motion and

rest come under our idea of necessary, and are so call'd. . . . So a
man striking himself, or his friend, by a convulsive motion of his
arm, which is not in his power . . . to stop, or forbear; . . . every one
pities him as acting by necessity and constraint. (II [xxi] 9)

Once again, of course, the reason we should pity such persons
is not that they would be acting under constraint, but that their
behaviors would be completely necessitated, and therefore not
actions at all. Especially to those familiar with Hume's criticisms
of this chapter, in his discussions both "Of Liberty and Necessity" and "Of the Idea of Necessary Connection," what is most
curious is Locke's actual failure to go on to emphasize that, notwithstanding that behaviors that are actions cannot have been
necessitated, since the agents must as such have been able to do
other than they did, still the aforesaid behaviors may themselves
necessitate. Actions may bring about effects, which are not themselves actions, making one alternative contingently necessary
and another contingently impossible.[10]
We know how Hume would have tried to dispose of this Lock-
ean contention, had Locke developed it. We know because, though
Locke did not, Hume did. Hume, like Popper, insisted upon the
perennial conceivability of alternatives: it must always be conceivable that what does usually happen one day will not. And, again
like Popper, Hume draws an invalid inference from this true
premise. Hume's inference is that, since there cannot be logical
necessities linking those events or sorts of events that happen to
be causes with those events or sorts of events that happen to be
their effects, there cannot be and are not objective necessities and
objective impossibilities in the nonlinguistic world. But this is
false, and our consideration of choice has shown how we can
know it to be false. It is precisely and only from our altogether
familiar experiences as agents making things happen, yet agents
always limited in the scope of their agency, that we can and must
derive two—if you like—metaphysical basics. This is the source
not only for our ideas of agency and of this kind of necessity but
also of our knowledge that the universe provides abundant application for both of these ideas. If anyone doubts this, I invite them to
devise completely nonostensive and mutually independent explanations of these terms, explanations that could benefit creatures
not themselves able and required to make choices and to deal

with often intransigently autonomous realities. Mine is the final
challenge of the archetypically incredulous man from Missouri:
"Show me!"

NOTES

1. For this rather obvious yet crucially important distinction
between evidencing and motivating reasons see, for instance,
either "Is Pascal's Wager the Only Safe Bet?" in *The Presumption
of Atheism* (London: Pemberton/Elek; New York: Barnes and
Noble, 1976), recently reissued as *God, Freedom and Immortality*
(Buffalo, N.Y.: Prometheus Books, 1984); or chapter 7, section 7
in *An Introduction to Western Philosophy* (Indianapolis: Bobbs
Merrill; London: Thames and Hudson, 1971).

2. For some development of this distinction between three
categorically different kinds of question see *A Rational Animal*
(Oxford: Clarendon, 1978), chapter 5.

3. Compare, for instance, the reckless claim once made by a
man who was in his day Britain's leading Freudian psychoana-
lyst: "The analyst must above all be an analyst. That is to say he
must know positively that all human emotional reactions, all
human judgements, and even reason itself, are but the tools of
the unconscious; and that such seemingly acute convictions
which an intelligent person like this possesses are but the inevitable effect of causes which lie buried in the unconscious levels of
his psyche." See Charles Berg, *Deep Analysis* (London: George
Allen and Unwin, 1946, p. 190). Such recklessly self-refuting
claims seem nowadays to be most common among practitioners
of what is defiantly miscalled the sociology of knowledge. They
are commonplaces, not only for the radical ratbags assailed in
chapter 1 of *Sociology, Equality and Education* (London: Macmillan; New York: Barnes and Noble, 1976), but also for the more
patient and hardworking yet no less incorrigibly perverse scholars of the Edinburgh Science Studies Unit, with whom I have
also tried to deal faithfully in "A Strong Programme for the
Sociology of Belief," in *Inquiry* (1982).

4. Compare "Another Idea of Necessary Connection," in *Philosophy* (1982).

5. The situation is complicated by the rarely noticed fact that
the development of the notions of unconscious motivation in-

volved not one but two conceptual innovations: it is not only a matter of attributing motivations to persons who are themselves unaware that they are so moved; but also of construing as expressions of such unconscious desires, purposes, and what have you, behaviors that are not actions and hence not under the conscious volitional control of the patient—compulsive symptomatic tics and psychogenic paralyses, for instance. See, again, *A Rational Animal,* chapters 8 and 9.

6. Compare, for instance, "Human Choice and Historical Inevitability," in the *Journal of Libertarian Studies,* 5 (1981).

7. See Norman Kemp-Smith *The Philosophy of David Hume* (London: Macmillan, 1949), pp. 116 ff. and passim; and note that the name phrase chosen by Kemp-Smith is not one of the several employed by Hume. On belief generally see H. H. Price *Belief* (London: George Allen and Unwin; New York: Humanities Press, 1969).

8. "Sincerity, Criticism, and Monitoring," in the *Journal of the Philosophy of Education* (1979):141-147, and a revised version in the *Proceedings of the IXth International Congress on the Unity of the Science* (New York: International Cultural Foundation, 1981), vol. 1, pp., 1019-1029; also particular applications in "Spend Less and Learn More," in D. Anderson (ed.) *Pied Pipers of Education* (London: Social Affairs United, 1981) and in "The Spending Cure,"in *Policy Review* (1982).

9. Contemplate the devastation wrought by firing off both barrels simultaneously in the first paragraph of Part 4 of the *Discourse on the Method:* ". . . on the grounds that our senses sometimes deceive us, I wanted to suppose that there was not anything corresponding to what they make us imagine. And because some men make mistakes in reasoning . . . and fall into fallacies . . . I rejected as unsound all the reasonings which I had hitherto taken for demonstrations." I give my own reasons for rejecting this argument type in chapter 9 of the *Introduction* mentioned in note 1, above.

10. See, for a filling of this gap, Max Black "Making Something Happen," in Sidney Hook (ed.) *Determinism and Freedom* (New York: New York University Press, 1958); reprinted as chapter 8 of Black's *Models and Metaphors* (Ithaca, N.Y.: Cornell University Press, 1962).

James H. Bunn

Flew on "Rationality and Unnecessitated Choice"

Let me state first what I consider to be Professor Flew's rhetorical strategy, for as with all acute strategies, though one sees it emerge during the course of the action, only afterward does one understand its accomplishments. Flew wants to carve out a position between naturalism on the one hand and the Hume-Popper position on the other by taking a bit of high ground from each. He argues that both sides are partially right but that each is crucially wrong with respect to cause and choice. He admits that the naturalists are correct when they posit the physics of causation. Of two definitions of "cause," "the sense in which we speak both of the causes of astronomical phenomena and of ourselves as agents causing movements of inanimate objects, causes truly do—*pace* Hume and the whole Humean tradition—bring about, and thus factually necessitate, their effects." But from this correct premise, it is incorrect to derive the kind of psychic determinism posited by the hard-core Freudians and the sociobiologists. As usual, the bind is best expressed by the founder. Sigmund Freud said, "needless to say, anyone who suffers a delusion is unable to recognize it as such." Flew then turns this bind against the premise.

Flew sees a parallel between two definitions of "cause," namely, two definitions of "determinism," and by extension a definition of "choice," via free agency, which rationally recognizes those constraints but mediates between the two categories while being unmitigated by either. His argument is that people experience the difference between physical and moral necessity, and they know how to act because they recognize the different kinds of choice available to them between the categories.

If I read the paper aright, Sir Karl Popper's extreme skepticism about the fallibility of knowledge is for Flew a more forbidding, if less popular, opponent than naturalism. Popper's indeterminism works well against scientific determinism. Here Popper rightly shows that if scientific determinism is true, then we cannot rightly know it, because we will have been constrained by our beliefs to accept it. Not being able to discuss scientific determinism rationally thereby undermines the inexorable logic from which it apparently springs. Flew argues, however, that Popper's skepticism is without limit. For him, Popper's "great mistake is to assume that knowledge presupposes infallibility; that, where we may conceivably be mistaken, there it is impossible for us ever to know. The truth is that we need only to be in a position to know and to be claiming to know something that is in fact true."

From John Locke's chapter on "Power" Professor Flew derives a theory of free agency that is based on common experience about the possibilities for choice in action. When one considers one's own power either to begin or to forbear, to continue or to end an action, from that understanding of the limiting conditions of one's own power there "arise the ideas of liberty or necessity." One recalls the two mafioso crooks: a bullet in the back gives one no alternative; that's physical necessity. But making him an offer he cannot refuse is a coerced necessity that provides only an apparently intolerable alternative. So Flew summarizes: "It is precisely and only from our altogether familiar experiences as agents making things happen, yet agents always limited in the scope of their agency, that we can and must derive two—if you like—metaphysical basics."

Now I should like to reinforce Flew's argument by commenting upon examples and analogies that he uses to ground this thesis about freedom and necessity. All the examples and analogies are of one kind: they are metaphors of imprisonment in which the inmates are would-be escape artists. I imagine that this metaphor is Flew's overriding rhetorical trope because his main job is to escape those new variants on the old argument from design: the physiologists and the psychic determinists. Indeed, his first example is Andy Capp, whose antics week after week display his ability to escape the well-meaning entrapments of Flo. Of course, he eludes her entrapment by underscoring his own incorrigibility, which certainly was the intent of Flo's entrapment in the first place. Even the colorless proposition *p* that follows is couched in the legal language of one's "warrant" for believing. By which of three magisterial powers is one authorized to believe that *p*? I am reminded of Ben Jonson's *Bartholomew Faire,* in which Justice Adam Overdo asks over and over, "By what warrant?"

In this context Flew gives an example of a false cause made by a criminologist: ". . . if causal theories explain why a criminal acts as he does, they also explain why he *must* act as he does, and therefore they make any reliance on deterrence seem futile or irrelevant." To which Flew responds with another example like Andy Capp. Asked by criminologists who were seeking the necessitarian cause for his multiple bank robberies, "Why," the robber responded, "Because that's where the money is."

Why do I call these examples and analogies "metaphors"? And of what possible pertinence is this discussion to the issues of free agency and necessity? Let me begin to answer by citing yet another example, this time from Hume, in what is perhaps the operative example for Flew's main argument about the difference between physical cause and psychical cause. The example is taken from Hume's chapter, "Of Liberty and Necessity" in *A Treatise of Human Nature:*

> When we consider how aptly *natural* and *moral* evidence link together, and form only one chain of argument, we shall make no scruple to allow, that they are of the same nature, and derived from the same principles. A prisoner, who has neither money nor interest, discovers the impossibility of his escape, as well when he considers the obstinacy of the gaoler, as the walls and bars, with which he is surrounded; and in all attempts for his freedom, chooses rather to work upon the stone and iron of the one, than upon the inflexible nature of the other.

Hume goes on to describe "a connected chain of natural causes and voluntary actions; but the mind feels no difference between them, in passing from one link to another." The prisoner infers only a chain of causes cemented together by an apparent physical necessity. The reader believes Hume's argument because he has metaphorically fused the jailer's inflexible nature with the nature of iron bars into an intertwined "chain" of evidence. Clearly one of the large accomplishments of Flew's paper is to have discriminated between Hume's conflation of two different causes and two different courses of action for those who would be free.

Now I would maintain that the strength of that argument in large part derives from the use of metaphor, which can be briefly defined as a figurative trope that is not literally true. Or to use Hume's language for a moment, metaphor conflates "moral" and "natural" evidence. The metaphor of imprisonment is a hypothetical constraint that is couched in the language of physical constraint. It is a metaphor of "inescapability." In other words, the metaphor of imprisonment, by being figuratively correct and literally incorrect at the same time, is based upon the same kind of category mistake that Hume uses to cement physical cause together with mental linkage.

Professor Flew shares with Andy Capp, as with all those who care for "truth-concerned criticism," a critical stance toward anything called an "inescapable" perception, belief, or conclusion. So a metaphor of inescapable imprisonment, just as a fiction of the locked room in miniature, arouses in them a corresponding desire to escape those limits. Hume used the metaphor of imprisonment to show that a prisoner arrives at an inference about physical necessity by cementing together the inflexibility of the wall and the jailer. Flew's metaphor of the mafioso, Andy Capp, and the goal-oriented bank robber show how to escape these hypothetical entrapments by seeing them as Blakean "mind-forged manacles," not as actual prison walls.

Now someone has said that the metaphor for all metaphor is kinship. That is, as Professor Max Black might say, metaphor describes family relationships. Metaphor is a figurative way of describing connections that are not literally connected. But the metaphor of imprisonment is a way of describing an isolated thing, some inescapable concept, *sui generis*. So a metaphor of imprisonment does violence to the very notion of metaphor's sense of relationship. Hence its intolerable feel. A metaphor of imprisonment inverts metaphor. If metaphor is a kind of category mistake that transfers meaning from one category of use to another in order to establish kinship with two previously unrelated things, then the metaphor of imprisonment is that category mistake that tries to cauterize meaning within one logical type, giving rise therefore to a willfulness for escape that will be inevitably successful in the realm of language. In short, any inescapable conclusion will eventually determine the premise that made it seem inevitable in the first place, for there will be a violent turn back upon the premise—a subversion.

In sum, for me the originality of Professor Flew's paper is its provision for ways of escape for those physical and psychic determinists who now no longer need to be bracketed by inescapable premises and conclusions. To paraphrase John Stuart Mill's essay *On Liberty,* these determinists are all the more in need of this kind of escape to originality the less that they are conscious of the want.

Alistair M. Macleod

Self-interest, Rationality, and Equality

An important preliminary task for the sponsor of a theory of rationality is to determine what the main kinds of thing are of which rationality can intelligibly be predicated. Theories (Type 1 theories, let us call them) for which it is beliefs and beliefs alone to which terms like *rational* and *irrational* are properly applicable will be very different, certainly in scope and probably also in structure, from (Type 2) theories for which actions and decisions can also be said to be rational and irrational. And both will be different from (Type 3) theories, which seek to make room in addition for rational appraisal of an agent's desires and preferences and of the ends, ideals, and principles associated with them.

While it is not my purpose to tackle this preliminary question here, it is important to my argument to try to fix the role played by the principle of self-interest within a theory of rationality by relating it, even if only in a crude and oversimplified way, to some of these issues. I shall claim that the principle of self-interest can be given recognition as a principle of rational decision-

I am grateful to Peter Hacker for discussing a version of this paper with me and to Lansing Pollock and other participants in the conference on Naturalism and Rationality (at SUNY, Buffalo in March 1985) for their helpful comments. Financial support to enable me to take part in the conference was provided by the Webster Foundation and by the School of Graduate Studies and Research, Queen's University.

making only within a Type 3 theory, the pretensions of two familiar (Type 1 and/or Type 2) contenders for the role notwithstanding. I shall then ask whether self-interest can be expected to serve as an omnibus principle of practical rationality. After identifying decision-problems to which it is powerless without supplementation to yield any solutions, I shall argue that a broadly egalitarian principle has a strong claim to recognition as the appropriate "successor" to the principle of self-interest as a principle of rational decision-making in these cases.

I

A theory of *practical* rationality, it might plausibly be thought, is bound to be part of either a Type 2 or a Type 3 theory. The hallmark, after all, of a Type 1 theory is the claim that rationality can be predicated with full propriety only of *beliefs*. It is arguable, however, that the proponent of a Type 1 theory might contrive to offer an account of what makes actions and decisions "rational" by (a) flagging this use of "rational" as one to be permitted only with misgivings, and (b) representing rationality—in this allegedly improper (or potentially misleading) sense—as a wholly *derivative* feature of actions and decisions, a feature they can be conceded to have only in virtue of the fact that the beliefs on which they are based can be said to be rational in a somewhat stricter sense. There is a famous passage in Hume that suggests he might have endorsed some such account.

> It is not contrary to reason to prefer the destruction of the whole world to the scratching of my little finger. It is not contrary to reason for me to choose my total ruin, to prevent the least uneasiness of an Indian or person wholly unknown to me. It is as little contrary to reason to prefer even my own acknowledged lesser good to my greater, and have a more ardent affection for the former than the latter. . . . In short, a passion must be accompanied with some false judgment, in order to its being unreasonable; and even then it is not the passion, properly speaking, which is unreasonable, but the judgment.[1]

It is probably better, however, to treat this sort of account as part of a Type 2 theory. For one thing, it is gratuitously restrictive to hold that beliefs are the only proper subjects of rationality-judgments when ordinary usage so readily sanctions talk about the rationality of decisions. Moreover, there is no incompatibility between the claim that rationality can be predicated properly of actions and decisions and the claim that this use of the term *rational* is wholly parasitic upon its application to the beliefs that serve to explain and/or justify what people do. This means, of course, that defenders of the view that so-called "practical" rationality is to be understood in terms of rationality in belief have little incentive to stick doggedly to the Type 1 theory.

There is, then, a Type 2 theory according to which rationality is a wholly derivative feature of actions and decisions, a feature they have simply in virtue of the relation in which they stand to the beliefs on which they are based. In the celebrated Humean version of this view, it is only a subclass of the underlying beliefs that can be denominated rational or irrational; and it is only these beliefs, consequently, that can serve as the "source," so to speak, of the rationality of an agent's decisions. Only beliefs about "matters of fact" or "relations of ideas" can be appraised as rational or irrational. The moral beliefs that often provide part of the basis for conduct, and the beliefs an agent may have concerning the worthwhileness of certain ends, fall wholly outside the domain of "reason."

This attempt to make the rationality of decisions parasitic upon the rationality of the beliefs that underlie them presents us with a curious puzzle. It is difficult to see how rationality can be successfully "transmitted" from beliefs to actions if only a subclass of these beliefs are held to be appraisable in rational terms. It is decidedly odd that beliefs about "matters of fact" and "relations of ideas" should be singled out as the only beliefs that must be shown to be rational when the rationality of conduct is under investigation. After all, moral beliefs and beliefs about ends worth pursuing play an important role in the decisions people make and are consequently indispensable to any reasonably complete attempt either to explain or to justify such decisions.

It is instructive to compare the attempt to derive the rationality of actions from that of the beliefs they presuppose with the attempt to ground the rationality of acceptance of some proposition r in the fact that r is deducible from the propositions p and q. In the latter context we know that it is rational to accept r only if it would be rational to accept *all* of the following propositions: (1) *If p and q, then r,* (2) *p,* and (3) *q.* Just as it would be bizarre to hold that the rationality of accepting *r* is a simple function of the rationality of endorsing the third of these propositions only—or, for that matter, of endorsing (3) together with (1), but (still) without any endorsement of (2)—so it is surely bizarre to hold that the rationality of an agent's decision can be a simple function of the rationality of the *factual* beliefs on which it is based. And just as it is of no assistance—should we be unable to represent (2) (also) as a proposition that it would be rational to accept—to point to the fact that credence is actually given to it by those who would like to be able to demonstrate the rationality of assent to *r*, so, too, it is idle to hope that the case for the rationality of a decision can be bolstered by pointing to the mere fact of an agent's commitment to the principles or ends presupposed by the decision.

II

Closely related to the view that the rationality of a decision is a simple function of the rationality of the (factual) beliefs it presupposes is the view that the rationality of conduct is a function of its consistency with the agent's preferences. According to John C. Harsanyi, for example, "rational behavior is simply behavior consistently pursuing some well-defined goals, and pursuing them according to some well-defined set of preferences or priorities."[2] Again, in his contribution to a recent collection of papers on utilitarian theory, David Gauthier quotes this passage with approval and then adds: "This conception is, in a large sense, instrumental; goals and preferences are themselves ultimately neither rational nor irrational."[3]

Instead of trying to forge a connection between rationality in belief and rationality in action, proponents of this type of view attempt to build on the essential connection widely presumed to exist between rationality and consistency. They do so by exploiting an interesting fact about consistency, namely, that it is a logical relation that cuts across the distinction between actions and beliefs. Not only can beliefs be both consistent and inconsistent with other beliefs, and actions with actions, but actions and beliefs—and actions and preferences, too—can be consistent and inconsistent with one another.

Impressive though the link is between consistency and rationality, its significance is easily misconstrued. While the consistency of two beliefs is a necessary condition of the rationality of accepting both, it is obviously not a sufficient condition: it may be perfectly rational to reject both despite their consistency. Again, it may be entirely rational to reject the conclusion of an argument even though it is the kind of valid deductive argument the conclusion of which cannot be rejected without inconsistency by anyone who accepts the premises. Similar remarks apply when we move to the cases covered by the "consistency with preferences" theory of rational conduct, even though now the relation of consistency is one that must hold not just between beliefs, or even between beliefs and actions, but between actions and preferences. Just as the consistency of a belief with other beliefs is no guarantee of its rationality, so the consistency of behavior with an agent's preferences is no guarantee of its rationality. And just as it is rational for an individual to accept proposition *r* (the conclusion of an argument of the form *If p and q, then r; p and q; therefore r)* only if it would be rational to accept *all* of the premises *(If p and q, then r; p;* and *q),* so, too, it is rational to perform action A1 (where this would serve in the circumstances to give effect to an agent's preferences) only if it can be shown, or assumed, that it is rational to seek to give effect to just these preferences.

III

The two accounts of rational decision-making that I have been reviewing have sometimes been taken—carelessly, no doubt—as accounts of what it is to act on the basis of self-interest. Thus it has sometimes been supposed that to act on the basis of self-interest is simply a matter of using one's knowledge of the relevant facts to select the most effective means of securing the achievement of one's ends, whatever these happen to be. Again, it is often taken for granted that there is no difference between pursuing one's long-term interest in a clear-headed way and giving effect over time to a consistent set of preferences.

Yet it is easy to see that neither will serve as an account of what it is to act on the basis of self-interest. For the view that the rationality of action derives from the rationality of the factual beliefs it presupposes, both actions that serve ill-advised, short-term objectives and actions that give effect to moral beliefs might qualify as "rational" in the sense defined by the theory; yet neither could plausibly be said to qualify because the principle of self-interest is satisfied. And as for the "consistency with preferences" account, it commits us to representing as "rational" not only the actions of those whose lives mirror their single-minded commitment to a stern, self-denying moral code but also the actions of those whose preferences, while consistent, do not serve to promote their long-term interest.

To show that the principle of self-interest is not to be confused with the principles discussed above is one thing; to show that it is a principle of practical rationality is another. This is because there are two different issues to be settled. The first is a question about the content and practical import of proposed principles for the making of decisions; the second a question about their status as putative principles of rationality. I have argued in sections I and II that neither the "rational empirical beliefs" theory nor the "consistency with preferences" theory offers a satisfactory account of what it is to make a rational decision. I have just argued, in the opening paragraph of this section, that the self-interest principle is not to be confused with either. If I am right about both matters, then at least the possibility is kept alive of self-interest qualifying as a principle of practical rationality.

I cannot explore here the large question of whether this is more than a mere possibility. I offer instead a rough sketch of what would have to be the case for self-interest to be given recognition as a principle of rational decision-making.

The key condition has to do with the rationality of aiming at promotion of one's long-term interest or well-being. This may be considered something of a truism, as Aristotle seems to have supposed. Or, as Derek Parfit has recently argued,[4] it may have to be regarded as in need of establishment, despite its centrality in the tradition of moral thought stemming from Aristotle. In any event the assumption that it is rational to pursue one's long-term interest or well-being is crucial to maintaining the view that decisions that give effect to the principle of self-interest are rational decisions.

Other conditions are less contentious. Thus, rational agents must make their decisions in light of the best available empirical evidence about their situation and about the likely consequences of the various options they have. Again, they must endeavor to secure the consistency of their decisions with one another and with their beliefs and commitments. When all these requirements are put together, what emerges is an account of rational conduct under the aegis of the principle of self-interest according to which a given agent *A* can be said to be acting rationally in doing *x* in given circumstancess only if all of the following conditions are fulfilled:

(1) that long-term interest 'or well-being is an objective it is rational for *A* to try to achieve.

(2) that it is rational for *A* to accept those (empirical) beliefs about present circumstances and the options they afford that are indispensable to the mapping of a strategy for the achievement of the objective in (1), and

(3) that *x* is the action most consonant in the circumstances both with the objective in (1) and with the beliefs in (2).[5]

It is in virtue of its inclusion of the first of these conditions that the self-interest view must be seen—unlike the views with which I have been contrasting it—as part of a Type 3 theory of rationality. For Type 3 theories, as was noted earlier, questions about the rationality of de facto ends and commitments must be faced, not side-stepped, suppressed, or disallowed. Rational conduct is thus not a matter of effective pursuit of the ends an agent happens to have, whatever these should turn out to be or involve. Rather, it is a matter of effectively pursuing ends the pursuit of which is rational. Again, rational conduct is not a matter of arranging for the successful implementation of the ideals and principles to which one happens to be committed, regardless of their content and import. It involves, rather, the successful implementation of ideals and principles *commitment to which is rational.*

When stated in this general way, of course, these theses do no more than put on the agenda questions about the criteria for determining the rationality of the ends people might pursue or of the ideals and principles to which they might commit themselves. The self-interest principle supplies one possible answer to these questions, namely, that it is rational for an individual to pursue those ends whose realization will best serve his or her long-term interest or well-being. Given the malleability of the notion of individual well-being (and of the cognate notions of interest, benefit, and advantage), this claim obviously cries out for further careful specification; and it is also to some extent controversial just how much determinate guidance the self-interest principle, circumspectly formulated, is capable of yielding. Nevertheless, within the limits set by judicious treatment of these issues, it at least offers what any principle of practical rationality worthy of the name must seek to provide: a basis for the assessment of individual decisions that does not treat the wants, preferences, and ends people have as brute givens.

IV

One reason it is important to see that the principle of self-interest is part of a Type 3 theory of practical rationality is that it suggests what sort of "successor" principle we need for situations to which the principle of self-interest is arguably inapplicable. Of these the most obvious are situations in which a *social* decision has to be made about the general shape of institutional arrangements and in which there is no feasible institutional set-up that would be maximally advantageous from the standpoint of every single individual.

To help determine whether the principle of self-interest can serve as an omnibus principle of practical rationality—and if it cannot, whether the reasons for its inadequacy point the way to selection of a suitable complementary principle—it is instructive to imagine a society the members of which are so situated that their real interests are in conflict. Despite the care they have taken and the ingenuity they have shown both in the drafting of their individual life-plans under the aegis of the principle of self-interest and in the identification of the institutional arrangements most conducive to their implementation, they find that ALPHA is the set-up that would suit individual A best, BETA the set-up ideally required from B's point of view, GAMMA the set-up needed to serve C's interests, and so on. In these circumstances, what collective decision about the design of the institutions under which they will all have to contrive to live would it be rational for them to endorse? And is there an illuminating connection between the decision and the principle of self-interest?

There is, it might be thought, at least one rather obvious way in which the principle of self-interest might be applied even here. Thus, *A* might argue that the preferred solution is to go for ALPHA, on the ground that only ALPHA will facilitate full-scale implementation of a life-plan carefully constructed by *A* in light of the principle of self-interest; and *B* and *C,* for their part, might put in strictly parallel plugs for BETA and GAMMA respectively. And, in a sense, all three would be right to claim that the principle of self-interest can properly be put to use in this way even though the question they face is one about the collective decision to be made about the institutional framework within which they will all have to live their lives: each, after all, must specify on what terms he or she will consent to be a party to a collective decision of this sort.

The trouble is that while putting the principle of self-interest to use in just this way would have enabled them, *under conditions of no conflict of interest,* to converge on a solution to the social decision problem, the solutions to which they are bound to gravitate in the circumstances supposed are *different* solutions. This means that when the interests of the individual members of a society pull in different directions—which is what we actually find in society as we know it—the principle of self-interest, invoked in the straightforward way described, cannot be expected to yield a basis for rational settlement of disputes about the design of social institutions. What is needed, and what we plainly do not have—yet—is a way of applying considerations of self-interest to our social decision problem that will enable us to claim that there is some determinate solution to it that is in *A's* interest *and* in *B's* interest *and* in *C's* interest.

Suppose, then, that we try to determine whether a rational solution can be found by arranging for *A, B,* and *C* to negotiate a deal with one another, a deal that reflects not only their sense of what it would be advantageous for each of them to secure if only their interests did not clash but also their relative power to extract concessions from one another by means of threats and counter-threats. Suppose, in short, that they try to secure a rational exit from the impasse in which they find themselves by representing the social decision problem they face as a *bargaining* problem, it being understood that each of them will then be committed to exerting whatever leverage he or she can to minimize the distance to be traveled in the direction of solutions favored by the others.

It need not be denied that a unique solution to this sort of bargaining problem is in principle obtainable, provided *A, B,* and *C* have access to enough pooled information—information, for example, about what they have the power to do in their dealings with one another and about the ways in which they would actually exercise their power in a wide range of possible circumstances. Thus, if they all know that *A* has much more power over *B* and *C* than either has over *A,* and that *A* can be expected to make full use of this power to push for a deal that is a close approximation to ALPHA, then it may well be the case that *B* and *C,* too, will be able to conclude that they can best promote their own interest by making substantial concessions to *A* at the bargaining table. Indeed, judicious use of the information at their disposal may well enable them to select just one of the ALPHA-like solutions (where these are solutions that deviate only slightly from the solution favored by *A)* as the solution that would *best* serve the interests of *each* in the circumstances. If, then, ALPHA 3 (say) were the unanimous choice of the parties, could it not be claimed that simple appeal to the principle of self-interest is all we need after all to generate a unique solution to our social decision problem when it is set up as a bargaining problem? And could it not be added that if the principle of self-interest can be presumed to be a rational principle, the solution generated in this way will also be a rational solution?

Both of these questions must be answered in the negative. It is perfectly true, of course, that on the proposed reconstruction of the problem—and of what is involved in the application of the principle of self-interest to the resolution of the conflicting views of *A, B,* and *C* as to the preferred solution—we do not get the sort of stalemate we got earlier. But the price is high, too high to enable us to claim either that it is the principle of self-interest on its own that has worked this magic or that uncontentiously rational considerations have dictated the solution. For without proper recognition of it as a criterion supplementary to the self-interest principle itself, we have permitted the *power* of the bargaining parties vis-à-vis one another—their power to extract concessions by the issuance of threats and counter-threats, for example—to play a crucial role in the selection of the preferred solution.

The only reason ALPHA 3 emerges as the favored set-up is that *B* and *C* are known by all to be no match for *A* if it comes to a showdown. But this means that the principle of self-interest—at any rate in anything like the form in which it might qualify as a principle of practical rationality—cannot *on its own* yield this result. A crucial part is also played by the idea that an exit can be secured from the impasse created by the conflicting interests of the parties by permitting the stronger to prevail. As for the suggestion that a solution generated in this way provides a *rational* solution to our social decision problem, it is strikingly at odds with the idea that in dispute-resolution settings appeals to *reason* are to be contrasted with appeals, however cunningly veiled or disguised, to *force*.

V

Is there, then, any rational solution to the social decision problem posed by the conflicting interests of *A, B,* and *C,* if the principle of self-interest cannot by itself generate the solution and if power considerations provide an unsatisfactory supplement? Consider the following argument. The principle of self-interest, in the form in which it can be invoked by *A* as a principle of rational decision-making, presupposes that protection and promotion of *A's* long-term interest or well-being is a rational practical objective: decisions based on self-interest will not be *rational* decisions unless this can be taken for granted.[6] In a precisely parallel way, protection and promotion of the long-term interest and well-being of *B* (and of *C)* must be assumed to be a rational practical objective: unless *B* (and *C)* can make this assumption, the decisions they make with a view to securing their own interest and well-being will not qualify as *rational* decisions even if they are admirably effective means to this end. However, it is wholly arbitrary for social decisions about the shape of a society's institutions to give systematic precedence to the interests of, say, *A* if no reason can be supplied for preferring *A's* claims to the conflicting claims advanced by *B* and *C.* Yet reasons of self-interest—the only reasons so far in sight—cannot be cited for doing so: the case for preferring *A's* claims to those of *B* (or of *C)* on grounds of self-interest is no more impressive than the case for preferring *B's* (or *C's)* claims to *A's*. Precisely because the claims they advance are identical in structure, any rational approach to our social decision problem must at least begin by assigning *equal* weight to the interests of *A, B,* and *C*. This means that it is presumptively rational for social decisions to be based on the principle that the interests of the members of a society are to be afforded equal protection.

In conclusion, it is worth emphasizing why this sort of egalitarian principle can be tagged as the natural "successor" to the principle of self-interest for situations in which the interests of the members of a society are in conflict. The reason is that it enables us to give continuing recognition—though now in a way that takes account of the special features of the problem of social decision-making under conditions of conflict of interest—to an assumption deeply embedded in the view that self-interest is a principle of rational decision-making. As we have seen, it is a condition of the rationality of actions that satisfy the principle of self-interest that it should be rational for individual well-being to be aimed at in the first place: unless the promotion of individual well-being can be represented as a rational practical objective, it will not be possible to represent as *rational* the decisions that are made to this end, no matter how effective these may be as means to its achievement. The principle that equal weight is to be assigned to the conflicting interests of *A, B,* and *C* in the design of the institutions that will provide the framework for their lives, clearly reflects recognition of this crucial presupposition of the use *A, B,* and *C* are presumed to be prepared to make of the principle of self-interest as a principle of practical rationality. Thus it commits us to endorsing the supposition—which is built into *A's* use of the self-interest principle—that importance attaches to the achievement of *A's* well-being. And it commits us, in precisely the same way, to endorsing the supposition that importance attaches to protection and promotion of the interests of *B* and *C* as well—something that is implicit in *their* use of the principle of self-interest. All that is really added by the principle of equality as a putative successor principle is the recognition that if importance is to be held to attach to securing the interests of *A and B and C,* then, in situations in which these are in conflict, the rational assumption for purposes of *social* decision-making is that *equal* importance attaches to protection and promotion of the interests in question. This is tantamount to endorsement of the principle that it is presumptively rational for institutions to be so structured as to afford all the members of society an equal opportunity to live satisfactory and fulfilling lives.

NOTES

1. David Hume, *Treatise of Human Nature;* Bk. II, Pt. III, Sec. III.

2. John C. Harsanyi, "Morality and the Theory of Rational Behavior," *Social Research* 44 (1977).

3. David Gauthier, "On the Refutation of Utilitarianism," in *The Limits of Utilitarianism,* edited by Harlan B. Miller and William H. Williams, (Minneapolis: University of Minnesota Press, 1982).

4. Derek Parfit, *Reasons and Persons* (Oxford: Oxford University Press, 1984).

5. It is to some extent artificial how the distinctions highlighted by these three conditions are drawn. It is easy to see, however, that it is a version of the second condition that is given prominence by the "rational empirical beliefs" account of rational decision-making and that the "consistency with preferences" account highlights a version of the third condition.

6. This is why, of course, I have been at pains to argue that an adequate theory of practical rationality must be a Type 3 theory.

Lansing Pollock

Self-interest and Moral Behavior

One of Professor Macleod's major concerns is to determine how far the principle of self-interest can take us in the development of a theory of practical rationality. He concludes that there are situations in which social decisions must be made where the principle of self-interest is inapplicable. Whether this conclusion is warranted will depend on what is meant by the principle of self-interest. When a person pursues his own interest, what is it that he is pursuing? I shall try to shed some light on this question by exploring two conceptions of self-interest; then I shall raise some questions about Macleod's conception.

I begin with what I call the value-neutral analysis of self-interest. According to this view, it is in one's self-interest to satisfy one's desires. Thus, we take a person's desires as a given and assume that it is in his interest to satisfy them. Pursuit of self-interest in this sense can be difficult. An agent will need to recognize when his desires conflict, and he may need considerable self-control in order to forgo immediate gratification. He will also require the necessary information for knowing what he must do to satisfy his desires. Thus, this analysis of self-interest allows us to criticize other agents. For example, we might criticize a friend for lacking the self-control to defer gratification, with the result that he satisfies a less important desire at the expense of a more important one. We could also criticize an agent for adopting ineffective means to his chosen end. However, while an agent is not immune from criticism on this conception of self-interest, he is the final judge of what he desires, along with the relative importance of his different desires.

The second conception of self-interest, which I shall call the normative analysis, is based on the assumption that it is in one's self-interest to live a good life. This view assumes that we have some beliefs concerning what it means to live a good life and that some desires are incompatible with these beliefs. Thus, persons may have desires that are not in their self-interest to satisfy. Consider the case of a teen-age girl who wants to quit school, become pregnant, and go on welfare. If we assume that these choices would not be compatible with living a good life, then it is not in her self-interest to satisfy these desires.

The value-neutral analysis and the normative analysis are clearly different. Is one better than the other? I prefer the normative analysis for the following reason. I assume that some persons desire things that are not good, and if these persons satisfy their desires, they will live bad lives. I do not want to say that it is in one's self-interest to live a bad life. But this is what the value-neutral analysis requires me to say. According to this conception, I must take a person's desires as a given and assume that it is in his self-interest to satisfy them, regardless of the content of his desires.

It would appear that Macleod also accepts the normative analysis of self-interest. He tells us that "the principle of self-interest can be given recognition as a principle of rational decision-making only within a Type 3 theory" (pp. 59-60)[1]. He also states that a Type 3 theory must provide "a basis for the assessment of individual decisions that does not treat wants, preferences, and ends people have as brute givens" (p. 66). In other words, the correct analysis of self-interest must provide for the evaluation of ends and not just means.

On the other hand, some statements by Macleod strike me as being inconsistent with the normative analysis. For example, I am puzzled by his reluctance to make a connection between acting in one's interest and acting morally (p. 64). If it is in one's interest to live a good life and if acting morally is good, then moral behavior would seem to be required by the pursuit of self-interest. I am also unsure of what Macleod means by the phrase "conflicts of interest." No doubt the desires of different individuals can conflict. Thus, the social arrangement that would allow *A* to satisfy his desires may be quite different from the social arrangement that would allow *B* to satisfy his desires. However, according to the normative analysis of self-interest, the fact that *A* and *B* have conflicting desires does not show that they have conflicting interests. They may, after all, desire things that are not good.

Finally, I am puzzled by Macleod's claim that the principle of self-interest is inapplicable when social decisions are called for. Since it is in my self-interest to act morally, it is also in my interest to respect the rights of others and to treat them fairly. And since it is in the interest of other persons to live a good life, the same reasoning would apply to them. Thus, the principle of self-interest seems to entail respect for rights and fair treatment. What else do we need to make social decisions? At this point one might object that I am making the unwarranted assumption that moral values are always overriding (i.e., more important than other values). This objection introduces a very large and difficult topic that I cannot pursue here. It is worth noting, however, that some very prominent philosophers have held that moral values are overriding, e.g., R. M. Hare, John Rawls, Alan Gewirth, Kurt Baier, and Bernard Gert.[2] Furthermore, most philosophers would agree that moral values are (at least) very important. If we accept this assumption, along with the normative analysis of self-interest, we can conclude that it is usually in one's interest to respect the rights of others and to treat them fairly.

NOTES

1. Alastair Macleod, "Self-Interest, Rationality and Equality." Page references are to his essay in this volume.

2. R. M. Hare, *Moral Thinking* (Oxford: Clarendon Press, 1981), pp. 53–60; John Rawls, *A Theory of Justice* (Cambridge: Harvard University Press, 1971), p. 135; Alan Gewirth, *Reason and Morality* (Chicago: University of Chicago Press, 1978), p. 1; Kurt Baier, *The Moral Point of View* (New York: Random House, 1965), pp. 148–150; and Bernard Gert, *The Moral Rules* (New York: Harper and Row, 1966), p. 135.

Part Two

Naturalistic Epistemology

Alvin I. Goldman

Epistemology and the
New Connectionism

I. INTRODUCTION

This paper illustrates my conception of how epistemology should be naturalized, by presenting a specimen of such naturalization. The paper is a condensed version of a chapter of my book, *Epistemology and Cognition,* earlier chapters of which lay out the foundations of this general conception. Let me begin by briefly summarizing some main points of the general conception, before turning to the specimen I shall examine here.

Epistemology is primarily a normative subject. In the first instance, it seeks to evaluate doxastic states like beliefs. But belief evaluation requires evaluation of things that *cause* beliefs, i.e., belief-forming methods, procedures, or processes. In particular, an important subclass of epistemic evaluations must assess *basic psychological processes* that cause beliefs. This is one reason epistemology needs help from cognitive psychology, or cognitive science. Cognitive science tries to specify the basic cognitive processes available to the human cognizer. It is then the task of epistemology to examine relevant properties of these processes, to see which processes (if any) deserve epistemic commendation.

One central term of epistemic evaluation is *justified*. A person's beliefs can be considered justified or unjustified. As a first approximation, I hold that a belief is justified only if it is caused by a psychological process that is generally *reliable,* i.e., a process-type whose set of belief outputs has a high truth ratio (say, 90 percent). This is somewhat oversimplified. Think of a cognitive process as potentially belonging to a *system* of cognitive processes, with interacting members. If a system has a high truth ratio, then it is *justificationally right,* or J-right. A belief is justified just in case it is generated by a J-right system of cognitive processes. (Even this is only an approximation of my view; but it will suffice for present purposes.) So an epistemologist who is interested in whether a belief is justified should be interested in the cognitive processes responsible for the belief; and, in particular, should be interested in certain *truth*-linked properties of those processes.

Justification is not the only term of epistemic appraisal. It is the chief one I will discuss, but others will be examined as well.

I have thus far concentrated on the dimensions and standards of epistemological evaluation. But now I want to think about *what* gets evaluated. In the first instance, I said, we evaluate beliefs and other doxastic states. But what, exactly, are beliefs? And what other doxastic states are there? This is a second class of questions for which epistemology should turn to cognitive science. *Belief* is a descriptive psychological term. But how useful, descriptively, is it? Elsewhere I argue that the term *belief* awkwardly straddles quite different psychological states; and this has some important epistemological consequences. A sophisticated epistemology, insofar as it is an epistemology of psychological states, should seek a precise and accurate descriptive terminology. It is this concern with psychological reality— especially connected with the notion of belief—that will occupy my attention in this paper.

My specific topic here is the theoretical representation of belief and uncertainty. Section II contains an (abbreviated) critique of the orthodox approach to this problem. Section III presents an alternative approach, borrowing the notion of a *winner-take-all* network from the Connectionist literature. Section IV proceeds on the assumption that winner-take-all networks provide a model of (at least some) belief-forming processes, and then inquires into the *evaluative* status of such processes.

II. ACCEPTANCE AND SUBJECTIVE PROBABILITIES

Many epistemologists deploy a *binary* notion of belief. A person either believes a proposition, or he does not. One label used for this notion is *acceptance*. Other epistemologists, however, think of belief, or credence, as a *graded,* or *quantitative,* notion. This is commonly expressed in the language of "subjective probabilities," or "personal probabilities." On this view, there are varying degrees of confidence one can have in a proposition, widely represented as points on the interval from 0 to 1.

The question I now wish to ask is: Are *both* of these credal state notions—binary belief and graded belief—psychologically legitimate? If not, which one is legitimate? If so, what is their *relationship?* In particular, are they two entirely different psychological categories (or continua)? Or do they somehow fit with one another into a single psychological category?

In my discussion I ignore the more popular controversy about belief that concerns the possession of *content.* Here I take content for granted. I shall make no attempt to elucidate the source of content, nor to say how content should find its place within a Connectionist framework.

From an introspective standpoint, the notion of acceptance, or unqualified belief, seems plausible. There seem to be many propositions people just believe without any (salient) doubt or reservation. At the same time, there are many cases in which we are *inclined* to believe a proposition, but feel some hesitancy. In some cases, we have tangibly qualified belief, prompting such verbalizations as *"I think* it is going to rain, but I'm not sure," or "It will *probably* rain, but it might not." Such cases seem to force the admission of graded beliefs.

Some writers admit both subjective probabilities and acceptance. Although they rarely explicitly address the psychological status of these states, they apparently view them as entirely distinct psychological categories. But this perspective is unsatisfying. The two kinds of states—binary belief and graded belief— seem too intimately tied with one another for this view to be plausible.

How, then, do we accommodate both sorts of states within an adequate psychology? A first attempt might be to identify acceptance with a subjective probability of 1.0. In other words, belief is identified with *maximal conviction*. There are three difficulties with this, however. Many propositions that a person can plausibly be described as "believing" are not accepted with *maximal* conviction. Second, it is standard theoretical practice, setting aside infinite domains, to reserve probability 1.0 for propositions that are true in all possible cases, i.e., for tautologies or necessary truths. But it then seems pathological for people to assign 1.0 to contingent propositions, which are not true in all possible cases. Yet people obviously *do* accept contingent propositions. So the proposed account of acceptance automatically imputes to people a pathological practice. Third, according to probability models, it is impossible (at least by use of Bayes' theorem) to revise a probability assignment of 1.0 conditional on the receipt of new evidence. So it would appear that the acceptance of, or belief in, a proposition would be unrevisable. Yet people clearly do revise their beliefs.

A second approach is to choose some threshold less than 1.0, e.g., .95, and say that any degree of credence at or above this threshold is (an unqualified) belief, or acceptance. One problem with this is that the choice of a threshold seems entirely arbitrary and artificial; whereas belief seems to be a psychologically natural and well-defined state, not carved out *artificially* from a continuous range of credal intensities. Second, this construal would unfairly ascribe inconsistent beliefs to people, a point that I will not elaborate.

Thus far I have worried about finding mutually comfortable niches for both subjective probabilities and acceptance. But now I want to turn to problems for the subjective probability interpretation of credal uncertainty. In other words, granted that there is *some* psychological reality to the notion of tentative, hesitant, or incomplete conviction, is this correctly or best described in terms of the probability calculus?

One problem is the empirical evidence against the notion that people conform their beliefs to the probability calculus. For example, it's a principle of probability theory that the probability of a conjunction cannot exceed the probability of any of its conjuncts. But people readily violate this conjunction rule (see Tversky and Kahneman, 1983).

Next, consider whether it is plausible that humans should have a psychological mechanism that fixes credal states in accord with the probability calculus. Remember, we are here considering subjective probability as a *descriptive* theory, one that is intended to hold for *all* human beings, whatever their age or educational background. Subjective credences must therefore be fixed by native mechanisms. But are there any native mechanisms that would make credal states behave like probabilities? An affirmative answer assumes there are native mechanisms for making arithmetic calculations of the kind needed for determining probabilistic relations. But native mechanisms do not seem to be adequate for even the simplest arithmetic. Most arithmetic needs to be culturally acquired, by explicit instruction; it is not programmed into the organism. Admittedly, there might be mechanisms that simulate arithmetic computation at a preconscious level, just as visual mechanisms apparently simulate mathematical operations in determining distance, or in computing the trajectory of a flying object. But there is no clear evidence of credence-fixing mechanisms that simulate the probability calculus in this way.

Many theorists of subjective probability might reply that the model is descriptively tenable as long as there is a clear procedure for ascribing such states to the organism on the basis of overt choice behavior, including expressed preferences or indifferences vis-à-vis gambles. A number of such procedures, of course, are proposed in the literature.

There are several problems with this approach. First, the mere fact that subjective probabilities *can* be imputed to a cognizer does not establish their *psychological reality*. Lots of different models of internal states and processes could be consistent with choice behavior. Second, in the present case, there are empirical problems about some of the preference axioms presupposed by the procedures. Third, the different proposed methods for "operationalizing" subjective probability are not equivalent. They would not yield the same assignments in the same cases.* Which of these nonequivalent operationalizations of subjective probabilities should be chosen? Clearly they cannot *all* correctly describe our inner mental apparatus. But this recognition makes one wonder whether *any* of them do.

In conclusion, there are numerous reasons for doubting that

---

*I owe this point to John Pollock.

subjective uncertainty can be correctly captured by applications of the probability notion. There is, of course, a widespread view to the contrary. However, this may merely arise from the allure of a precise mathematical tool—the probability calculus—which dangles the prospects of a tidy and elegant theory. This makes it extremely tempting to try to devise a workable application. But there are scant grounds for thinking that any such theory *does* capture psychological reality.

It should be stressed here that I do not question the ability of people to understand probabilistic concepts and to take propositions about chances as the *contents* of their mental attitudes. One facet of uncertainty, which I do not dispute, is the acceptance of "propositionalized" probabilities. I only query probabilities as measures of credal intensities (the approach of subjective Bayesianism). This probabilistic construal of psychological uncertainty is what I wish to reject, and ultimately replace with a better model.

III. ACCEPTANCE AND WINNER-TAKE-ALL NETWORKS

In the spirit of psychological realism, what might be a better way to model credal uncertainty, and how could we achieve an integrated model of acceptance as well as uncertainty? Recent work in the Connectionist theme suggests a promising avenue. In particular, I wish to draw on a paper by Jerome Feldman and Dana Ballard (1982), and a related paper by Lokendra Shastri and Jerome Feldman (1984). Their approach includes a particular kind of neural network—the "Winner-Take-All" network—which provides, I shall argue, a fruitful way of conceptualizing acceptance and uncertainty.

New Connectionism's approach to cognition has two main emphases. First, it assumes that enough is known about brain structure to offer a serious constraint on hypotheses about cognition. It is a necessary exercise for anyone proposing a cognitive theory to provide an argument to show that the brain could work in the way the theory requires (see Rumelhart and Norman, 1981). Second, Connectionism assumes that an important array of neural processes are parallel as opposed to sequential; this parallel processing involves the use of massive numbers of neural units and connections.

One critical argument for this approach appeals not only to basic properties of neurons but considerations of computational speed as well. The basic computation speed of neurons is a few milliseconds. But they must account for complex cognitive behaviors carried out in less than a hundred time steps. However, current artificial intelligence and simulation programs, which are largely sequential, require millions of time steps. Hence, these sequential models seem inadequate (see Feldman and Ballard, 1982).

Feldman et al. develop a standard model of an information processing "unit," based on the current understanding of neurons. A unit may be used to model anything from a single neuron (or neuron-part) to a major subsystem of neurons. The exact realization of a unit is left intentionally vague. Attention is focused on the computational properties of units and networks of units.

Units communicate with the rest of a network by transmitting a simple value. A unit transmits the same value to all units to which it is connected. The *output* value is closely related to the unit's *potential,* and is best described as a level of activation, such as firing frequency. A unit's potential reflects the amount of activation it has been receiving from other units. For concreteness, think of a unit as a single neuron having multiple dendrites (neural impulse receivers), or dendritic "sites," each of which receives inputs from other neurons. This is illustrated in figure 1 (see page 86).

All inputs are weighted and combined in a manner specified by *site functions* and a *potential function,* in order to update a unit's potential. The computation behavior of units can be described in terms of these main variables:

p: a continuous value called *potential*
v: an *output* value (approximately 10 discrete values)
i: a vector of *inputs* $i_1, i_2, \ldots, i_n$

Two functions define the values of potential and output at time t+1 based on the values at time t:

$$p_{t+1} \leftarrow p\ (i_t, p_t, q_t)$$

$$v_{t+1} \leftarrow v\ (i_t, p_t, q_t)$$

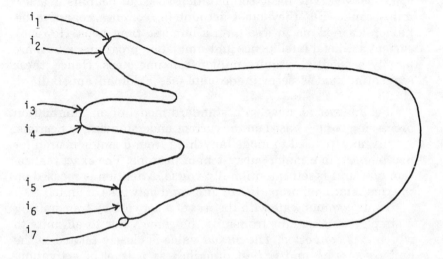

Figure 1.

The arrow notation is borrowed from the assignment statement of programming languages. The value at time t+1 (to the left of the arrow) is determined by the values of the variables at time t (represented by the expression to the right of the arrow). Time is broken into discrete intervals. The variable q ranges over a small set of states that a unit can be in; for purposes of this exposition, though, these states can be ignored. Also, while the output function relates the output, v, to several variables, Feldman et al. frequently treat it as just the rounded value of p, the potential. I shall follow that practice here.

A unit does not treat all inputs uniformly. Units receive inputs via connections, or "links," and each incoming link has an associated *weight*. A unit weighs each input using the weight on the appropriate link. A weight may have a *negative* value. This corresponds to an *inhibitory* link. This is important, since inhibition is a basic neural mechanism, and many of the constructions that interest us are networks featuring *mutual inhibition,* a phenomenon widely found in nature.

To illustrate these ideas, let a unit be a neuron with dendrites that receive inputs. Each dendrite can be thought of as an alternative enabling condition: if it receives enough inputs, it activates the neuron. The firing frequency of the neuron might be the maximum of the firing rate at any one of its dendritic sites. The formula for this unit's potential could be written as follows:

$$p_{t+1} \leftarrow p_t + \text{Max} \, (i_1 + i_2; \, i_3 + i_4; \, i_5 + i_6 - i_7)$$

This is shown in figure 1. The minus sign associated with i_7 indicates that it is an inhibitory input.

Drawing on these ideas, let us illustrate a configuration of symmetric units that mutually inhibit one another. Consider Figure 2, containing two units, A and B, each with two input sites.

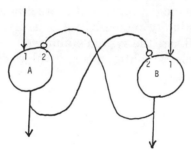

A_1 receives an input of 6 units, then 2 units per time step
B_1 receives an input of 5 units, then 2 units per time step

t	P(A)	P(B)
1	6	5
2	5.5	4
3	5.5	3.5
4	6	3
5	6.5	2
6	7.5	1
7	9.5	0
8	Saturation	0

Figure 2.

Suppose the initial input to site A-1 is 6, after which that site receives 2 inputs per time step. Suppose B-1 receives an initial input of 5, and then 2 inputs per time step. Notice that at site 2 each unit transmits an inhibitory input to its mate. Suppose further that the weights at the sites are as follows: The weight at site 1 is 1, and the weight at site 2 is -.5. Then at each time step, each unit changes its potential by adding the external input value and subtracting half the output value of its mate. So we have the equation:

$$p_{t+1} = p_t + i_1 - (.5) i_2.$$

Finally, assume that the output variable v takes the discrete values: 0, . . . , 9; and that v is always the rounded value of the potential, p. The result, as indicated in the table of figure 2, is that the potential and output of unit B are gradually reduced to 0, while unit A gradually increases its potential and output to a saturation point. There the system stabilizes.

Another symmetric configuration involves *coalitions* of units, shown in figure 3.

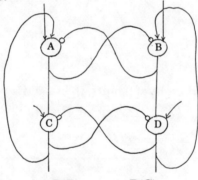

t	P(A)	P(B)	P(C)	P(D)
1	6	5	6	5
2	6.5	4.5	6.5	4.5
3	7.5	3.5	7.5	3.5
4	9.5	1.5	9.5	1.5
	Sat	0	Sat	0

Figure 3.

The idea here is that units A and C form a coalition with mutually reinforcing connections. This coalition competes with another coalition comprised of B and D. Competition between the coalitions is determined by their mutual inhibition. As in the previous example, such mutual inhibition results in convergence toward a stable state, but here the convergence is faster: convergence occurs in only four time steps. This system is described by the following equations and specifications:

$w_1 = 1$, $w_2 = .5$, $w_3 = -.5$

$v = \text{round } (p)$

$p_{t + 1} = p_t + i_1 + .5\,(i_2 - i_3)$

A and C start at 6; B and D start at 5

A, B, C, and D have no external input for $t > 1$.

Of special interest to me are Feldman and Ballard's *winner-take-all* (WTA) networks. These exhibit the properties of convergence and stable states illustrated in figures 2 and 3. The basic idea motivating WTA networks, as Feldman and Ballard explain, is that cognitive systems make *decisions*. This includes behavioral decisions, such as turning left or right, and fight-or-flight decisions; but also cognitive decisions, such as the interpretation of ambiguous words or images. *I* am interested in WTA networks because I view them as promising models of *acceptance*, or (binary) *belief*, in general.

The critical property of a WTA network is that *only the unit with the highest potential (among a set of contenders) will have output above zero after some settling time.* An example of a WTA network is one that operates in one time step for a set of contenders each of which can read the potential of all the others. This is an extreme example, but it suffices for illustrative purposes. Each unit in the network computes its new potential according to the rule:

$$p \leftarrow \text{If } p > \max\,(i_j), \text{ then } p; \text{ otherwise } 0.$$

In other words, each unit sets itself to zero if it knows of a higher input. This general idea is illustrated in figure 4.

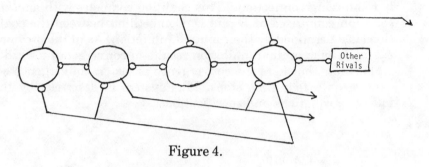

Figure 4.

Winner-Take-All: each unit stops if it sees a higher value

The inhibitory connections guarantee that each unit stops if it "sees" a higher value. This is fast and simple, though probably not terribly realistic. However, there are other ways in which a WTA network might be realized.

The basic idea of acceptance, as I view it, is that a proposition is accepted only when all rivals, or contraries, are rejected. This is well modeled by the idea that all rival hypotheses, or interpretations, have their activation levels reduced to zero. This does not imply that these competing hypotheses cannot later be reactivated. But acceptance marks the emergence of a *decisive* winner, not a hypothesis that merely has *more* strength than its competitors. At the same time, belief must also be a reasonably *stable*, or *settled*, state. If one's attitude is continually fluctuating, one does not yet have a belief. Roughly, this account of belief was endorsed by C. S. Peirce, who viewed belief as a "calm" and "satisfactory" state, in the nature of a "habit" (see "The Fixation of Belief" and "How To Make Our Ideas Clear," in Peirce, 1955.)

This account of acceptance carries with it a plausible account of its complement, *uncertainty,* which is to be viewed as a condition of continuing competition among rival alternatives whose relative attractiveness—here interpreted in terms of activation-level—is still in flux. It is an *unstable* state, that has not yet converged on any one contender. This depiction of uncertainty is phenomenologically appealing. Uncertainty is irresolution or indecision, a condition in which competing ideas battle one another without one clearly besting the others.

Apart from introspective appeal, this approach has the virtue of unifying the treatment of cognition and *choice* (or volition). The phenomenon of uncertainty is as central to the *volitional* domain as it is to the *doxastic*. The difference, of course, is that volition, or choice, is directed at behavioral alternatives, competing plans of *action* rather than hypotheses or propositions. But here, too, I propose, uncertainty consists in the absence of a clear-cut winner. There is continued oscillation among the set of contenders; or at least multiple contenders are kept "on hold" while deliberation continues. As long as such rivalry persists, there is the feeling of hesitancy, of tentativeness, of "not having made up one's mind." Felt uncertainty is the sense of *continuing competition* among contenders, while acceptance is the victory of one contender over all others. This parallel treatment of volitional decision fits well with the plausible conjecture that the same types of computing mechanisms subserve decision-making in both domains.

Perhaps the clearest cases of cognitive acceptance occur in perception. But I believe that the nonperceptual domain also tends to favor categorical, doxastic choice. While doxastic uncertainty, or indecision, is more common here than in the perceptual domain, there is a built-in preference for finding "winners." Thus, contrary to what the standard subjective probability model suggests, acceptance is a natural, highly prevalent doxastic state, not a radical or pathological state, as judged by the normal operating characteristics of the system. This idea was anticipated by Peirce, who viewed uncertainty, or "doubt," as an "irritation" of which the system seeks to rid itself by replacing it with belief.

Several other features of the neuropsychological models proposed by Feldman et al. suggest properties of doxastic activity different from those implied by typical subjective probability approaches. First, although their models do have a place for degrees of confidence—represented by the magnitude of a unit's output value (e.g., firing frequency)—there is no assumption that the degrees of confidence among a set of contenders must *sum* to a fixed value. This contrasts with the probability model, in which the sum of all mutually exclusive possibilities must equal 1.0. Second, mutual-inhibition networks tend to depress the activation level of most units, which can result in rapidly changing levels of confidence until some stable point is reached. I think this accounts for the familiar fact that people commonly find it difficult to specify precise degrees of confidence on the basis of introspection, or even to make comparative assessments of confidence. Typically, the activation levels associated with competing alternatives change too quickly. This contrasts with subjective probability approaches, which usually assume definite degrees of confidence.

At this point an objection arises. Surely people are *sometimes* capable of making precise probability estimates. This presumably explains their ability to settle on precise betting odds. How are these activities compatible with my remarks? The crucial point here is that judgments of probability need not always (or typically) be expressions of subjective confidence. They may be assessments of objective chance, i.e., *beliefs* in propositions about chance. (This is what I earlier called "propositionalized" uncertainty.) In making probability estimates of tomorrow's weather, a patient's prospects for recovery, or the outcome of a horse race, people assess objective chances, for which known (or believed) *frequencies* provide relevant clues. Where probability estimates are anchored to frequencies, rather than introspected credal intensities, definite numerical values are more easily formulated and accepted.

I have here sketched a model of acceptance and uncertainty that I regard as psychologically plausible. Its account of uncertainty is better than that of standard subjective probability models. Its neat accommodation of acceptance, which seems to be a psychologically robust phenomenon, also gives it superiority over those models. Finally, it fits within a general framework that can make claims for neural realism.

IV. ACCEPTANCE, JUSTIFICATION, AND PRUDENCE

The kind of model I have been sketching of acceptance and uncertainty is purely *descriptive*. Yet my introductory remarks characterized epistemology as an *evaluative* subject. It is time to turn— very briefly—to evaluative issues.

Let us now assume that human cognition widely employs WTA mechanisms, so categorical *belief* is widespread. What evaluative assessment should be made of these beliefs and of the mechanisms that generate them? In particular, can these processes yield *justified* (or warranted) beliefs? Recall my proposal that a belief's being justified depends on its being caused by a process (or a system of processes) with a high truth ratio. So the question of justifiedness becomes: does the process associated with a WTA mechanism have a high truth ratio? Is it "reliable"?

My main answer, at this juncture, is that the question cannot be answered without more information; but high reliability does not seem to be precluded. What further information is required? First, we need a more exact specification of the WTA process(es). Does the slightest difference in strength between two rival units reduce the weaker rival to zero? That is what the model sketched in section III provides. But alternatives to that model are readily available. There might be a constant d such that a given unit's strength is reduced to zero only when the strength of some rival unit exceeds it by at least d. If d is fairly large, it is hard for a unit to become a winner, thereby forestalling rash beliefs. Obviously, the exact value of such a d-parameter is a critical determinant of the truth ratio for any WTA mechanism.

Second, we need more information about rivalry, or competition. This may be illustrated with a lottery example. Suppose there is a 1,000 ticket lottery and S considers the proposition, "Ticket #1 will lose." Which propositions are its rivals? (For convenience I will speak of propositions as rivals, rather than the units that represent the propositions.) If rivals are only the *contraries* of a proposition, then presumably this proposition will be much stronger than all of its rivals. But suppose the rivals of proposition P include any proposition Q *negatively relevant* to it—that is, any proposition Q such that the probability of P given Q is smaller than the prior probability of P (see Lehrer, 1974). Then "Ticket #2 will lose," "Ticket #3 will lose," etc., will all be rivals of "Ticket #1 will lose." Since all these rivals are presumably tied in strength, no rival will be reduced to zero, and none will be accepted.

A third question to raise about a WTA process is how it performs when information is sparse. Although the evidence may favor one hypothesis over all rivals, its evidential support may nonetheless be (intuitively) weak. Does it still get accepted because all rivals have zero strength? Such a mechanism would not be conducive to a high truth ratio. (This problem is mentioned by Shastri and Feldman, 1984.)

Clearly, more needs to be known about WTA processes, and

about other cognitive processes they complement, before firm conclusions can be drawn about justificational rightness. However, the discussion suggests one conclusion: WTA networks *might* pass the test for justificational rightness.

Until now I have directed attention to the question of epistemic justifiedness, and its associated standard, reliability. But there are other standards of appraisal that should also interest epistemologists. Two that I would like to consider are *power,* or the range of questions of interest to which one can get true answers, and *speed,* the ability to get correct answers quickly. Let me briefly examine some implications of a WTA mechanism for speed and power. (Notice that while the desiderata of power and speed are distinct from reliability, all involve the acquisition of *true* belief.)

Any facet of a WTA mechanism that *delays* acceptance obviously works against speed. For example, the larger the d-parameter, the more it will take for the mechanism to reject rivals. Hence, it will take longer, on the average, for the mechanism to select a winner. Similarly, the more the cognitive system seeks and creates competing coalitions, which might give an initially favored hypothesis a run for its money, the slower the system will be in selecting a winner. Of course, both of these traits would enhance reliability, but there would be loss in speed.

It seems likely that the human system is speed-sensitive, not just reliability-sensitive. In language understanding, for example, the hearer processes sentences very rapidly, normally selecting a unique grammatical parsing and a unique semantical interpretation for each sentence, even where there are (in principle) several alternative parsings and readings. (Of course, if there is a special language module, this fact may not say much about doxastic decisions in other domains. But it is certainly suggestive of a design that is oriented toward speed considerations.)

The core of a WTA device may also be seen as sensitive to considerations of power. The fundamental impact of a WTA device is to remove clutter from active memory. As long as rivals are competing with a given hypothesis, active memory will be cluttered with items requiring processing resources. This makes it more difficult to move on to *other questions* that could be answered. Selection of a *winner* settles an issue, and allows the mind to proceed more quickly to the rest of its agenda, enabling it (in principle) to solve a larger number of problems.

What I have said thus far shows that a WTA mechanism is congenial to the desiderata of speed and power, but not incompatible with achieving high reliability. But other epistemologists have not viewed the idea of "acceptance" so favorably. It is time to mention a kind of objection that might be raised against any such doxastic act, more specifically, against a process that selects one hypothesis as a winner while reducing the strength of rival hypotheses to zero.

As background, notice that many theorists are attracted by what may be called a *pragmatic* criterion of evaluation. An example of a pragmatic criterion is one that evaluates cognitive processes by their impact on desire-satisfaction. Decision theory stresses that a cognizer's subjective probabilities are among the factors that determine the choice of behavior. And behavior, of course, may be more or less successful in obtaining outcomes that the agent desires. Now it may be suggested that an optimal cognitive system is one that so selects behavior as to optimize (the agent's) desire satisfaction. Is a WTA mechanism optimal according to this standard?

One problematic feature of a WTA mechanism leaps out in this context. It is in the nature of such a mechanism to reduce the strength of all but one of a set of competitors to zero. But does this not entail a loss of critical information, and an attendant tendency for nonpragmatic, or nonprudential, choices? Consider this example: You are driving on a two-lane road, and are pressed for time. There is little traffic in the opposite direction. You are now caught on a hill behind a slow truck. Should you try passing the truck, even though you cannot see over the hill? The sparsity of traffic going the opposite way suggests that the hypothesis "A car is coming over the hill" is much weaker than the hypothesis "No car is coming over the hill." It seems, then, as if a WTA mechanism might *reject* the former hypothesis and *accept* the latter. And once these decisions are plugged into a *behavioral* decision matrix, it looks like a decision to *pass* the truck will be made. Yet this seems likely to be a contra-pragmatic, contraprudential choice. If the objective probability of a car coming is, say, .15, and if you act this way repeatedly in similar situations, the long-run performance of these mental mechanisms will probably lead to a very bad (long-term) payoff.

There are several possible ways of countering this objection, granting (for the sake of argument) the appropriateness of a pragmatic criterion of evaluation. First, an acceptance process does not necessarily preclude the retention of probabilistic information. A person could accept propositions about objective chance as the content of beliefs, and use these beliefs in behavioral choice. In the driving example, one could accept the proposition, "The chance that a car is coming in the opposite lane is .15." Thus, an acceptance mechanism potentially has a device for satisfying the indicated prudential desiderata. Admittedly, this must involve belief contents that invoke an *objective* probability notion, the use of which is philosophically problematic. But if sense *cannot* be made of objective probabilities, it is unclear that the prudential criticism can be properly motivated in the first place. Certainly the objection being considered relies on objective probabilities.

Second, there is another possible mechanism that would avert the bad consequences of acceptance. Suppose there is a cognitive mechanism that is sensitive to possible payoffs with *extreme values* (very rewarding or very threatening outcomes). This mechanism heightens the activation level of any hypothesis H that is believed to make some extreme payoff likely. Such heightened activation level would tend to prevent such a hypothesis from being rejected, would keep it "in contention," and hence keep it from being ignored during behavioral choice. In the foregoing example, the threat of a fatal accident heightens the activation level associated with "A car is coming." This keeps it from being rejected, and keeps its negation from being accepted. Thus, the choice of the "don't pass" option is promoted. (I don't have a specific model to present about how the choice would then be made. But many such models could readily be constructed.)

I suspect that human beings *do* have some such mechanism. Indeed, it may be just the mechanism that accounts for wishful thinking and for fearful thinking. The present analysis shows how such a mechanism can have prudential merit—even if it has attendant liabilities regarding its reliability. If a cognizer *believes* hypotheses largely because they would, if true, fulfill his fondest dreams or deepest fears, these beliefs are unlikely to have a high truth ratio. But forestalling the rejection and submergence of such hypotheses may well have the indicated prudential trade-off. An acceptance mechanism with built-in sensitivity to extreme values may thereby pass the test of prudential effectiveness.

This proposal is obviously rather speculative. But these are examples of the evaluative issues that epistemology should raise, on the assumption that WTA mechanisms do, indeed, inhabit the human brain.

Finally, suppose it were concluded that any acceptance mechanism is, on the whole, inferior to a subjective probability mechanism. Still, human beings may well be *stuck* with an acceptance mechanism. Why, then, expend theoretical energy exploring the properties of mechanisms it might be nice to have, if we do not in fact have them? Why spend time bemoaning the actual machinery of our minds if there is nothing we can do about it? Why not seek the best procedures that are realistically available to human cognition? If acceptance mechanisms, or WTA mechanisms, are basic, wired-in features of our cognitive architecture, epistemology should be concerned with their optimal utilization. It should not expend too much energy over subjective probability models, which, while arguably "ideal," are not realizable by human beings. At any rate, this is how "naturalized" epistemology, on my view, would look at the matter.

REFERENCES

Goldman, A. I. *Epistemology and Cognition* (Cambridge, Mass.: Harvard University Press, 1986).

Feldman, J. A. and D. H. Ballard. "Connectionist Models and Their Properties," *Cognitive Science* 6 (1982):205–254.

Lehrer, K. *Knowledge* (Oxford: Oxford University Press, 1974).

Peirce, C. S. *Philosophical Writings of Peirce,* J. Buchler, ed. (New York: Dover Publications, 1955).

Rumelhart, D. E. and D. A. Norman "Introduction," in G. E. Hinton and J. A. Anderson, eds., *Parallel Models of Associative Memory* (Hillsdale, N. J.: Erlbaum, 1981).

Shastri, L. and J. A. Feldman "Semantic Networks and Neural Nets" (University of Rochester Computer Science Department, Technical Report 131, 1984).

Tversky, A. and D. Kahneman "Extensional Versus Intuitive Reasoning: The Conjunction Fallacy in Probability Judgment," *Psychological Review,* 90 (1983):293–315.

Christopher Cherniak

Rationality and Anatomy

Professor Goldman's paper addresses two important ideas: a compatibilist treatment of the notions of acceptance and degree of confidence, and a "neurally realistic" model of the foregoing. In this brief and preliminary discussion, I want to focus on the latter, that is, on the basic idea of neuroanatomically and neurophysiologically realistic models of rationality, and on their philosophical significance. One can argue that the fact that human beings are in the finitary predicament of having fixed limits on their cognitive resources of memory and of computation time (*homo sapiens* do not have God's brain, nor a Turing machine's potentially unlimited spatio-temporal resources, and so on) has epistemologically interesting consequences. And one can go on to claim further that a psychologically realistic model of, for instance, the structure of human memory (e.g., taking account of the fact that our working memory has a very limited capacity relative to our long-term memory) has similar philosophical relevance. Can a philosophically interesting realism be extended down yet another level, to brain anatomy and physiology?

Besides the fact that the nervous system consists of discrete nerve cells, probably the most fundamental fact of its anatomy is its massive parallelism: For example, each retina contains about 130 million receptors, funneling into an optic nerve of about 1 million fibers, which then begins to fan out into a brain of 100 billion neurons. Since 1980, various workers in artificial intelligence (notably Geoffrey Hinton, Jerome Feldman, and Dana Ballard[1]) have focused on the brain's parallelism, especially as it contrasts so sharply with the one-operation-at-a-time bottleneck of standard von Neumann-architecture sequential computing machinery. However, parallel computation is no free ride. It has a cost: it is "nonadaptive," since at each instant, it can make no use of results of all the computations then in progress. In addition, the brain computation models now emerging entail not just massive parallelism, but also massive interconnection of neurons; hence the name "New Connectionism." One worries a little, though, about the false-dawn history of Perceptrons in the 1950s repeating itself here. Or again, neoconnectionists like to point to cheap chips as a harbinger of practical parallel machine architecture; but very large-scale integration (VLSI) layout is a notorious snakepit of deep and fascinating difficulties for interconnecting "many"—e.g., a mere hundred thousand—simple components. Let us explore a little more neuroanatomical realism in our models.

UNLIMITED INTERCONNECTIONS

A winner-take-all (WTA) network, a typical neoconnectionist device, requires only $(n - 1)^2$ mutually inhibitory interconnections among its n neurons. (Feldman and Ballard's example of a WTA network has a wiring error; some connections are missing.[2]) Some of the other Feldman-Ballard connectionist devices require enormously larger numbers of connections.[3] But we shall begin with the ultimate heuristic fantasy, absolutely unlimited interconnectability. That is, imagine all dendrites and axons in neural networks as *infinitely thin;* their total value and synaptic contact area to a given neuron are always zero. We also shall employ the simplest model of a neuron, as just a standard "and," "or," or "not" logic gate, with a cell body the diameter of a proton—that is, absurdly, but not infinitely, small. It is important to be aware that there are still severe computation constraints, particularly on formally correct algorithms for decidable portions of logic and mathematics.

For example, weak monadic second-order theory of successor (WSLS) is a decidable fragment of elementary arithmetic; there is no multiplication operator, no addition except of a constant, but quantification over sets is possible. A typical (true) WSlS formula is, "$\forall n \exists m(m < n+1)$." In 1975, Albert Meyer proved that the decision problem for WSlS has "super-exponential" computational complexity. In addition, Meyer and Larry Stockmeyer showed, in effect, that just deciding truth or falsehood of any WSlS statement of 617 symbols or less in length must require a "neural network" of the above idealized variety that could not be densely packed into a sphere of 20 billion light-years radius—the size of the known universe, to the "relativistic horizon."[4] (The ultimate speed limit of the velocity of light for signal propagation imposes a fundamental size-speed tradeoff on computers: There must be worst cases where the running time of this machine would be at least twice the age of the universe. The machine would also suffer from an appalling clock-skew problem.)

The moral of this story is that even a connectionist free lunch for a brain the size of the universe would not eliminate, or in some cases even much reduce, computation constraints. Formally correct decision procedures for logic and mathematics just seem to be computationally intractable *simpliciter,* whether executed on a standard von Neumann-architecture sequential machine, or on massively parallel machines.

ANATOMICAL REALISM

Let us proceed, by successive approximations, to a less anatomically idealized model of a neuron. A moderate maximal interconnectionist scenario would presumably be that every neuron in the brain can directly connect to every other brain neuron. In terms of anatomy, rather than only the laws of physics, just how impossible would that be? The typical human cranial volume is 1.4 liters; estimates of a decade ago were that the brain contained only about 10 billion neurons. The average volume of a single neuron would then be about 10^{14} cubic nanometers. [A nanometer (nm) is a millionth of a millimeter (10^{-6} mm); e.g., the length of a visible light wave is around 500 nm.] We consider an "all-dendrite cell," in which the *entire* volume of the neuron serves just to receive interconnections, in the form of synaptic boutons or terminals from other cells. A typical synaptic bouton's contact area equals a square about 1,000 nm on a side, but let's start with a bouton that has a "synaptic footprint" of a square only 100 nm on a side, so the contact area will be 10^4 square nm.

We also assume a cell with the maximum physiologically feasible surface-to-volume ratio; a cell in the shape of a single fiber, rather than a sheet of equal thinness, would have a greater surface area. The fiber can no longer be infinitely thin, but let us say it has a square cross-section with the area of only 1 synaptic bouton. (Thus, each 4 synapses onto the surface of this fiber will require 1 "bouton cube" of the fiber's volume—that is, a 100 nm-edge cube, of 10^6 cubic nm volume.) The maximum "fan-in," i.e., the largest possible number of input connections to the surface of such an all-dendrite cell, would therefore be about 4×10^8 (400 million) synapses. The *memento mori* point of this back-of-the-envelope exponentiation is that, for the above, still anatomically idealized neuron, not all 10^{10} brain cells could each synapse on each other; only 1 in 100 could interconnect to a given cell. This type of maximal interconnectionism is *deeply* impossible.

Let us briefly consider one last, more anatomically realistic model of a neuron. What would be the upper bound on brain cell interconnection? First, more recent estimates of the total neuron population of the human brain are 100 billion, not 10 billion.[5] Second, perhaps only one third of the cranial volume consists of neurons: Some 90 percent of brain cells are glial cells, involved in neuron maintenance; there are Schwann cells, constituting the myelin "insulating" sheath on many axons (to increase conduction velocity), and the brain of course contains an extremely extensive circulatory system. Third, a real cell cannot be all dendrite: Following the standard tripartite division of dendrite, soma, axon, we might allow one third of a "typical" neuron's volume for its cell body and other structures exclusively involved in cellular nutrition and maintenance (the brain is the most metabolically active tissue in the human body). And we can allow another one third for the functions of the axon, that is, rapid long-distance conduction of impulses and making synaptic contact with other neurons. Dendritic volume per neuron is then about 10^{12} cubic nm. Fourth, we will assume the actual area of the typical synaptic bouton, namely, 10^6 square nm.

Finally, let us still suppose that the dendritic volume is in the form of a single fiber averaging just one bouton in width. Then about 4×10^3 synapses can connect to the surface of each cell. And in fact, this neuronal model turns out to agree with anatomical reality in that this synapse-to-cell ratio is of the same order of magnitude as is actually observed in the human brain.[6] This agreement in turn raises some question about whether the observed interconnectedness may be close to the absolute, theoretically possible limit in the way that the sensitivities of the human eye and ear, for example, are known to approach their theoretical limits.

LOCAL INTERCONNECTIONISM

So, anatomical reality would permit at most only a set of about 4,000 neurons to be maximally interconnected, e.g., with *just* the mutually inhibitory wiring of a WTA network. If anatomy is destiny in this way, neoconnectionist allusions, such as Geoffrey Hinton's, to the brain's millionfold parallelism would benefit from explicit qualification regarding limits to growth of interconnections: only moderate interconnectability is possible. One additional point can be extracted from neuroanatomy concerning the structure of these interconnections: they cannot be homogeneously distributed. Instead, throughout the nervous system, there is strong *local* interconnection, and relatively weak interconnection of more remote areas. For example, in retinas—whether horseshoe crab or human—lateral inhibition of surrounding receptors radiates out from a stimulated receptor, somewhat as in a WTA network. However, the strength of this lateral inhibition is inversely proportional to the distance of a given receptor from the excited receptor. Some straightforward modeling of the retina suggests a directly corresponding drop-off in anatomical connections from the stimulated receptor with distance.[7]

And if we proceed inward to the visual areas of the cerebral cortex, there is the same pattern of local more than global interconnection. In the 1950s Roger Sperry and his associates showed that vertical cuts—indeed, *cross-hatching*—into the visual cortex of cats and monkeys did not affect their visual pattern discrimination abilities.[8] (While the cross-hatching entirely severed interconnections within the cortex between adjacent areas averaging less than 1 mm square, the more limited "vertical" deep fiber tracts interconnecting remote cortical areas remained intact.) David Hubel and Torsten Wiesel's findings[9] of a "columnar" structure to the anatomy and function of the visual cortex (with columns about half a millimeter in diameter) again indicate predominantly local surface interconnections.

WORKING MEMORY LIMITATIONS

The anatomical hypothesis of moderate local interconnectionism in fact fits with an intuitive conclusion: that in comparing alternative propositions for acceptance, human beings cannot consider 1,000 candidates. Instead, people consider much smaller sets of propositions. The above discussion suggests that using a strongly interconnected WTA network to compare simultaneously many alternatives would be an anatomical impossibility. After all, neurons (or neuron groups) have other synaptic tasks besides just mutually inhibiting each other—e.g., receiving external input, recurrent (i.e., self) inhibition, and so on.

And this point—that WTA networks must be quite small, in that a person can consider conjointly only a relatively small number of propositions—also seems to gain some further confirmation when we turn to temporal, as opposed to spatial, limitations of the nervous system. Impulse conduction velocity along an axon here stays below a 55 mph speed limit, unlike the speed-of-light signal propagation in an electronic computer. (This in itself entails an interesting "cerebral clock-skew" problem for coordinating events across the brain.) Neoconnectionists[10] point out that the "neuronal cycle time" for an elementary operation within the brain must then be on the order of a few milliseconds. Reaction time experiments indicate that the computation time for a single decision is a few hundred milliseconds. The conclusion drawn is that decisions have to be computed in around 100 time steps.

Let us now consider the cognitive task of determining only the truth-functional consistency of a set of propositions. This is known as the "satisfiability problem" in computational complexity theory (it is a member of the class of NP-complete computational problems, which are strongly conjectured to be intrinsically intractable[11]). And let us imagine a mind using the familiar truth-table method for consistency-checking (no other algorithm is faster for worst cases), where one truth-table line can be tested per neuronal cycle. The number of lines in a truth table is 2^n (rather than n^2), where n is the number of logically independent ("atomic") propositions in the set of formulas being evaluated. Now, $2^6 = 64$, $2^7 = 128$, and $2^8 = 256$. So, the largest number of independent propositions that can be evaluated in this way for consistency within the 100 time-step limit is around 7.

We thus return from limits on computation time to space, at least psychological space. For, it is another possibly interesting coincidence that about seven "chunks," or meaningful units of information (whether randomly chosen digits, syllables, or words), is the well-known capacity of human short-term working memory, in contrast to the virtually unlimited capacity of long-term memory; the title of George Miller's classic review article on this point was, "The Magical Number Seven, Plus or Minus Two: Some Limits on Our Capacity for Processing Information."[12] What is significant here is not that we might thereby have uncovered any sort of confirmation of the physiological reality of formally correct consistency-testing methods for small sets of propositions. (I have in fact argued elsewhere that, for more complex logic tasks, people seem to use formally incorrect heuristics involving prototypical examples.[13]) The point of interest is that this limitation on human working memory capacity, derived from temporal features of the nervous system, seems to converge with the WTA network limitations that emerged earlier from neuroanatomical connectivity constraints.

PHILOSOPHICAL IMPLICATIONS

What has such a local connectivity constraint to do with philosophy? To bring out its epistemological—in particular, normative—import, it is helpful to return to the last part of Professor Goldman's paper, where the concluding point might be stated as: Philosophers ought to explore rationality standards that are realizable by a human brain, rather than a Cartesian simple substance, or whatever. The discussion here has suggested that, when we apply such a neuroanatomical realizability constraint to neoconnectionist models themselves, we uncover the basic fact that the maximum number of propositions that can be conjointly considered (whether for comparing probabilities, or consistency-testing) is stringently limited. We may thus have some better understanding of the depth of the impossibility of a human being simultaneously processing a set of propositions much larger than "the magical numer seven," the observed short-term working memory capacity. In this sense, the actual may approach the ideal, and not just be an accident of our particular anatomy.

Massive parallelism is no free lunch; neural interconnections are themselves a seriously limited resource. The anatomical constriant that strong interconnection can only be relatively local entails a cognitive cost, that WTA networks (e.g., as models of belief) must involve correspondingly restricted sets of alternatives. As an important example, such a limited "span of awareness" in turn will entail preference intransitivities, contrary to standard decision-theoretic models[14] That is, human beings will be constitutionally unable at one (specious) moment always to notice that alternative A is better than B, and B is better than C; as a result, they will sometimes inconsistently rank C over A.

The points that have emerged here are: (1) Such behavior is not mere "noise," or minor exceptions to normal behavior; it seems a symptom consistent with some fundamental local connectivity constraints. (2) Consequently, with a realistic connectivity model, preference intransitivities also do not seem an inexplicable freak of nature; in contrast, Donald Davidson has described how he quit empirical research in decision theory because he could not account for subjects' observed intransitivities in terms of a standard ideal decision-theoretic model.[15] (3) Finally, a limited-connectivity account justifies some of the ways of Mother Nature to humans: That is, neuroanatomical reality suggests another entire level of global rationale for moderate (not unlimited) inconsistency in a cognitive system. Rather than being baffling irrationality, it may be an unavoidable compromise with our very anatomy. Anatomical, as well as psychological, reality is then philosophically relevant, in that one cannot otherwise fully understand human rationality. Also, the anatomy tells us something about what we *ought* to do with regard to our choice of epistemic strategies. In this way, even for epistemology, anatomy matters.

NOTES

1. See, for example, G. Hinton and J. Anderson, eds., *Parallel Models of Associative Memory* (Hillsdale, N.J.: L. Erlbaum, 1981); and J. Feldman and D. Ballard, "Connectionist Models and Their Properties," *Cognitive Science* 6 (1982):205-254.

2. See fig. 12, p. 229, op. cit.

3. See, for example, pp. 237-238, op. cit.

4. A Meyer, "Weak Monadic Second-Order Theory of Successor is Not Elementary-Recursive," in A. Dold and B. Eckmann, eds., *Lecture Notes in Mathematics,* no. 453, (New York: Springer-Verlag, 1975). L. Stockmeyer and A. Chandra, "Intrinsically Difficult Problems," *Scientific American* 240 (1979): 140–159. See also D. Knuth, "Mathematics and Computer Science: Coping With Finiteness," *Science* 194 (1976):1235–1242.

5. See, for example, D. Hubel, "The Brain," *Scientific American* 241 (1979): 44–53 (especially pp. 46, 49); and C. Stevens, "The Neuron," op. cit. pp. 53–65 (especially p. 55). Also useful for the following discussion is the neurology section of P. Williams and R. Warwick, *Gray's Anatomy,* 36th British ed., (Philadelphia: W. B. Saunders, 1980).

6. See Hubel, op. cit.; Stevens, op. cit.

7. See, for example, T. Cornsweet's discussion of psychophysical data on the modulation transfer function of the retina (especially p. 360), in his *Visual Perception* (New York: Academic Press, 1970).

8. R. Sperry, N. Miner, and R. Meyers, "Visual Pattern Perception Following Subpial Slicing and Tantalum Wire Implantations in the Visual Cortex," *Journal of Comparative and Physiological Psychology* 48 (1955):50–58.

9. For a recent review, see D. Hubel and T. Wiesel, "Brain Mechanisms of Vision," *Scientific American* 241 (1979):150–162. On the local nature of cortical connections, see especially p. 152.

10. E. g., Feldman and Ballard, op. cit., p. 206.

11. For a review of some philosophically relevant aspects of complexity theory, see my "Computational Complexity and the Universal Acceptance of Logic," *Journal of Philosophy* 81 (1984): 739–758.

12. *Psychological Review* 63 (1956):81–97.

13. See my "Protoypicality and Deductive Reasoning," *Journal of Verbal Learning and Verbal Behavior* 23 (1984): 625–642.

14. As I have pointed out in "Rationality and the Structure of Human Memory," *Synthese* 57 (1983): 163–186.

15. See "Psychology as Philosophy" (especially pp. 235–236), in *Essays on Actions and Events* (New York: Oxford University Press, 1980).

Erwin M. Segal

The Limits of Reductionism
A Discussion of
"Epistemology and the New Connectionism"

The paper by Professor Goldman implies that the way to study doxastic states such as belief is to explore "basic, wired-in features of our cognitive architecture." Such study, however, tells us very little about belief. Beliefs are controlled by variations in events outside of the organism that can be only partially correlated with wired-in neurological features. They are affected by one's social history and academic education. It is even possible to change beliefs with arguments. One must consider the variables that affect beliefs before attempting to identify the psychophysiological mechanisms that support them. If proposed physiological mechanisms are to be explained, they must be consistent with psychological phenomena. For example, if one can assign subjective probability to an event, and there are no known physiological mechanisms that can be used to assign subjective probability, too bad for those mechanisms.

Goldman implies that there must be one basic universal neurological mechanism that causes beliefs in humans. However, the evidence for such a position is nonexistent. The evidence that simple excitatory-inhibitory, winner-take-all (WTA) mechanisms are the primary basis for beliefs is still worse. WTA mechanisms are probably important; they probably play an important role in perception, comprehension, and action; but as currently described, they are often incompatible with a person's belief.

The cognitive domains to which connectionist models in general, and WTA mechanism in particular, seem to be most easily applied are those in which a given local input may be interpreted differently depending upon how it relates to its neighbors, either at the same cognitive levels or at different ones. The purpose of connectionist models is to resolve ambiguity quickly and silently. By so doing they usually lead to a reasonable interpretation of some stimulus situation. A few examples may clarify the function of this interpretation.

Most American readers would have no problem reading aloud and comprehending the following sentence (modified from Waltz and Pollack, 1985):

1. Phil shot two bucks in the north wood.

The words are all simple to comprehend and easy to pronounce. One does not notice that several letters have different pronunciations in different word contexts. For example, "h," "s," "o," "t," and "w," all have multiple pronunciations in this short sentence. These letters are unambiguous units at an alphabetic level, but feed into multiple representations at a phonetic level. How does one explain why we pronounce "o" as "oh" in one location and as "oo" in another? At another structural level, all the words in the sentence, with the possible exception of "the," have multiple meanings: either as a function of their orthography, their pronunciation, or both. In spite of the ambiguity, at least on the first reading, only one interpretation enters consciousness. Why is "fil" perceived as a man's name in one context, and an action of putting something in a container in another? This is due to the context within which it appears, and the structure of the information in memory to which it relates. Theories using parallel connectionist systems are, in part, attempts to build mechanisms that result in these psychological phenomena.

Similar psychological phenomena can be seen at even a higher structural level. By making what seems to be a minor change—substituting one locative noun phrase for another at the end of the sentence—the perceived meaning of the sentence is changed. In most contexts

2. Phil shot two bucks in Atlantic City

conveys a different action and object than that conveyed by

the first sentence. The different meanings normally occur without the ambiguity being noticed.

Another example of a situation in which parallel interactive mechanisms may be proposed is depicted in figure 1.

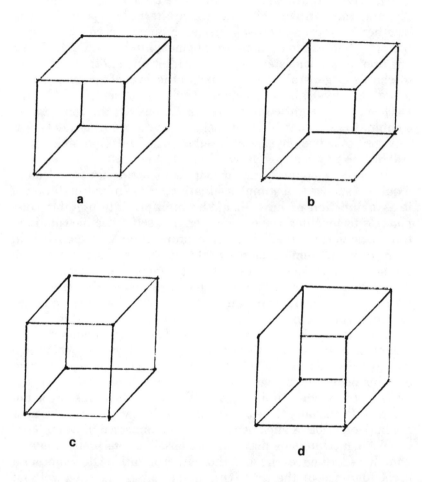

Figure 1.

The two "boxes" designated by 1a and 1b are most often perceived to be configured differently from each other. The back wall of 1b is located in the same relative position as the front wall of 1a. Each visible outside wall in 1b is a partially occluded inner wall in 1a and vice versa. In order for these different percepts to occur, corresponding identical local stimuli have to be interpreted differently; in particular, the two Y-like intersections in the middle, and the "arrows" opposite them alternate depending upon whether they are viewed as inside or outside corners. Possible percepts that lead to a consistent physical interpretation facilitate one another, inconsistent percepts inhibit one another. Proposed mechanisms generally iterate beneath the level of awareness until a stable, physically consistent structure is perceived. In the Necker (1c) all eight corners are ambiguous. Of the 256 possible combinations of outside and inside corners, we alternately perceive only the two physically possible ones. The impossible figure (1d) has no physically consistent resolution of its corners.

In general, connectionist mechanisms are designed to lead to a quick response to a stimulus situation, or to an interpretation of it as a function of how all of the multiply interpretable components fit together. Belief, however, is a self-reflective condition that depends on analyzing some proposition or experience in terms of what seems to be relevant to it. An analysis may lead to the same conclusion as an automatic response, but not necessarily. Moreover, reflective outcomes are potentially reversible. By receiving new relevant information one's belief may change, regardless of whether the phenomenal experience is affected.

Illusions are situations in which WTA mechanisms may be seen to be at variance with reality. By rational or empirical analysis most people come to believe that the perceptual experience of an illusion is untrustworthy. Is the moon larger when on the horizon than when it is high in the sky? Do roads on a hot summer day usually have a layer of sparkling water on them near the horizon? Does a stick bend when it is immersed in water?

WTA mechanisms may support possible interpretations of a stimulus situation, even when those interpretations do not occur a preponderance of the time. Organisms often must act without having time to think. Birds at my feeder often fly away to escape a predator even when none appears. Animals frequently check possible food sources without finding food. Complex situations do not allow one to wait to react until the consequences of the stimulus situation have a very high probability of occurring. There is no reason to believe that humans are different from other animals in this regard.

Many perceptual situations have uncertain consequences. Alternatives can be anticipated. People carry umbrellas if they believe it may rain, or sweaters if they believe the weather may become cooler. Most of us will not pass on a two-lane road if the opposing lane is visually obscured regardless of the paucity of oncoming traffic. We are aware that both of the following propositions are possibly true: "A car is approaching" and "A car is not approaching." Some of us buy lottery tickets although we "know" that we will not win, because we also believe a win is possible. Although most people are not able to derive a consistent probability calculus over alternative events, they believe that alternative outcomes are possible. Although one outcome may be much more likely than another, a low probability outcome can be expected to some degree and thus anticipated.

Beliefs cannot be solely controlled by "basic, wired-in features of our cognitive architecture." People are not always rational, but they may learn to be more rational than they are. Amos Tversky and Daniel Kahneman (see Kahneman, Slovic, and Tversky, 1982) have collected a large amount of data showing that people often use strategies to arrive at beliefs that are not logically valid. This is not evidence that beliefs are automatic consequences of some automatic process, but rather that certain heuristics used by many people may lead to conclusions that are grossly in error. One heuristic they have investigated is representativeness. An outcome is judged more likely to be a member of a class if it is more similar to a typical member of the class. This heuristic may lead one to commit a conjunction fallacy. For example, a personality sketch of "Bill" led most subjects to conclude that he was more likely to be an accountant who played jazz for a hobby than just someone who played jazz for a hobby. However, when some of the subjects were asked "to consider the argument that, 'the probability that Bill is both an accountant and a jazz player cannot exceed the probability that he is a jazz player, because every member of the former category is also a member of the latter,' [m]ore than two-thirds of the subjects . . . agreed after some reflection, that their answer was wrong" (Tversky and Kahneman, 1982, p. 95).

Belief states are often learnable and reflective, and justified by a reasoned consideration of varied information. WTA mechanisms are fast and automatic, and designed to explain the resolution of ambiguous local stimuli. They are not the same. The major problem with any enterprise that explains belief by focusing on characterizing the neurological mechanisms within an organism is that the focus is at the wrong level of description. Although the processes within the body must be ontologically consistent with belief states, they are epistemologically and structurally independent of them. Beliefs must be characterized by constraints in the environment. To the extent that they are a function of argument and information, a theory of belief states must be established as a function of the kinds of information and arguments that lead to such states. Any other enterprise is secondary.

REFERENCES

Kahneman, D., P. Slovic, and A. Tversky, eds., *Judgment Under Uncertainty: Heuristics and Biases* (New York: Cambridge University Press, 1982).

Tversky, A., and D. Kahneman, "Judgments of and by Representativeness," in D. Kahneman, P. Slovic, and A. Tversky, eds., *Judgment Under Uncertainty: Heuristics and Biases* (New York: Cambridge University Press, 1982).

Waltz, D. L., and J. B. Pollack, "Massively Parallel Parsing: A Strongly Interactive Model of Natural Language Interpretation," *Cognitive Science* 9 (1985): 51–74.

Hilary Kornblith

Naturalizing Rationality

I

Questions about rationality ask how we ought to arrive at our beliefs. Such questions may be asked from either of two perspectives; I will call them the internal and the external perspective. The goal of this paper will be to make clear the content of the normative question about belief acquisition when viewed from the internal perspective.

An analogy with moral theory is useful here. When evaluating an agent's conduct, there are two importantly different perspectives from which we may view the question, "How ought the agent to act?" The external perspective has us ask this question: What does the objectively correct moral theory dictate that the agent should do in his current circumstances? The internal perspective, however, has us ask this question: What should the agent do in his current circumstances by his own lights? These questions may, of course, come apart, for agents frequently have moral beliefs that are objectively false.

I have received helpful comments on an earlier version of this paper from Mark Heller, Christopher Maloney, Duncan MacIntosh, David Shatz, George Sher, William Wilcox, and audiences at Syracuse University and the Buffalo Conference. I am sorry to say that time pressure has not allowed me to take account of many of these suggestions to the extent I would like. My work has been supported by a generous grant from the National Endowment for the Humanities.

We overlook an important aspect of moral evaluation if we fail to adopt either of these perspectives. If we adopt only the external perspective, we have no idea whether the action under evaluation manifested moral integrity. If we adopt only the internal perspective, we have no idea whether the action was morally acceptable. A fully adequate evaluation of conduct requires that we assess it from both the internal and the external perspectives.

Things are much the same in epistemology as they are in moral philosophy. When we ask how an agent ought to arrive at his beliefs, we may adopt either the external or the internal perspective. As in moral philosophy, we overlook an important kind of evaluation if we fail to adopt either of these perspectives. The internal perspective tells us only how things stand from the agent's point of view; the external perspective tells us only how things actually stand.[1]

II

Identifying the internal perspective was once an easy task. It no longer is. In order to explain why there is a problem about identifying the internal perspective, I will begin by presenting briefly René Descartes's account of it. Descartes's theory of mind makes the internal perspective easily locatable. Unfortunately, it will turn out that it is the most implausible features of Descartes's account of the mind that make it easy for him to locate the internal perspective. This will leave us with a problem: How may we locate the internal perspective within the constraints of a reasonable theory of the mind?

In the first Meditation, Descartes lays out the method of doubt. He is concerned to find those things about which it is impossible to be in doubt; those things about which it is impossible to be mistaken. By the end of the second Meditation, Descartes has met with some success. He has found that he can be mistaken about neither the fact of his existence nor the contents of his present states of mind. These successes set the problem for the remainder of the Meditations: What additional knowledge can be projected from this base?

This statement of the problem allows us to locate the internal perspective. According to Descartes, the mind is endowed with certain faculties that allow for infallible self-perception. By the end of the third Meditation, the scope of infallibility is expanded to include epistemic principles: Whatever is clearly and distinctly perceived is true. At this point, Descartes has marked a significant difference between two mental faculties. On the one side we have perception of the external world, which is subject to error. On the other side is introspection, which is not only infallible, but known by an infallible method to be infallible. The internal perspective is the perspective of the infallible faculty of introspection.

Descartes's epistemic principles were designed to guarantee truth, but this need not be required to make sense of the internal perspective in the way Descartes did. We may allow for epistemic principles that, while fallible, guarantee justification, so long as the epistemic principles themselves are infallibly known to guarantee justification. Even on this weakened Cartesian view, the internal perspective is bound up with an infallible faculty of introspection.

This linking of the internal perspective with an infallible faculty allows us one way of understanding the importance of the internal perspective. Descartes is concerned with what we may call the Problem of Doxastic Advice: What is the best advice we can give to a truth-seeking agent? Consider the following advice: Believe whatever Dan Rather says. This may, in many respects, be quite good advice. Indeed, let us assume that Rather never makes a mistake. In this case, it is excellent advice. Nevertheless, this kind of advice fails utterly to perform the job Descartes wants doxastic advice to do. There are two reasons for this failure. First, the truth-seeking agent may not have access to what Dan Rather says. Second, even assuming such access, the truth-seeking agent may not have any reason to believe that Rather is a reliable source of information. From the external perspective, the advice to believe whatever Rather says is excellent, but from the perspective of a truth-seeking agent it may be either useless or reckless.

Descartes's solution to the Problem of Doxastic Advice is intimately tied to his views about the powers of the faculty of introspection. He believes it is possible to give doxastic advice that is both usable by every agent and infallibly known by every agent to be good advice. This is possible, on Descartes's view, not only because the faculty of introspection is infallible, but also because the mind and the principles of proper reason are wholly transparent to it. There simply are no features of the mind or of proper reason that are not wholly and infallibly accessible to introspection. There is thus a level at which doxastic advice may be pitched so that it is impossible for either of the problems to arise that arose for the advice to believe what Dan Rather says. The proper level for such advice is the level of facts accessible to the faculty of introspection.

The importance of the internal perspective on this view is thus that it provides us with a level at which to pitch doxastic advice so that we may solve the Problem of Doxastic Advice once and for all, for all agents. This is so even if one adopts the weakened Cartesian view on which epistemic principles do not guarantee truth.

Although this explains the importance of the internal perspective for Descartes, it does not help us. Recent work in philosophy of mind, philosophy of language, and epistemology has shown the untenability of claims to incorrigibility. Moreover, the thesis of the transparency of both the mind and the principles of proper reasoning to infallible introspection is clearly absurd.

We are thus left with a problem. Both the importance and the location of the internal perspective are easily seen on Descartes's view, but this view rests on an account of the mind that is clearly untenable. What, then, are we to make of the internal perspective once we reject Descartes's extraordinarily optimistic assessment of our mental faculties?

III

My own motivation for seeking to make explicit the content of the internal perspective is not only different from Descartes's but diametrically opposed to it. His account of our mental faculties forces him to view the content of the internal perspective as the same for all agents; it is thus that he is able to give a single solution to the Problem of Doxastic Advice. On the contrary, it seems clear to me that different agents regard different modes of belief acquisition as reasonable; the content of the internal perspective shifts from agent to agent. Indeed, on my view it is precisely because of this shift that the internal perspective takes on the importance it does. Because internal perspectives differ

among agents, full evaluation of belief acquisition requires that
we adopt not only the external perspective but the perspective of
the agent in question as well.

Given this motivation, the internal perspective seems easily
locatable. An agent arrives at his beliefs in the way he ought to,
as viewed from the internal perspective, just in case he arrives at
his beliefs in the way he believes he ought to. The internal perspective is thus identified with the agent's beliefs about proper
belief acquisition.[2] Just as there is some plausibility to the view
that, in some sense, one ought to act as one believes one should,
this view about the internal perspective is just the view that there
is a straightforward sense in which one ought to arrive at one's
beliefs in the way one believes one should. Obvious as this suggestion is, I will argue that it does not provide us with an adequate
account of the internal perspective. There are, I believe, numerous
objections to this suggestion.[3] I will focus on one of these.

It is certainly possible to hold a belief and yet, at the same
time, believe that one is unjustified in holding that very belief. I
have heard many people say quite sincerely, "I believe that God
exists, but by my own lights, I am not justified in believing that
God exists." There is no contradiciton here. It is not that such a
person believes both that God does and does not exist. Rather,
such a person believes that God exists, regards this belief as
unjustified, and finds that so regarding the belief does not make
it go out of existence. What I want to suggest is that this may
happen not only with the belief that God exists, but also with the
belief that certain ways of arriving at one's beliefs are correct.
Thus, I will argue that an agent's belief that certain ways of
arriving at one's beliefs are correct may itself be unjustified by
the agent's lights. If this is so, it is incorrect to identify the internal perspective with the agent's beliefs about correct ways of
acquiring beliefs.

An autobiographical example will be useful here. I have many
beliefs about correct means of acquiring beliefs, and I often present and defend my views about belief acquisition in seminars. In
one semester, I was defending a certain view about proper belief
acquisition, when a student presented an extraordinarily cogent
attack on this view. The attack was so cogent that I was convinced that I was no longer justified in my belief about proper
belief acquisition. In spite of this, and without my realizing it, I

subsequently defended various other positions by showing how they followed from the undermined view. Each time this was pointed out to me, the error was obvious. Nevertheless, I was not aware of the error as I was making it.

On the basis of my behavior, I had to acknowledge that I still believed in the view about proper belief acquisition, which, by my own lights, my student had so effectively undermined. Although I thus believed that a certain method of belief acquisition was proper, this very belief was not, by my lights, justified. Moreover, although I believed a certain method of belief acquisition to be proper, this method was not one that I could endorse from the internal perspective.

It is thus clear that the internal perspective cannot be identified with the agent's beliefs about proper belief acquisition. Nevertheless, my example may suggest that the difficulties with this view may be repaired with only minor modification. Difficulties seem to arise when a belief about proper belief acquisition is held by the agent to be unjustified. Let us say that in such a case the belief about proper belief acquisition is undercut by a higher-order belief. We may now reformulate the thesis. The internal perspective of an agent should be identified with those beliefs about proper belief acquisition that are not undercut by higher-order beliefs.

Even this reformulation, however, will not work. Although my example shows that an agent's belief about proper belief acquisition may fail to constitute part of his internal perspective when he judges that very belief to be unjustified, this is not the only way in which such a belief may fail to reflect his internal perspective. Consider the following kind of case. Mary is reading a book on epistemology, and because of the author's smooth style, she comes to accept uncritically one of his suggestions about proper belief acquisition. Mary has no beliefs about this belief of hers, and so it is not undercut by a higher-order belief. Nevertheless, this new belief does not sit well with her other beliefs. As soon as Mary considers the matter, and she will do so shortly, she will reject her hastily acquired belief.

The belief Mary hastily acquires is never part of her internal perspective, in spite of the fact that it is not undercut by higher-order beliefs. If we wish to explain what Mary ought to believe by her own lights, it would be a mistake to appeal to beliefs such as this.

Our initial suggestion, that the internal perspective be identified with an agent's beliefs about proper belief acquisition, was inadequate. It failed to take into account that a belief may be undercut and thus fail to reflect the agent's perspective even if the agent does not explicitly believe it to be unjustified. The internal perspective obviously bears some relation to the agent's beliefs about proper belief acquisition. But this relation is not one of identity, nor is it the simple transformation suggested by the reformulation just considered.

IV

What, then, is the relation between an agent's beliefs about proper belief acquisition and his internal perspective? One suggestion worth exploring is that the internal perspective is achieved through some combination of conservative modifications of the agent's beliefs about proper belief acquisition, where the result of these modifications is a coherent account of the way beliefs ought to be acquired.[4] In evaluating this suggestion we will need to ask first, what this suggestion has to recommend it; and second, whether the crucial notions of coherence and conservatism can be explained with any precision.

That this suggestion has much to recommend it is easily seen, for the problems that arose for earlier accounts are easily dealt with on this view. Beliefs about proper belief acquisition need not constitute part of the internal perspective, for they may fail to cohere with other relevant beliefs the agent holds. Moreover, it is clear that a belief may fail to cohere with others even if it is not believed to be unjustified. Indeed, one may come to see a belief as unjustified precisely because one notices its failure to cohere with other beliefs. This account thus seems to avoid the difficulties of other views, while at the same time giving a plausible account of the connection between an agent's beliefs about proper belief acquisition and the nature of the internal perspective.

That the account is initially plausible should encourage us to try to make it more precise. What exactly is required for a belief to cohere with other beliefs? What exactly does the stricture of conservatism require? How may we recognize changes that are not conservative enough? While a complete answer to these questions may be too much to ask for, something more than an appeal to unexplained notions of coherence and conservatism is clearly required. In what follows, I will argue that attempts to elucidate the internal perspective by appeals to coherence and conservatism are doomed to failure. I will focus my discussion on the notion of coherence, but the points I make apply equally to conservatism.

The notion of coherence has been widely used in epistemology, but attempts to explain what coherence consists in are typically very sketchy. We are often provided with little more than metaphors or synonyms: a belief is said to cohere with others if it "fits in" with them or if it is appropriately "consonant" with them. Such accounts do very little explanatory work. My objection to using coherence to make sense of the internal perspective is not, however, that attempts to explain what coherence is are overly vague, but rather that any attempt to explain what coherence is will make that notion unsuitable for making sense of the internal perspective.

In order to see why this is so, one need only consider this question: Is it possible for one of an agent's beliefs to cohere, or fail to cohere, with others without the agent realizing this? It seems clear that the answer to this question must be yes. However coherence is to be explained, it is a relation that may hold between a belief and a set of beliefs quite independently of an agent's believing that it holds. Were this not so, an agent could not discover that a belief of his fails to cohere with others, and *a fortiori* such discoveries could not serve as a reason for rejecting beliefs that fail to cohere. Whether a belief thus coheres with others may be hidden from an agent: it my be difficult for him to determine since he is likely to have many false beliefs about coherence.

The direction that I mean to push this argument should be clear. Coherence is too external a relation to provide an account of the agent's internal perspective. Whether an agent's beliefs cohere is no more an internal matter than, for example, whether they are reliably produced. It is not that coherence relations are unknowable, but simply that they are often external to the agent's point of view. Just as it is now a commonplace that unreliably produced beliefs may be quite reasonable from the agent's point of view,[5] it is equally clear that beliefs that fail to cohere may be reasonable from the agent's point of view. The relation of coherence is ill-suited to the job of explaining the internal perspective.

A defender of the coherence account may argue that my attack on coherence shows too much. If the argument against a coherence account of the internal perspective is simply that relations of coherence are not infallibly introspectible, then, although the charge is accurate, it will also eliminate all other attempts to elucidate the internal perspective. The failure of Descartes's program has surely shown us that nothing is infallibly introspectible. Thus if the argument against the coherence account succeeds, it does not show that such an account fails; rather, it shows that there is no internal perspective to give an account of.

In response to this charge, let me make clear that I am not simply claiming that the fault with a coherence account is that coherence is not an infallibly introspectible relation. Rather, I am claiming that coherence is just as external a relation as various other well-known external relations, such as reliability. It is clear that whether a belief is reliably produced can give us no purchase on the agent's perspective on belief acquisition. I am claiming that coherence relations are in the same boat with reliability. This is not because such relations are not infallibly introspectible, but, instead, because they are too distant from the agent's perspective.

In order to see why this is so, we need to consider Christopher Cherniak's recent work on computational complexity.[6] Perhaps the best way to gain an understanding of the issues here is by way of an example. Consider the game of chess. On hearing that computers may be programmed to play chess, many people assume that it must be an easy matter to write a program that assures that the computer will always win, or at least that it will never lose. Here is how such a program might work. Let us assume that the computer's opponent moves first. There are twenty possible opening moves for the opponent, and twenty possible responses for the computer. All the programmer need do, it seems, is have the computer work its way through the following tree diagram. At the top, we list the opening move of the opponent; under it we draw branches for each of the twenty possible responses. Under each of these responses, we draw branches for each of the opponent's possible countermoves; and so on. Some of these branches will end in a win for the computer; others will end in a win for the opponent; still others will end in a draw. The computer must at each point choose moves that do not appear on branches that end in a win for its opponent. In this way, it can never lose.

Obvious as this idea is, it cannot be carried out. There are several problems with developing such a program. I will focus on one of these: the problem of combinatorial explosion. After one move by each player, the computer must account for four hundred different possible positions. After three moves by each player, the number of positions to be accounted for exceeds sixty million. The number of such positions increases exponentially, and it is quickly out of reach for any computer that now exists or will ever exist.

There are numerous significant mathematical problems that, although a decision procedure is available for solving them, run into the problem of the combinatorial explosion. Interestingly, many of these are quite simple. As Cherniak points out,

> Of course a decision procedure exists for tautological soundness—for example, by use of truth-tables. But while a tautology decision procedure is in principle possible, it now appears to be inherently "computationally intractable," and in some sense to be extremely unfeasible as a practical matter, e.g., to require computations for relatively simple cases that would exceed the capacities of an ideal computer having the resources of the entire known universe.[7]

What this means is that if coherence requires even as little as logical consistency, determining whether one's beliefs meet the coherence requirement is likely to be beyond the abilities of any agent who might ever exist. In light of this, one can hardly claim to explain the internal perspective in terms of coherence. Moreover, it will hardly do at this point to claim that the problem may be avoided by denying that coherence requires consistency. Surely the burden of proof is now on the defender of the coherence account to show that determinations of coherence are computationally tractable. Indeed, the importance of Cherniak's point is surely this: *any* holistic relation will likely run into problems of computational complexity if one attempts to apply it to sets as large as that of any human's set of beliefs.[8]

Of course one may seek to avoid this problem by suggesting that it is not actual coherence that allows us to explain the internal perspective but rather beliefs about coherence. Such a suggestion might look like this: The internal perspective is achieved through some combination of modifications of the agent's beliefs about proper belief acquisition, where these modifications are believed to be conservative and to result in a coherent account of the way beliefs ought to be acquired. But this cannot be right either. As we saw earlier, an agent may hold a belief that he, at the same time, judges to be unjustified. This may happen with the belief that certain other beliefs cohere with one another. Indeed, an agent who realizes how difficult it is actually to determine coherence relations and yet finds himself with beliefs about coherence nonetheless may well judge these very beliefs to be unjustified. This is just to say that from the agent's perspective he ought not to have this belief. And this is just to say that beliefs about coherence cannot be used to define the boundaries of the internal perspective.

V

What, then, is the internal perspective on belief acquisition? In this section, I will present an answer to this question, and in the section that immediately follows, I will defend this answer against a number of objections.

Let me begin with a definition. An *epistemically responsible agent* is one whose beliefs are regulated by a desire for true belief. Such regulation may occur in two quite different ways. On the one hand, the desire for true belief may inhibit various other desires from playing a deleterious role in belief acquisition and retention. On the other hand, the desire for true beliefs may play a role in regulating the agent's action. Each of these roles calls for brief discussion.

In some agents, the desire that the future be bright is so strong that it plays a prominent role in their acquisition and retention of beliefs; they come to believe that the future will be bright precisely because they desire it. In other agents, the desire to be well liked is similarly efficacious. Such examples may be multiplied indefinitely. What they have in common is that in each of these cases, the agents' beliefs are not regulated by the desire for true belief. The epistemically responsible agent is not subject to such shortcomings.

The desire for true beliefs must do more in the responsible agent than simply inhibit wishful thinking. Actions of various sorts may be regulated by the desire for true beliefs, and although belief formation and retention are not subject to direct voluntary

control, actions that are subject to such control may have a pronounced effect on the contents of an agent's beliefs. We may
divide such actions into two categories: actions, such as seeking
and gathering evidence, which are designed to exploit processes of
belief acquisition and retention that are already in place; and actions that are designed to modify those very processes. Attempts
to overcome prejudice may be an example of this second category.

The desire for true beliefs thus plays a number of distinct roles
in the epistemically responsible agent. There is no reason to
think, however, that such an agent will be constantly thinking
about the acquisition of true belief. Kantians in ethics have rightly pointed out[9] that a life of action regulated by a recognition of
duty does not require that one's every thought be turned toward
duty, nor that one's every action have as its sole motivating force
the desire to do one's duty. By the same token, the life of an
epistemically responsible agent is not dominated by self-conscious
efforts to acquire true beliefs.

By what kinds of processes will an epistemically responsible
agent acquire and retain beliefs? It should be clear that this is an
empirical question; it will depend, among other things, on what
kinds of processes of belief acquisition and retention such an
agent starts off with. Since an epistemically responsible agent is a
slightly idealized human being, it will depend on what processes
of belief acquisition and retention we start off with. In short, the
answer to our question will turn on the nature of our innate intellectual equipment.

In saying that this question is empirical, I do not mean to
suggest that I will not deal with it; indeed, I will turn to this
question shortly. At this point, however, we need not inquire into
the details of our idealized agent's intellectual equipment. All that
is currently relevant is the idealization itself.

What I want to suggest is that the internal perspective should
be identified with the perspective of the epistemically responsible
agent. An agent should arrive at his beliefs, internally viewed, in
whatever manner would result form his beliefs being regulated by
a desire for true belief.

We may best understand the merits of this view by turning
directly to a consideration of some objections.[10]

VI

In dismissing the coherence account of the internal perspective, I argued that the relation of coherence is too distant from the internal perspective to provide us with a proper account of it; in a word, coherence is too external. The same objection, it seems, may reasonably be made to the present account. The perspective of the epistemically responsible agent is too distant from the perspective of any real agent.

I have already admitted that it is an empirical question, and one not easily answered, as to how an epistemically responsible agent would arrive at his beliefs. It is clear that this question cannot be answered by simple introspection, and it is equally clear that we are all likely to have numerous false beliefs about the processes of belief acquisition that would be sanctioned from the perspective of an epistemically responsible agent. These facts by themselves do not show a defect in the present account, however. As we have already seen, once we acknowledge that there is no faculty of introspection with the powers Descartes attributed to it, these supposed defects will be shared by any account.

This much granted, some explanation is needed of the sense in which any account may explain an internal perspective, for in the absence of any such explanation, we may be better off denying that there is an internal perspective to be accounted for. The present account lends itself to precisely such an explanation.

However the distinction between things internal to an agent and those external to an agent is to be drawn, it is clear that an agent's desires are internal to the agent. Dualists and materialists may disagree about the status of an agent's body, but we may all agree that there is a change internal to the agent when his desires change. The desire for true beliefs is thus something internal to an agent. By the same token, the effects of this desire, and the effects it would have were it to regulate his beliefs, are rightly called internal. It is thus that we may speak of the epistemically responsible agent's perspective as internal; that is, it is internally generated.

Of course this by itself does not distinguish the perspective I favor from other internally generated perspectives: those generated by the desire for coherent belief, belief immune from doubt, or belief meeting any other requirement. No doubt those who favor one of these other perspectives will want to argue that my account lacks any real substance; it fails to give agents instructions on proper belief acquisition. The advice I am offering—one should regulate one's beliefs by a desire for truth—seems about as useful as the stockbroker's advice to buy low and sell high.

It is true that the suggestion that agents should regulate their beliefs by a desire for truth is completely neutral on how this goal is to be achieved. I take this to be an advantage rather than a defect of the view. Someone who wishes to defend some more substantive advice—for example, the suggestion that we should be moved by a desire for coherent belief—must show how this strategy flows from the desire for truth. Failing this, it is hard to see how any more substantive suggestion than my own would be an answer to the question, "How ought we to arrive at our beliefs?"

What I am suggesting is that even those who prefer a more substantive account than I have offered should agree that my account is correct as far as it goes. The only question that remains at issue is this: By what processes would an epistemically responsible agent—an agent whose beliefs are regulated by a desire for true belief—arrive at his beliefs? It is to this question that I now turn.

VII

Because agents differ in their beliefs, their inferential habits, and their circumstances, the demands of epistemic responsibility will vary from agent to agent; there is no one way in which epistemically responsible agents will arrive at their beliefs. Nevertheless, there are certain inferential habits that are at least extremely widespread. A brief examination of these tendencies will allow us to see the processes by which many responsible agents will arrive at their beliefs.

I will begin with the role of vivid data in inference. Richard Nisbett and Lee Ross introduce the notion of *vividness* as follows: "Information may be described as vivid, that is, as likely to attract and hold our attention and to excite the imagination to the extent that it is (a) emotionally interesting, (b) concrete and imagery provoking, and (c) proximate in a sensory, temporal, or spatial way."[11] Numerous studies, as well as anecdotal evidence, suggest that vivid data have a far more pronounced effect on human inference than data that are not vivid, and this effect is largely independent of the objective relevance of the data. Here, even more than elsewhere, a good example is worth a thousand arguments. I can do no better than to quote Nisbett, Borgida, Crandall, and Reed:

> Let us suppose that you wish to buy a new car and have decided that on grounds of economy and longevity you want to purchase one of those solid, stalwart, middle-class Swedish cars—either a Volvo or a Saab. As a prudent and sensible buyer, you go to *Consumer Reports,* which informs you that the consensus of their experts is that the Volvo is mechanically superior, and the consensus of the readership is that the Volvo has the better repair record. Armed with this information, you decide to go and strike a bargain with the Volvo dealer before the week is out. In the interim, however, you go to a cocktail party where you announce this intention to an acquaintance. He reacts with disbelief and alarm: "A Volvo! You've got to be kidding. My brother-in-law had a Volvo. First that fancy fuel injection computer thing went out, 250 bucks. Next he started having trouble with the rear end. Had to replace it. Then the transmission and the clutch. Finally sold it in three years for junk." The logical status of this information is that the N of several hundred Volvo-owning *Consumer Reports* readers has been increased by one, and the mean frequency of repair record shifted by an iota on three or four dimensions. However, anyone who maintains that he would reduce the encounter to such a net informational effect is either disingenuous or lacking in the most elemental self-knowledge.[12]

Anecdotes of this sort can be multipled indefinitely. In addition, there has been some experimental evidence confirming the pronounced effect of vivid data on inference.[13] There can be little doubt about the existence of this phenomenon.

Classic studies on the effects of base rate information were done by Daniel Kahneman and Amos Tversky.[14] One such study[15] was conducted as follows. Two groups of subjects were asked to read the following paragraph.

> Tom W. is of high intelligence, although lacking in true creativity. He has a need for order and clarity, and for neat and tidy systems in which every detail finds its appropriate place. His writing is rather dull and mechanical, occasionally enlivened by somewhat corny

puns and by flashes of imagination of the sci-fi type. He has a
strong drive for competence. He seems to have little feel and little
sympathy for other people and does not enjoy interacting with
others. Self-centered, he nonetheless has a deep moral sense.[16]

One of these groups was asked to estimate the likelihood that
Tom should become a graduate student in each of nine different
fields. The second group was asked to judge Tom's similarity to
graduate students in each of the nine fields. Finally, a third
group, which did not read the description of Tom, was asked to
estimate the percentage of graduate students in each of the fields;
these last figures constitute the judged base rate. Although base
rate information should play a prominent role in predicting Tom's
chosen field of study, these predictions closely tracked the judgments of similarity; indeed, the correlation here was .97. Base rate
information played no apparent role, in spite of the subjects' belief, as elicited in questioning, that personality information is of
little use in accurately predicting a student's choice of graduate
field. Indeed, subjects estimated that predictions based on personality information would correlate with chosen field of graduate
study to a degree of .23. In short, subjects believed that personality information is a poor predictor of field of study, but based their
predictions entirely on such information, ignoring the base rates.
This is typical of the effect of base rate information on inference.

One more example from the psychology of inductive inference
deserves mention. Statisticians have long been familiar with the
law of large numbers: the larger the sample drawn from a given
population, the more likely that sample is to reflect the characteristics of the population. As Tversky and Kahneman[17] note, "People's intuitions about random sampling appear to satisfy the law
of small numbers, which asserts that the law of large numbers
applies to small numbers as well." Human beings tend to draw
inductive inferences from remarkably small samples with strikingly high confidence.[18]

These three examples—the role of vivid data, the role of base
rate information, and the law of small numbers—indicate three
inferential tendencies that are extremely widespread. Nevertheless, one might doubt whether this tells us anything about epistemically responsible agents. Wouldn't agents who are motivated
by a desire for true belief overcome these tendencies? Don't these

studies, and others of their ilk, show us nothing more than the existence of widespread epistemic irresponsibility?

There is reason to think that both of these questions should be answered in the negative. First, it should be noted that the occasion for testing our inferences from sample to population against an entire population are extremely rare. Feedback on the accuracy of our inductive inferences is typically indirect at best. Moreover, on those occasions where we do get feedback on our inductive inferences, the inductive strategies I have already described, as well as a host of others like them, go to work in producing our assessment of our own performance. As a result, responsible attempts to check on one's inferential accuracy will often result in apparent confirmation of one's ability to get at the truth. Responsible agents who start off with tendencies like those described will not, in the typical case, be in a position to recognize their faults.[19]

How then will responsible agents reason? How ought we, as viewed from the internal perspective, to arrive at our beliefs? The answer, it seems, is that we will and should arrive at our beliefs in something of a slapdash manner.

VIII

In closing, I would like to put my account in a broader perspective. My way of approaching questions about rationality—about how we ought to arrive at our beliefs—is by introducing a certain idealization, the epistemically responsible agent. Such an agent's beliefs are regulated by a desire for truth; in other respects, epistemically responsible agents are exactly like other human beings. In light of current evidence of our inferential tendencies, I have offered a certain picture of what epistemically responsible belief acquisition comes to. The suggestion is, quite simply, that rational belief acquisition is far less truth-conducive than is typically thought.

There is, I am confident, room for other accounts of rationality using idealizations other than the one I have suggested. In particular, we will at least need an account of some kind of external perspective on the question, "How should we arrive at our beliefs?" Nevertheless, I believe the account presented here offers one useful approach to questions about rationality.

NOTES

1. I have said more about how these two perspectives fit together, or fail to fit together, in "Ever Since Descartes," *The Monist* 69 (1985).

2. A suggestion similar to this is made by John Pollock in his "A Plethora of Epistemological Theories," in *Justification and Knowledge,* George Pappas, ed., (Dordrecht: Reidel, 1979), pp. 93–113.

3. Many of these objections are made in Barbara Winters "Inferring," *Philosophical Studies* 44 (1983):201–220.

4. A close relative of such an account is presented in Laurence Bonjour's "Externalist Theories of Empirical Knowledge," *Midwest Studies in Philosophy* 5 (1980):53–73. Bonjour there presents one kind of coherence theory that is designed to give an account of the internal perspective. My criticism of coherence theories applies to Bonjour if it applies to anyone.

5. This is now a commonplace as a result of Bonjour's persuasive argument in ibid, note 4.

6. "Computational Complexity and the Universal Acceptance of Logic," *Journal of Philosophy* 81 (1984):739–758.

7. Ibid., p. 743.

8. Considerations like this suggest that Jerry Fodor's account of the fixation of belief in *The Modularity of Mind* (Cambridge, Mass.: Bradford Books; MIT Press, 1983) must be incorrect. Fodor expresses skepticism about our ever understanding the mechanisms of belief fixation because, he claims, (1) we can only come to know the workings of modular mental processes, and (2) belief fixation is holistic and not modular. Even if we grant (1), we ought to reject Fodor's skepticism because, as Cherniak's work shows, belief fixation could not be holistic. Robert Cummins has also suggested a modular account of belief fixation in his review of *The Modularity of Mind* in *Philosophical Review* 94 (1985):101-108.

9. See, e.g., Marcia Baron, "The Alleged Moral Repugnance of Acting from Duty," *Journal of Philosophy* 81 (1984):197–220.

10. I have developed this view at greater length in "Justified Belief and Epistemically Responsible Action," *Philosophical Review* 92 (1983):33–48.

11. *Human Inference: Strategies and Shortcomings of Social Judgment* (New York: Prentice-Hall, 1980), p. 45.

12. "Popular Induction: Information is Not Necessarily Informative," in Kahneman, Slovik, and Tversky, eds., *Judgment Under Uncertainty: Heuristics and Biases* (Cambridge: Cambridge University Press: 1982), pp. 112–113.

13. For a review of the literature, see Nisbett and Ross, op. cit., chapter 3.

14. "On the Psychology of Prediction," "Judgment Under Uncertainty: Heuristics and Biases," and "On the Study of Statistical Intuitions," all in Kahneman, Slovik, and Tversky, op. cit.

15. "On the Psychology of Prediction," loc. cit.

16. Ibid., p. 49.

17. "Belief in the Law of Small Numbers," in Kahneman, Slovik, and Tversky, op. cit.

18. See also Hillel Einhorn and Robin Hogarth, "Confidence in Judgment: Persistence of the Illusion of Validity," *Psychological Review,* 85 (1978):395–416.

19. I have made this case in greater detail for the example of hasty generalization in "Justified Belief and Epistemically Responsible Action," loc. cit.

Duncan MacIntosh

Rationalizing Naturalism
On Hilary Kornblith's "Naturalizing Rationality"

Peoples' fallibility seemingly allows Kornblith to counterexample the view that "one's own lights" are some of one's beliefs or self-aware procedures for belief formation; similarly, that they involve one's beliefs having certain properties, like coherence, or reliability. One can lack sufficient awareness of and control over these beliefs, procedures, and properties for them to constitute belief-formation's subjectively rational element. Thus neither the reliability, the coherence, nor the desired reliability or coherence of one's beliefs are unconditional features of subjective epistemic rationality. They belong to the external perspective on doxastic aptness. Instead, subjective rationality merely involves having one's beliefs regulated by the desire for truth. One need not actually have any true beliefs or make any licit inferences.

Some objections:

1. If fallibility respecting some condition falsifies any theory

This is a reconstruction of a partly extemporized talk. While I think it reproduces the spirit of my comments, it has benefited from subsequent thinking, and I hope, then, that it is clearer than it was when presented. I am grateful to Victoria McGeer, Douglas Butler and Professor Kornblith himself for discussion of these issues, and to the Social Sciences and Humanities Research Council of Canada for the doctoral fellowship support I enjoyed during preparation of this commentary.

135

of the internal perspective featuring it, then likewise, surely, for Kornblith's. My beliefs can be regulated by desires I do not know I have—among them Kornblith's favorite, the desire for truth— and would not countenance if I did. How, then, would such beliefs have issued from my subjective sense of justification? Moreover, since I might not be authoritative on what desires I have, on whether I act accordingly, or on what conduct would serve them; and since I might be unable to get myself to act on them even if I do know them, how does my internal perspective essentially involve me intentionally acting in a way that is successfully regulated by a desire for truth?

Is it rational to desire the true? Internal or subjective rationality will be explained by relating it to that desire only if that question is an internal matter. It may not be. For how is it subjectively irresponsible or irrational to fail to value truth or regulate one's beliefs by the desire for it?

Other counterexamples (effectively externalizing the desire for truth): Suppose you believe I will give you all the truths if you will desire only the false. If you then desire the false, you are not epistemically rational according to Kornblith; but if you desire the true, your beliefs will not here be motivated by a desire for the true (at least not after your initial desire modification). Indeed, surely one can be a subjectively rational believer without having desires at all, and even desiring *not* to know—as when wanting to avoid acquiring information useful to an enemy in the event of capture. While busily guarding one's ignorance, through a slip-up in the telephone lines at the CIA office, one overhears the very information one was trying to avoid. Surely, in spite of this, it might be (epistemically) rational by one's lights to believe that information. So the desire requirement seems not unconditional.

2. I think subjective rationality requires greater epistemic competence than Kornblith requires. He requires beliefs to be regulated by a desire for the truth, but not necessarily for coherence (even though coherence is a necessary property of truth). Now, while one can desire something without knowing all its properties, I do not think one is *regulated* by it unless *sufficiently* informed on the object for it to be *identified as* the object of one's desire. If I believe that the truth is the *incoherent,* for instance, and then seek it out, how does a desire for the true operate here at all? My beliefs would effectively be regulated by a desire for the

false, though not obviously irrationally. Yet without *some* beliefs, desires have no effect at all: they cannot guide, because they are inert as motivators except in belief-desire complexes. Thus, perhaps one cannot desire truth or be regulated by that desire until one knows enough about it that desiring it could be distinguished from desiring anything else.

Moreover, in evaluating someone's credal rationality and epistemic responsibility, it must first make sense to attribute beliefs to him; and while I cannot defend this here, many people (e.g., Donald Davidson) see no sense in ascribing beliefs systematically false, incoherent, or unjustified. Thus from the conditions on the felicity of belief-imputations derive the constraints of general doxastic soundness and inferential licitness that Kornblith eschews as constitutive of subjective rationality.

Another problem: Responsibility entails awareness and approval. Generally, we cannot hold you responsible, epistemically or otherwise, for beliefs you merely think you have. Apparently, then, a minimal epistemic competence (a requirement of some true beliefs and licit inferences) is needed for epistemic responsibility and subjective rationality.

3. By (1) above, even desires would have to be external matters in the limit of Kornblith's standard. But then, perhaps *nothing* remains as the internal perspective. To some, this may not be an unwelcome conclusion. The skeptics hold that there is no justification for any belief, while ultra-naturalists would take the failure of the internal as part of the happy and overdue fall of folk psychology, epistemology, and semantics. There are no propositions, so no beliefs as attitudes toward them, so *nothing to be justified* (or not).

Moderates might say that only the external remains to epistemology. We can ask what inferences are objectively licit, but knowers may never have subjective justification, though they may form beliefs by reliable processes, and though objectively speaking, various inferences are mandated.

This I think is premature and a seriously faulted doctrine, for I think "ought" locutions make sense only when conceived as subject-directed and executable in acts with subjective antecedents as reasons. An argument may be sound, a proposition well-warranted, but to say that objectively one ought to believe accordingly is presumably to assert more. What work is "ought" doing in these cases? It is *enjoining* beliefs or asserting their *aptness*.

Now, in ethics (the source of Kornblith's analogy), there are constraints on what it can be true that one ought to do. It must be both doable ("ought" implies "can"), and something that would be an act by the concept of act in the circumstances. Acts are behaviors issuing from reasons. Complete reasons for acting are belief-desire complexes. One is only acting if one is aware of and has some pro-attitude to one's behavior and if the behavior would not have happened except given the former two conditions. Similarly, in epistemology, if I ought to believe something, I must be able to believe it in result of the right antecedent beliefs and desires. A desire is rationally acquired if it follows by a practical syllogism from one's antecedent desires plus background beliefs, or plus appropriately acquired new beliefs. A belief is rationally acquired if arrived at by a deduction from one's antecedent beliefs and/or by its seeming true in the situation given one's background beliefs.

Does this not limit enjoinable acts and beliefs by conditions too contingent and subjective to have analyzed the objective and ideal nature of the enjoinment? No. Rather, the objective sense of ought pertains to what *ideal* agents ought to do under ideal conditions, and to what *ideal* knowers ought to believe under ideal conditions for knowledge. Thus, were I so powerful as to be able to cure cancer, then I ought to, and were I so good at finding things out that I would find a certain truth obvious while in a certain evidential predicament, then I ought to believe it when in that predicament. Indeed, these principles may hold objectively. (Though, if so, I do not think anyone yet knows why.)

Perhaps an ideal epistemic agent is one who can milk a situation of all its absolute informational content (Fred Dretske's notion); who can appreciate all its nomic and deductive associations. Similarly, epistemically ideal conditions for a fact might be ones from which an ideal epistemic agent could get knowledge of it. But real people may be in less favorable conditions, or have less efficient (but perhaps no less rational) epistemic faculties, and what *they* ought to believe is commensurately diminished.

This leaves the so-called objective ought still contingent on conditions varying with the agent and his circumstances, but the situation is no worse, surely, than in ethics, even if there are objective, universal moral principles categorically enjoinable. No moral principle holds in all cases—only where there is no excuse for not meeting its standard. One need only cure the world of cancer if one can. Likewise, one must believe *p* only if one can.

Well, if the objective ought is just that holding of ideal agents and epistemic subjects in ideal evidential circumstances, strictly speaking, there is no external ought. Someone who cannot believe the truth (because lacking the subjective justifications needed to make acquiring the belief an act) need not; likewise, even the ideal epistemic agent need not believe the truth without motivating reasons for him to believe it given his informational predicament. For even were he somehow to acquire the enjoined belief, his believing would not properly constitute a responsible act; would not be a belief acquired as a result of his being an epistemically responsible agent. To enjoin having it would be to enjoin one not to be an agent—to prescribe a contradiction.

So it remains, then, to give an account of epistemic subjectivity—of the internal—even in the so-called objective case, since it proves simply a more ideal instance of the subjective case for ordinary epistemic agents.

If (per Davidson) beliefs must generally be accounted reliable to be attributed at all, and if (per me) some degree of epistemic competence is needed for epistemic agency and felicitous doxastic advising, the subjective or internal may just be the faculty of belief-formation itself. It would consist of brute capacities to get truths by perception and make appropriate inferences, and of yet other beliefs and belief-formation processes generated in conjectures over those perceptions and testable in subsequent ones. Thus, one's subjective perspective is the view on truth afforded one by one's brute capacities augmented by one's evolving theories.

What, then, is the status of Kornblith's counterexamples? They are not, as he thinks, proofs of the doxastic contentlessness of the internal perspective on truth. They simply illustrate occasional (i.e., nonsystematic) *failures* of doxastic faculties and processes. They do not locate the features *of* which they are failures in the exclusively external.

This is especially welcome when we think to what we were driven by Kornblith's arguments. Their unstinting application left no subjectivity in epistemology. What, then, of that quotidian phenomenon of things *seeming* thus and so to people? Perhaps the very existence of opinion is the *reductio ad absurdum* of Kornblith's line.

Robert G. Meyers

Naturalizing Epistemic Terms

Just what is it to naturalize epistemology? Presumably it is to make epistemology consistent with naturalism, but 'naturalism' itself is not used in one clear sense. At the most modest level, a naturalized epistemology would allow us to attribute knowledge to nonhumans. A highly intellectualistic conception of knowledge might require reasoning processes that are so sophisticated that only humans (and perhaps not even all humans) could ever know anything. Such a theory would divorce humans from the rest of the animals and deny continuity in the animal kingdom. Seen in this light, a naturalized epistemology would be judged in part by the extent to which it helps us understand how the capacity for knowledge could have evolved from lower biological organisms. I will assume without argument that epistemology should be naturalized at least to this extent.

A theory of knowledge might be naturalistic in this sense and still accept mind-body dualism. A more extreme form of naturalized epistemology would rule out this possibility and require that it be materialist. (A wag once said that 'naturalism' is the name a Vermonter like Dewey would give to materialism.) We might distinguish three versions of materialism. (1) The first and most extreme form would eschew all epistemic notions on the ground that they are misleadingly mentalistic, and substitute only purely physical or behavioral locutions. A theory of knowledge developed along these lines would be an epistemic counterpart of extreme

141

forms of behaviorism in psychology, which attempt to treat what we normally classify as mental solely in terms of behavior, avoiding mentalistic terms completely. (2) We could continue to talk of awareness, justification, and knowing but seek definitions of these terms in non-normative, physicalistic language. Unlike the first option, this would be a reductive program rather than an eliminative one. Or (3), we could try to specify physical and psychological conditions for epistemic terms without claiming that epistemic locutions express or are reducible to physical notions. This would be a nonreductive and noneliminative program: noneliminative in that it would continue to countenance the standard epistemic vocabulary, and nonreductive in that it would not claim that epistemic terms are synonymous with some expressions containing only physical terms.

Something can be said for each of these versions of materialism, but it seems to me that the third is the most promising. If we hold that epistemology should be type (3) materialism, the relation between the theory of knowledge and psychology would be analogous to that between biology and, say, chemistry. These are distinct sciences and so have different principles and vocabularies, but biological entities are not distinct from chemical entities. A frog is not after all a distinct being over and above the mass of molecules that occupies the same place. As Wilfrid Sellars puts it, we have to distinguish between the postulated *entities* of two sciences and the theoretical *principles* (i.e., laws) of the sciences.[1] Although the sciences refer to the same range of entities and thus in this sense are unified, the principles need not be. The principles of biology may be discoverable only by "techniques and procedures appropriate to dealing with biochemical substances." Furthermore, the laws of one science may not be reducible to the laws of the other science; that is, it may not be possible to define the terms of the less basic science in the more basic one. For Sellars, this does not mean that the objects obey different laws in biology and chemistry, but only that the vocabulary of one is not reducible to that of the other. Since they are laws of physical entities, they are physical laws even though they are expressed in nonreducible biological terms.

I think the same thing might be true of the relation between epistemology and psychology. Although they employ different terminology, use different procedures, and present us with very different principles, we need not conclude that they are about different entities. In particular, we need not conclude that talk of knowing and justification commits us to a mental domain distinct from the physical, as a dualist epistemology holds.

In what follows, I will assume that Sellars's conception applies to the relation between epistemology and psychology. One might think that this assumption gives the epistemologist free reign, but this is mistaken. The biologist is not free to multiply entities as he wishes, but must conform to other sciences (or have strong reasons for not doing so). Similarly, epistemology cannot postulate entities willy-nilly either. In particular, it cannot postulate states that cannot be identified in some way with physical states.

I will assume that these two senses of naturalism are clear enough: first, epistemology should not make it impossible for us to understand how knowledge could arise from evolution. Or to put it differently, it should not make knowledge too difficult an achievement for the so-called lower creatures of the world. (Note that it need not make it possible for the lowest creatures. It is not clear that mosquitoes know anything. The kind of creatures that worry me are those from cats and dogs up to human children.) Second, epistemology should attempt a unification (to use Sellars's term) of entities with psychology and physics, although not necessarily a unification of methods or principles.

It is clear that traditional epistemology has not been naturalistic in either of these ways. The reason is its *justificationist* character. As I will use the term, a justificationist holds that knowledge is either (i) an intuitive state or (ii) derives from such states by certain modes of argument or inference.[2] Intuitive states are states in which something is self-evident or given to the mind. The justificationist holds that these are the source of all warrant since they are the only cases in which the knower "sees" the object of his knowledge and does not have to infer its properties. An important feature of these theories has been the claim that justification is immanent to the mental: beliefs can be justified only by cognitive mental states in which something is intuited; they are not justified by noncognitive, physical states.

Justificationist theories are the rule in traditional epistemology. René Descartes holds that we are justified in holding a proposition only if we can intuit it or deduce it from premises that we can intuit. Deduction transmits the luminous character of these premises to other beliefs that are not seen to be true immediately. Beliefs that are not self-evident or justified by deduction from self-evident premises, fall short of knowledge, even though it might be rational to accept them in some lesser sense. John Locke and Gottfried Leibniz held less austere versions of the theory. They agreed that inductive arguments can generate knowledge even though they do not guarantee their conclusions.[3] In more recent versions of the theory, intuition is replaced by talk of the given (at least for knowledge of empirical truths), and the modes of argument are expanded to include hypotheses or what C. S. Peirce called abduction.

These are minimal requirements for a justificationist theory. A further requirement is usually added, namely, that knowledge can exist only if we are able to show that our modes of argument are reliable. It is not enough, for example, that deduction and induction actually be reliable; we must also be able to show that they are. This was not thought to be a problem in the case of deduction, because (so it was claimed) each step in a deduction is itself self-evident. But it created a first-class crisis in the case of induction. Since inductive principles are neither intuitive nor a priori, they can be justified only by generalizing from experience even though this begs the question by assuming induction itself. The result is skepticism about most of what we think we know.

Justificationist theories are nonnaturalistic in both the biological and the materialist senses I discussed earlier. For one thing, intuition and givenness are sophisticated achievements that seem quite rare in the animal world. Animals do not gain information about their surroundings by attending to experience, but act more or less spontaneously to unconscious cues.

The theory is also dualistic and so nonnaturalistic in the other sense in that the first steps to knowledge are irreducibly mental. This is clearest in the case of the given. Those who defended the given did not deny that the awareness of sense data was preceded by physical states in the brain or by events in external objects. What they held was that acts of givenness do not depend on any previous *cognitive* or *mental* states. There may be a chain of events starting with the object and proceeding through the brain, but this does not make the sensation inferential since the given is, by definition, the first cognitive or mental event in the chain.[4] What we have is a stimulation of the sense organ, then internal brain events, and finally the initial mental event or sensation itself. The direct knowledge on which everything else depends has *physical* antecedents, but no mental ones. The theory is thus committed to a sharp distinction between the physical and the mental. If the distinction is graded, there would be no clearly cognitive starting points and the justificationist program would be mistaken. In fact, it is the tacit assumption of dualism and a determinate notion of the mental that made the theory of the given so seemingly obvious. H. H. Price and C. I. Lewis, for example, found it incredible that anyone should deny that there was a given precisely because they were convinced that, at some point in the chain from external object to perceptual belief, a physical event must cause a mental event that is a cognitive starting point for our other knowledge.

If this is right, a naturalized epistemology cannot accept the given or, by parity of reasoning, a justificationist account of knowledge. The question is whether it can accept epistemology itself. What happens to the notions of knowledge and justified belief if we give up justificationism? As I suggested earlier, the most promising program is a theory developed along the lines of type (3) materialism. We would have to specify physical conditions under which beliefs can provide evidence for other beliefs without appealing to irreducible mental states like intuitions or acts of givenness.

Two ways have been suggested in the recent literature. (a) Taking a hint from the common assumption that knowledge must be nonaccidental, i.e., that S cannot know that p if it is a coincidence that he has a true belief that p, some people have argued that a person has knowledge that p provided he would not have believed as he does if p were not true. (b) The second proposal is to treat beliefs that result from reliable processes as sources of evidence for other beliefs. If we treat a reliable process as one that results in true output more often than false, we have a nonmentalist condition for evidence and so do not have to appeal to something like the given. For reasons I will not go into, the reliability theory seems more promising and is the one I will restrict myself to here.[5]

How does this account naturalize the notion of justified belief? As we saw, the justificationist restricts justification to beliefs resting on cognitive states. No allowance is made for the possibility that a belief can be justified under some specified set of non-cognitive conditions. The reliability theory allows us to liberalize this account: we can hold that a belief that results from a reliable process is justified even though the process is not itself cognitive or mental but, roughly speaking, an input-output mechanism in which only the output, i.e., the belief, is cognitive. This does not commit us to a determinate notion of the mental or to the given, i.e., to the theory that the process at some point contains an irreducible mental first, and so is consistent with materialism. It also allows us to accept a more plausible picture of knowledge in the biological world, since reliable epistemic mechanisms are on a par with other biological mechanisms and do not require highly intellectual skills.

Nevertheless there are problems. First, the theory allows for the possibility of reliable mechanisms other than the ones we now recognize. Suppose S wakes up with an ability like that of the rocking-horse winner in D. H. Lawrence's story: he can predict the winners at the local race track simply by having a certain distinctive feeling about them. If his ability is genuinely reliable, we would have to conclude that his beliefs about the winners are justified. Furthermore, we would be committed to this conclusion even if he had no evidence of his successes, i.e., even if he had no metabeliefs about his ability. Some people have found this to be counter-intuitive.[6]

As I understand it, the problem is not simply that S has an unusual ability or one that we cannot understand easily. For all we know, such abilities are physically possible and have not come about because the proper combination of causes is not present, much in the way that vision was possible long before the genetic and evolutionary conditions appeared to bring it about. The problem is rather that it would be irrational for S to base other beliefs on his hunch without reason to think he was clairvoyant; hence, he cannot be justified in thinking this or that horse will win.

There are several ways to get around this problem. The most straightforward way is to distinguish between S's being justified in accepting p and it being rational for him to do so. This allows us to admit that it would not be rational for him to act on his belief even though it is justified for him. This option moves us even further from a justificationist account since, traditionally, what we are justified in believing and what it is rational to believe have been taken to be identical.[7] Obviously this is sketchy. The main point is that this would lead to a broad distinction between the theory of justification and the theory of rationality. The reliability theory is an attempt to explain justification (and thus knowledge) along naturalistic lines, whereas rationality (so the naturalist would claim) is a more complicated notion.

In general, I think this is just the sort of distinction we want to make in order (a) to extend knowledge to nonhumans while (b) acknowledging our differences. Rationality, for instance, involves doxastic ascent and evaluation of the sources of our premises, whereas knowledge is a "lower" capacity. Rabbits and owls cannot reflect on their abilities and past successes even though many of their perceptual skills are more sophisticated than ours. The self-reflection necessary for evaluating sources seems unique to us and, in its way, our own contribution to the array of knowledge-gathering skills. If we distinguish between rationality and justification, we might be able to sort out these intuitions in the proper way while also accepting naturalistic predelections.

A second problem has been raised by Putnam.[8] He thinks that "the prospects for actually *finding* powerful generalizations about all rationally acceptable beliefs" are poor and hence that 'rational', 'reasonable', and 'justified' are not natural-kind terms like *gold*. As a result, he is skeptical of the possibility of treating epistemic locutions in terms of reliability. (He also argues that the theory assumes a correspondence theory of truth, whereas he thinks truth is "an idealization of rational acceptability," but I will not discuss this argument.)

I think this objection is instructive, but mistaken at the perceptual level. Within the kind of naturalized epistemology I have in mind, terms like 'rational', 'reasonable', and 'justified' are further removed from observation than the terms describing perceptual mechanisms; they are theoretical terms, if you like. The theory holds that S is justified in believing that p provided his belief results from the proper operation of a certain sort of mechanism M under conditions C. The mechanism is a source of beliefs that serve as premises for other beliefs under some set of unspecified conditions that epistemology would try to provide by considering examples. These conditions might include references to the lighting in the case of vision or to the absence of conflicting beliefs in the case of memory.[9] The reliability of these sources would be established by generalizations about the relation between the input and the output. Given that the sources are reliable, a justified belief would be one accepted on the basis of the source (in conditions *C*). What the likely sources are and how they relate to the sense organs and other biological mechanisms would be empirical questions whose answers we could not know beforehand. In fact, for all we know, new sources such as clairvoyance might evolve or even be artificially created (by mad scientists, for example).

Given this background, our prospects of finding strong enough generalizations to sort and rank reliable mechanisms are not poor, as Putnam maintains. In fact, we would be surprised if there were not such generalizations. Indeed, we already have a good idea what the short list would be; it would include perception with all its specific modalities, memory, and testimony, but not clairvoyance or tealeaf reading. Reason, innateness, and religious illumination would find avid defenders, although I think further clarification would be needed before we could even raise the question of their reliability in a clear way. In other words, we already know in general which sources are reliable overall, which are not, and which are controversial. What we lack is a fine-grained understanding about how the reliable sources operate; in particular we lack a theory about the conditions under which they yield justification. As a result, I find Putnam's pessimism unfounded at the level of noninferential knowledge.

Putnam's doubts about reliability are more plausible when we consider inferential justification. Although it is likely that we will find generalizations that will support reliability at the perceptual level, I do not think we will find them for cases in which belief rests on complicated argument. This raises a third problem for the reliability theory: the problem of explaining inferential knowledge. Perceptual mechanisms turn stimulations into beliefs relatively independently of other beliefs (although not completely so, of course). Cases in which belief rests on other beliefs as premises are more complicated and are less likely to reflect generalizable mechanisms. There are causal explanations of beliefs at every level, but the fact that a belief has a causal explanation is not enough to make it justified or knowledge; even superstitious beliefs and unsound inferences have explanations, but this alone does not make them justified. What the reliability theory needs to make its case are mechanisms in which true beliefs as input yield true beliefs as output more often than not. Yet, once we get beyond the perceptual level, it is not clear that sufficiently strong generalizations can be found to support these claims.

It might be argued that we can posit inferential mechanisms of sufficient power if we can show that true beliefs of sort F usually bring about true beliefs of sort G. This would allow us to take F-type beliefs as reliable indicators of the truth of G-type propositions. However, this ignores the role of background beliefs in inferential justification. Suppose I hear what sounds like a snow plow and infer without looking out the window that it has snowed. Whether my belief is justified or not depends on what else I know. If I know that it is too warm for snow but temporarily overlook this, my belief is not justified even though hearing what sounds like a snow plow is a reliable indication that it has snowed. Yet if I have a different set of background beliefs, the inference could well be justified. Furthermore, even if we could link belief types to deal with low-level inferences, it is not likely that we could find generalizations to warrant higher-level inferences, such as proofs of theorems in geometry.

Another problem with the reliabilist account of inferential justification is that there seem to be counterexamples to the claim that the proper causal genesis is sufficient to justify a belief. If S learns a theorem in class, but is unable to provide an argument for it or even to remember that he once learned it, it is unlikely that we would say that he knows that it is true. Yet the process by which he came to believe the theorem might still be a reliable process. These cases are not decisive, but they suggest that, whatever the plausibility of a reliability theory of noninferential knowledge, inferential justification is better explained in terms of the quality of the arguments one is able to provide for the belief.

It might be argued that the reliability theory can meet this problem simply by requiring that the believer be able to defend the conclusion with a *reliable* form of argument. The problem with this is that we cannot explain the reliability of arguments in the straightforward way we explained the reliability of perceptual mechanisms; that is, we cannot explain them as input-output mechanisms, but rather must resort to notions of validity and evidential support as well as to the believer's background beliefs and their justification, and this is not compatible with the reliability theory.

Because of this, I would suggest that the reliability theory of noninferential justification be supplemented with a more justificationist account of inferential justification. The account I have in mind holds that S is inferentially justified in accepting p only if he is able to defend p in accordance with certain conditions that would have to be specified by the theory. The account is still causal, since the belief would have to have been caused (or causally sustained) by the ability in order for it to be justified. But it would not be a reliability theory in the sense in which this is usually understood. The reason is that it would take inferential justification to rest on what the believer is able to do at the moment and not on the reliability of the process that resulted in his belief. In Goldman's words, it would be a *current time-slice theory* as opposed to a version of historical reliabilism.[10] However, the theory would not be a justificationist theory either. The reason is that it can hold that the premises S needs to defend p can be justified by reliable perceptual mechanisms instead of because they are given to the mind. In general, we might call this an *ability* theory. To be justified is to have certain kinds of abilities. In the case of noninferential knowledge, the abilities are input-output mechanisms; in the case of inferential knowledge, they are abilities to provide certain kinds of arguments. The theory does not have to hold that the premises on which inferential knowledge rests are justified by some cognitive state, but rather can be justified because certain noncognitive conditions obtain.

There is no time at the present to develop this theory, but I would like to make two points. First, I do not think we can plausibly hold that inferential justification is simply a function of the strength of one's argument, i.e., of the positive evidence he can muster for it. The knower must also be able to rule out nontrivial alternatives to his belief as well. This talk of alternatives suggests the theory (or rather theories) of relevant alternatives that have become popular in discussions of reliability, but it is not quite the same notion.[11] If S believes p on the basis of certain positive evidence e yet cannot rule out hypothesis h even though e supports h equally, he is *not* justified in accepting p on the basis of e. In order for him to be justified in accepting p, he must also be able to provide evidence that rules out h. The same thing is true of every significant alternative to p. He does not have to be able to rule out every possible alternative explanation of e, however.

An example might help. Suppose I believe that the driver in a fatal crash committed suicide; I offer as evidence the fact that no skid marks were found at the scene. If I am unable to disconfirm the equally plausible hypothesis that he fell asleep at the wheel (and so could not brake before going off the road), I would not be justified in thinking he killed himself. The reason is that falling asleep at the wheel is a nontrivial alternative to the belief that he committed suicide in this case. But I would not have to rule out the hypothesis that there are no skid marks because gremlins disabled the brakes just as he applied them, then returned them to normal so we could not tell. Although these remarks need considerable detail, they point to stronger requirements for inferential justification than are often offered, but weaker than the traditional claim that knowledge must be certain. They are also in line with the idea that a justified belief has to be beyond reasonable doubt although not beyond all possible doubt.

The second point is whether a theory of inferential justification of this kind is consistent with naturalism. If we consider the weak sense of naturalism that I began with (the kind that requires only biological continuity), the answer would seem to be that it is inconsistent. Few animals are able to defend their beliefs. (Note that by defending beliefs, I do not mean being able to express one's premises to others; it is enough if the creature could express them to himself.) I do not think this is a problem, however. The ability to give arguments characterizes higher-level beliefs, i.e., those further removed from perception, and infants and nonhumans seem to have little inferential knowledge at this level. In fact, one might argue that the theory allows us to intellectualize knowledge just at the point where it is unlikely that infants and nonhumans have it. As a result, I do not think the theory violates our conception of humans as animals, but rather, it might well explain our differences from the other animals.

The more serious issue is whether the theory is incompatible with type (3) materialism. I am not sure of the answer to this question. On the one hand, as I have already remarked, the theory can be developed alongside a reliability theory of noninferential belief, which is more clearly naturalistic. It need not, in other words, be committed to the claim that such beliefs are warranted by intuition or self-evidence. The central question is whether the normative criteria for evidence and the criteria for nontrivial alternatives can be explained in a naturalistic framework. I suspect that this problem is no more difficult than the more general problem of accounting for belief, action, and other mental notions with a naturalistic theory. I do not mean to suggest that these other problems are easy. (Actually I do not know what to say about them, although I tend to be sympathetic to a materialist account of mental functions.) What I mean is that I do not think the epistemic problems are different in kind from some of the other more obvious difficulties naturalism has to get around. If this is right, these epistemological issues do not pose special problems for materialism (as I assume the theory of the given does), although I must say I would be hard-pressed to prove this.

NOTES

1. Sellars, 1963, p. 21.

2. This is a stronger sense of 'justification' than one often encounters in the literature. Goldman, 1979, p. 114, for example, takes a justificationist theory to hold that justification depends on one's state at the time and not on the history of the belief. He calls this a *current time-slice theory.* My sense of 'justificationism' can be called *strong justificationism*—nothing important turns on my use of the phrase. Later I will suggest a time-slice theory to deal with inferential justification.

3. See John Locke, *An Essay Concerning Human Understanding,* Bk. IV, chap. ii, sec. 14, and Gottfried Leibniz, *New Essays,* Bk. IV, chap. ii, sec. 14.

4. This is a rough statement of the view. Price and Lewis (as well as Locke) thought that sensations could be influenced by other beliefs and so were not cases of givenness simply because they were sensations. Their view was that we can determine by introspection which elements are "contaminated" and which are "pure," i.e., given, so that any contamination was eliminable. See Price, 1950, p. 9. In more contemporary terms, they held (1) that some observation terms are not theory-laden and (2) that we can tell by introspection which these are.

5. On (a), see Dretske, 1978, and Nozick, 1981. On (b), see Goldman, 1979, and Shatz, 1983, among others. Both of these

approaches can be treated as reliability theories. Theory (a) can be interpreted to hold that S's belief that p is a reliable indicator that p is true if and only if he would not have believed that p if it had not been true. I will restrict the term 'reliability theory' to reliable-process theories, however. The reason this theory seems more plausible than (a) is that we can imagine circumstances in which S would not believe p unless p is true, even though S lacks knowledge (is not justified). Schmitt, 1983, p. 221, gives this example: S believes e, and e entails p, but he does not believe p on this basis. Rather, the evidence jars a childhood memory that forces him to believe p. We can imagine circumstances in which he would not have believed p unless p were true, yet S is not justified in accepting p.

6. Among those who have found it counterintuitive are Bonjour, 1978; Sosa, 1983; and Shatz, 1983. I have discussed Bonjour's objection in Meyers, 1981, pp. 75-76.

7. Schmitt, 1983, accepts the counterexample but holds that the reliability theory is a theory of knowledge rather than of justification. This means that S's beliefs about the winners can be knowledge even though he is not justified in holding them. This may be a verbal variant of the suggestion I am making. If he means by 'justified belief' what I mean by 'rational belief', the difference is verbal. Note that, if we accept Schmitt's view, we have to hold that noninferential knowledge need *not* be justified although we would not have to hold that it is *un*justified either, i.e., we would have to hold that S's having noninferential knowledge that p does *not* entail that S is justified in believing p. A precedent for this is the Wittgensteinian view that justification does not apply to the lower level, but only to higher levels. See Chisholm, *Theory of Knowledge*, 1966, pp. 29-30.

8. Putnam, 1981, pp. 114-115.

9. For a discussion of the sort of restrictions I have in mind, see Chisholm, 1982, pp. 146-147; for details on perceptual mechanisms, see Goldman, 1976.

10. Goldman, 1979, p. 114.

11. See Dretske, 1978; and Nozick, 1981.

REFERENCES

Bonjour, Lawrence. "Can Empirical Knowledge Have a Foundation?" *American Philosophical Quarterly* 15 (1978).
Chisholm, Roderick M. "Theory of Knowledge in America," in *The Foundations of Knowing* (Minneapolis, Minn.: University of Minnesota Press, 1982).
———. *The Theory of Knowledge* (Englewood Cliffs, N. J.: Prentice-Hall, 1966).
Dretske, Fred. "Epistemic Operators," *Journal of Philosophy* 67 (1970):1007-1023.
———. "Conclusive Reasons," in *Essays on Knowledge and Justification,* ed. G. S. Pappas and Marshall Swain (Ithaca, N.Y.: Cornell University Press, 1978).
Goldman, Alvin I. "Discrimination and Perceptual Knowledge," *Journal of Philosophy* 73 (1976):771-791.
———. "What Is Justified Belief?" in *Justification and Knowledge,* ed. George S. Pappas (Dordrecht: D. Reidel, 1979).
Lewis, C. I. *Mind and the World Order* (New York: Dover, 1956).
Meyers, Robert G. "Sellars' Rejection of Foundations," *Philosophical Studies* 39 (1981):61-78.
Nozick, Robert. *Philosophical Explanations* (Cambridge, Mass.: Harvard University Press, 1981).
Price, H. H. *Perception* (London: Methuen, 1950).
Putnam, Hilary. "Philosophers and Human Understanding," in *Scientific Explanation,* ed. A. F. Heath (Oxford: Oxford University Press, 1981).
Schmitt, Frederick F. "Knowledge, Justification, and Reliability," *Synthese* 55 (1983):209-229.
Sellars, Wilfrid. *Science, Perception and Reality* (London: Routledge and Kegan Paul, 1963).
Shatz, David. Review of Swain, *Reasons and Knowledge. Journal of Philosophy* 80 (1983):542-554.
Sosa, Ernest. "Nature Unmirrored, Epistemology Naturalized," *Synthese* 55 (1983):49-72.

John T. Kearns

Meyers on
"Naturalizing Epistemic Terms"

After following Professor Meyers's paper with great interest, I am afraid I do not really understand what he is up to. The project he describes in his introductory remarks is either ridiculously easy or terribly difficult. We cannot say which it is because he fails to resolve the "ambiguity" by working on the project. Instead, he describes a different project, which he fails to work on as well.

Professor Meyers motivates the discussion of naturalistic epistemology by expressing a longing for an account of knowledge that makes human knowledge continuous with the knowledge or cognitive capacities of nonhuman animals. He suggests that the researcher who wishes to achieve such continuity is free to select the concept of knowledge that best suits his purposes. If Meyers is serious about this, then the task is ridiculously easy.

We can avoid creating a gulf between the knowledge that nonhuman animals have and the knowledge that people have by defining 'A knows that p' to mean A *is breathing and p is true*. Given this concept of "knowledge," there is no difference between what dogs know and people know. Though, of course, both dogs and people know everything.

My proposed definition of 'know' is not serious, but it is worth considering this worthless definition to see *why* it is worthless. What is wrong is this: If I wish to give an account of knowledge, I am not free to select or shape the concept of knowledge as I see fit. An account of knowledge must be an account of knowledge as this is commonly understood. If I wish to give an account of something else, I can do so. If the something else has not got a name, I can give it one. But I must not tell people I am giving an account of knowledge.

Of course, there may already be different kinds of knowledge, or different concepts of knowledge. Someone may wish to argue that one kind is more interesting, or more important, than the others. Perhaps he can insist that the favored kind is more important precisely because it allows for continuity between humans and other animals. This could be a legitimate procedure, but it will surely be quite difficult to articulate the chosen concept, establish the human-nonhuman continuity, and make the case for the fundamental character of this knowledge. This is not what Meyers has done, or tried to do.

In this paper, Meyers uses his introductory remarks to provide a reason for abandoning what he calls Justificationist theories in epistemology. He has done nothing whatever to show that the approach he favors does better than the approach he rejects. For he has said nothing at all about what is surely the most fundamental issue when it comes to continuity between the knowledge of humans and other animals—this is the issue of whether non-human animals can engage in propositional thinking. It seems absolutely clear that in order to believe something, one must be capable of propositional thinking. She must be able to grasp what it is for something to be the case—she must be able to think *that* so and so. It is far from obvious that dogs and cats can engage in propositional thinking. But unless nonhuman animals can do this, there is no way to establish an important continuity between animals and humans. The issue of which epistemological theory is correct will be totally irrelevant.

Many people will affirm with great confidence that animals have beliefs. None of them, so far as I know, can explain what they (or the animals) have in mind. Recently, John Searle, in his book *Intentionality,* has insisted that cats and dogs, or, at least, dogs, can and do have beliefs. He has tried to explain what such beliefs might amount to. But the careful reader will note that, by the end of his book, Searle has assigned properties to beliefs that seem to require linguistic abilities on the part of any believing subject.

Perhaps I am being unfair to Professor Meyers. Many people

have described reliabilist approaches to epistemology as naturalistic, so I should not require that he be the one to show that, or why, this label is appropriate. And instead of accusing him of not carrying out either the easy or the difficult task that his remarks suggest, it may be more appropriate to consider what he is really up to. But if we look past his comments on naturalism, and on the appropriate way to account for the appropriate sort of knowledge, we are left with various statements of his preferences. Meyers favors reliabilism when it comes to foundational beliefs, but he thinks Justificationist approaches have something to offer when it comes to inferential beliefs. And he would like to see a distinction made between what a person is justified in believing and what it is rational for her to believe. Meyers has described an epistemological theory without developing it, or solving any of the problems that confront such a theory. In his discussion of the features that an epistemological theory ought to possess, Meyers vacillates between appealing to familiar concepts and calling for new ones. (He appeals to an ordinary concept when he says "it is unlikely we would say that" a student knows a theorem when its proof is forgotten, though he clearly calls for new conceptions of justification and rationality.)

It is one thing to engage in traditional epistemological inquiries, trying to solve traditional problems as they have traditionally been conceived. It is something different to call for a new epistemological enterprise. It is not possible to develop a traditional theory and carry out a new enterprise at once, but Meyers acts as if it were. By relying on old concepts while he is calling for new ones, Meyers shows that he is not entirely clear about what he is trying to do, or what he is calling for others to do. I think it is important to get clear about conceptual issues before trying to achieve substantive results. Professor Meyers has not done this. But many of those called reliabilists have not done so either.

Reliabilism claims that a belief is justified if it is produced by a reliable procedure or mechanism, even if the belief's owner does not know what the mechanism is and cannot come up with any reason for thinking it is reliable. Reliabilism is unsatisfactory because it gives a bad answer to a question put in terms of the ordinary concept of justification. Reliabilism just does not explain what it is for a belief to be justified, as we ordinarily understand this. Reliabilists also fail to describe a new concept, or propose a new question for which reliabilism might be a good answer.

Murray Clarke

Reliability and Two Kinds of Epistemic Justification

Stuart Cohen has recently taken the externalist, reliable process account of justification to task.[1] Cohen thinks there is an ineliminably normative aspect to justification that the reliable process account of justification is unable to do justice to. Since Cohen's case is persuasive, it is important that reliabilists come to terms with it.

I propose a conciliatory solution to the internalist-externalist debate concerning the nature of epistemic justification. I shall argue that externalists (such as Alvin Goldman, Hilary Kornblith, and Fred Schmitt)[2] are explicating what I shall call *objective* epistemic justification, while internalists (Laurence Bonjour[3] and Stuart Cohen) clarify a different notion, *subjective* epistemic justification. Both notions are essential to a complete rendering of the term *justification* since, as it turns out, we employ at least two distinct kinds of "ordinary standards" in assessing the justificatory status of our beliefs.

I

Goldman's basic reliable process account has it that a "reliable cognitive process" is a belief-forming process that generally (e.g.,

I would like to thank Bruce Freed, Alvin Goldman, Hilary Kornblith, and Charles Lambros for helpful comments on earlier versions of this work.

and roughly, 90 percent of the time) produces true beliefs. Later, a "background" clause is added. Finally stated, his account reads:

> If S's belief in p at t results from a reliable cognitive process, and there is no reliable or conditionally reliable process available to S which, had it been used by S in addition to the process actually used, would have resulted in S's not believing p at t, then S's belief in p at t is justified.[4]

There is an indirect link between reliability (i.e., justification) and truth on this account. This is so since a reliably formed belief emerges from a process that generally produces *true* beliefs.[5]

Cohen's approach is simply to deny the alleged probabilistic connection between reliability (i.e., justification) and truth. He tries to demonstrate this by showing that reliability is not even necessary for justification. Cohen accomplishes this apparent refutation of Goldman's account of justification using two interesting counterexamples.[6]

In his first example, Cohen asks us to suppose that the evil demon hypothesis is true in world W and that S, an inhabitant of W, believes some proposition P on the basis of what he takes, on apparently good inductive grounds, to be a reliable process, say the process of perception. Let us refer to this believed-to-be-reliable process as R. The machinations of the malevolent demon are such that our experiences, and S's, are just as they would be if our cognitive processes were, in fact, reliable. S assumes R to be reliable on these grounds. On Goldman's account, however, R is *not* reliable, due to the evil demon, and S is not justified in believing P. This, Cohen rightly points out, is counterintuitive. If S has every reason to believe that R is reliable—if, so far as S is able to tell, his inductive grounds are good—then he is justified in believing P, despite the fact that R is in fact not reliable (due to the presence of the evil demon). Cohen concludes that Goldman's account fails to accord with our intuition that S is justified since his belief is appropriate *given the available evidence*.

A possible response to Cohen's putative counterexample is to deny the intelligibility of the example. One could insist, for example, that S simply would never come to believe that R is a reliable process in the demon world. Surely, we might argue, R could not be thought reliable by S if an evil demon was manipulating this world, for there would then be inductive inconsistencies that S would notice. Alternatively, if the evil demon was manipulating S to believe R reliable, such manipulation would only be successful on the supposition that the demon had, unwittingly, actually made R reliable. (Here we suppose the demon to be evil, but stupid!)

I do not find either response plausible for the following reason. All Cohen need say is that the demon has the requisite ability to make R actually unreliable while systematically misleading S in such a way that S takes R to be reliable. Construed in this way, there is no logical impossibility involved. S is justified in believing P on the basis of R, and R is not reliable. Reliability, it would seem, is not necessary for justification.

II

Is there any plausible reliabilist response to be made to Cohen? As will become evident, I think the answer is yes. Let me first introduce a distinction that I think goes to the heart of the debate, namely, that between *objective* epistemic justification and *subjective* epistemic justification.[7] My claim will be that the present debate rests on a confusion of two equally legitimate kinds of justification, where Goldman is explicating objective justification and Cohen subjective justification.

Now for the distinction. Imagine the following situation:[8] A man sincerely believes it is morally permissible to drown baby girls. He reasons that since it is morally permissible and since his family is impoverished, he can only continue to support them if he kills his daughter. He commits the act. Though we enlightened souls rightly find his act atrocious from our perspective, we would be inclined to admit that, *given his beliefs,* he acted in a morally justifiable and rational fashion. This sort of example, John Pollock claims, has been traditionally used to distinguish two senses of *should* in ethics, an objective sense and a subjective sense. Our man is *subjectively* justified in killing his daughter; he (subjectively) "should" have killed her. Objectively, however, he "should not" have killed her.[9]

Pollock thinks, and I concur, that an analogous distinction is at work in epistemology. It is, roughly speaking, the difference between what a person should believe, given what are *actually* (metaphysically) good reasons for belief, and what he should believe, given *his* (possibly mistaken) beliefs about reasons for belief. The former is the objective sense of *should* while the latter is the subjective sense of *should*.

My claim with respect to Cohen's evil demon example, then, is that Cohen's objection to Goldman is predicated on an appeal to subjective epistemic justification. It is this concept that Cohen takes Goldman's project to flounder on. This is why Cohen's use of the evil demon example *appears* so damaging to Goldman's reliable process account of justification. Were Goldman attempting to explicate the subjective brand of epistemic justification, then Cohen's objection would be devastating. But this, clearly, is not Goldman's project. He intends to explicate the objective sense of epistemic justification. Cohen refers to subjective epistemic justification as "normative justification."[10] Objective epistemic justification is nonnormative since the term *justification* is clarified in nonepistemic terms. "Good reasons" for belief reduce, according to Goldman, to beliefs that are "probably" true, given that they were formed by means of a reliable process. The result is a nonnormative explication of "justification" in terms of a metaphysical probability condition. This is not to say that justification has somehow become a nonnormative concept on this account, but rather that, and only that, the normative concept of epistemic justification is explicated in nonnormative terms.

Recall that a "reliable cognitive process" is one that generally produces true beliefs. Goldman does not commit himself to either a frequency or propensity account of probability here, in keeping with his view that our "ordinary conception" of justification is vague in this respect. Note, also, that one could have an objectively or nonnormatively justified belief that *is* false on Goldman's account. This follows from the fact that the probability that the functioning of a reliable process will result in a true belief is less than 1.0. There is a difference, then, between a reliably formed belief and a certain belief. By analogy, my car is reliable, but this fact is consistent with the fact that, *occasionally*, it will not run. We do not think it unreliable on these grounds and neither should we refer to a process, such as perception, as "unreliable" even if its use, *occasionally*, results in false beliefs. The point is that beliefs formed by reliable processes are objectively justified even if, occasionally, they are false. There is a sense, however, in which objective justification *is* normative. This is the fact that the agent "ought" to believe something that is reliably generated. But this is not to the point. The point is that the term *justification* is defined in nonnormative or nonepistemic terms. It is this aspect of the "normative" that Goldman is concerned to eliminate from his account of epistemic justification.

Goldman, unfortunately, does not make this point as clear as one would like in his "What is Justified Belief?" There he suggests that his explanation is just of our "ordinary standards" of justification. As he notes:

> I do not try to prescribe standards for justification that differ from, or improve upon, our ordinary standards. I merely try to explicate the ordinary standards, which are, I believe, quite different from those of many classical, e.g., "Cartesian," accounts.[11]

The term *ordinary standards* is left undefined because justification is a somewhat vague concept. He later notes, however, that:

> justification is not a purely categorical concept, although I treat it here as categorical in the interest of simplicity. We can and do regard certain beliefs as more justified than others.[12]

Independently of whether or not *justification* is a categorical term, however, I think we have *two* "ordinary standards" of justification: conditional (on the subject's background beliefs) or subjective epistemic justification and, in contrast, objective or categorical epistemic justification. The latter notion ought to be used in an analysis of knowledge, while both notions are needed for an analysis of justified belief. (I will say more about this in my concluding remarks.)

Another way to characterize the distinction is to say that subjective justification is conferred when S believes what any "representative," typical, or normal agent would believe under exactly the same circumstances. Objective justification, on the other hand, is conferred when S believes what any epistemically competent person who does have complete information concerning the reliability of a process R—but who does not know that p—would believe were he or she in exactly the same circumstances as S.[13] It is the latter sort of notion that Goldman wishes to explicate. Failure to separate these two senses of "epistemic justification" gives Cohen room to operate.

III

The question I now wish to address is: What *is* the relationship between these two types of justification? The objective sense of epistemic justification is construed by Schmitt as the objective frequency that a reliable process, R, displays in producing true beliefs. Justification, we are to suppose, is indirectly linked to truth insofar as a reliable process is defined as a process that generally has, as output, true beliefs.[14]

There is no direct nor indirect natural connection to truth on the subjective account of epistemic justification. The agent is required only to do the best he can given the inputs available to him and is deemed justified or unjustified on *that* basis. This explains why this is the wrong type of justification for an account of knowledge: there is an insufficient link to truth. It makes the acquisition of a true belief too much a matter of chance to qualify as the sort of belief acquisition procedure involved in knowledge. There is, it would seem, a world of difference between a justified belief and knowledge. The belief need not be true in the former case while, in the latter case, it *must* be true. We need an account of justification that is weak enough to allow false beliefs but strong enough to account for knowledge. Internalist accounts, I suspect, are too weak for knowledge since they guarantee no link, not even an indirect one, to truth.[15]

The second of Cohen's examples will help to clarify these points. In order to bring out the normative aspect of justification, he offers an example that appears to suggest counterintuitive results when viewed from the perspective of Goldman's reliable process account. Imagine an evil demon world, W, with two reasoners, A and B, in it. A is a good reasoner because he reasons in accordance with the canons of inductive logic: he is a good Bayesian. Good reasoning, according to Goldman, is a paradigm example of a reliable process. Others include standard perceptual processes, remembering, and introspection. B is *not* a good reasoner, for he engages in confused reasoning, wishful thinking, guesswork, and so on. These are processes that Goldman, as everyone else, considers unreliable. Both A and B believe that p; A for good reasons, B for poor reasons. Cohen correctly points out that, despite the fact that A utilizes a process that Goldman deems reliable, neither A nor B would be justified on Goldman's account.

No one could ever possess a justified belief in an evil demon world, *ex hypothesi,* on the reliable process account. Yet, says Cohen, it is clear that there is a crucial difference between *A* and *B,* a difference, moreover, that Goldman's account is insensitive to. *A* is epistemically justified, while *B* is not. Using my terms, Cohen's point is that *A* is subjectively justified, while *B* is not. Cohen concludes that justification is properly construed as essentially normative or subjective in nature. Reliabilist accounts collectively fail insofar as thay fail to bring out this normative sense of justification.

How ought we to resolve this dilemma? The answer, I think, is conciliatory: there is something right about both Goldman's and Cohen's accounts of justification. The following analysis of Cohen's second evil demon example captures what is right about each analysis. Neither *A* nor *B* is *objectively* justified in accepting *p* due to the presence of the evil demon; however, *A* is subjectively justified in accepting *p* while *B* is *not* subjectively justified in accepting *p.*

A is subjectively justified in accepting *p* because *A* is a good reasoner, *B* is *not* subjectively justified in accepting *p* because *B* is not a good reasoner. Surely Cohen is right about *subjective* justification: the differences between *A* and *B* are crucial and the reliabilist has no means, it would seem, to mark this difference. On the other hand, neither *A* nor *B* is objectively justified in accepting *p* due to the presence of the evil demon. Goldman is equally right about *objective* justification: so long as the evil demon undermines the reliability of the processes that lead *A* and *B* to believe *p,* neither is objectively justified, and *neither* has knowledge.

I conclude that both Goldman and Cohen have half of the analysis correct. My view is better, though, since it takes what is right about each approach and combines their insights into a complete account. A complete account of justification must explicate both senses of justification. The internalist, subjective sense of epistemic justification is important and legitimate but so is the externalist, objective reliable process sense of epistemic justification. The dilemma is resolved.

IV

We are now in a position to complete the examination of the relationship between these two notions of justification. A plausible naturalistic explanation for the existence of objective justification is that it would be a miracle of sorts if we continued to survive despite utilizing objective, radically *un*reliable processes. If perception were not reliable, one might ask, how could we ever survive as a species, or, for that matter, how could any species survive? It seems totally implausible to suppose that we could have survived.

If this proposed naturalistic explanation is cogent, then one can see how the notions of objective and subjective justification are interrelated. Beliefs that are important to our survival *must* be formed on the basis of reliable processes. Our subjective, normative justification-assessments for accepting these important beliefs must, historically, have been close enough to the actual, objective probabilities involved to have allowed our survival.

One might object to my account on the grounds that I have unnecessarily multiplied senses of the term *justification*. Surely, it might be argued, we need to apply Occam's eraser[16] and settle on one sense of justification. The main argument against this view has two parts:

(1) The internalist guarantees no link through the justification condition to truth. So internalist justification is inadequate for an account of knowledge.

(2) Externalist accounts stumble on the sort of examples Cohen uses concerning the evil demon. Externalist, reliable process accounts of justification are therefore also flawed.

In short, both internalist and externalist accounts are incomplete. It would seem only sensible to extract what is right from each account even if we thereby disappoint Occamites. Moreover, it is the *objective* account that is required for an analysis of "knowledge." A person undertaking this latter task would utilize one account of justification as a condition of knowledge, while accepting that there is another legitimate sense of the term *justification* that is applicable for other purposes. Objective justification provides the indirect link to truth that we need for an account of knowledge. Moreover, it can account for some cases where we want to allow that a belief is reliably (objectively) formed, yet false. The subjective account captures the remaining cases where we want to allow that a particular belief is justified, in the sense of being rationally held, while abstaining as to the truth of the belief.

In short, I think it is a mistake to try to provide a uniform account of justification that somehow tries to bridge these two senses of epistemic justification. This is so because, as Cohen's second example highlights, we may be willing to ascribe subjective epistemic justification to a proposition that a person believes, while not ascribing objective epistemic justification to the acceptance of that same proposition.

The point of requiring that true beliefs be justified *is just* that justification provides a link, indirect but close, to truth. The reliable process account of justification captures this linkage and, for this reason, remains a very compelling account.

NOTES

1. Cohen's paper is "Justification and Truth," *Philosophical Studies* 46 (1984):279-295.

2. Goldman's paper is "What Is Justified Belief," in *Justification and Knowledge,* edited by G. S. Pappas (Dordrecht: D. Reidel Publishing Company, 1979), pp. 1-24; Kornblith's paper is "The Psychological Turn," in the *Australasian Journal of Philosophy* vol. 60 no. 3 (September 1982):238-254; Schmitt's paper is "Reliability, Objectivity, and the Background of Justification," in the *Australasian Journal of Philosophy,* vol. 62 no. 1 (March 1984):1-15.

3. Bonjour's paper is "Externalist Theories of Empirical Knowledge," in Peter A. French et al., editors, *Midwest Studies V: Studies in Epistemology* (Minneapolis: University of Minnesota Press, 1980), pp. 53-73.

4. Goldman, op. cit., p. 20. On page 13 Goldman says that a process is "conditionally reliable when a sufficient proportion of its output-beliefs are true *given that its input-beliefs are true."*

5. The basic account (clause 1) has it that a "reliable cognitive process" is a belief-forming process that generally produces true

beliefs. The "background belief" aspect (clauses 2, 3, and 4) elimi-
nates the possibility that a cognizer could have available to her
both a belief that the reliable process R was unreliable and that
she still would be justified in believing that p, where p is generated by R.

6. Since Cohen attacks the notion of a reliable process in
general, his criticism applies to Kornblith and Schmitt as well
since they accept the basic reliabilist account.

7. John Pollock draws a similar distinction in "A Plethora
of Epistemological Theories," in *Justification and Knowledge,*
edited by G. Pappas, op. cit., pp. 110-111.

8. Ibid., p. 110.

9. Pollock notes that the subjective sense of "should" is equivalent to Brandt's "putative sense of should" in his *Ethical Theory*
(New York: Prentice Hall, 1959). The distinction is between what a
person should have done, given the *actual* (possibly unforeseen)
consequences of his actions (his *objective* obligation) and what he
should have done, given his *beliefs about the consequences of his
actions* (his *subjective* obligation).

10. Cohen (1984), op. cit., p. 282.

11. Goldman (1979), op. cit. p. 1.

12. Ibid., p. 10.

13. The notion of a representative cognitive agent occurs in
Bruce Freed's "Failing to Know the Necessary," *Philosophical
Work in Progress,* The University of Western Ontario, no. 17,
May 1984.

14. Reliabilists do not give precise probability estimates here
since they believe that objective justification is a somewhat vague
notion. Schmitt suggests, for instance, that we assess the same
situation in the same way even if we would construe the likelihood
of p in widely divergent ways. See his 1984, p. 24, n.10.

15. This last claim may be thought an overstatement. It
might be argued, on quasi-evolutionary grounds, for example, that
if there were no connection at all between epistemic justification
and truth, then there would be no point to the concept of epistemic
justification, and we would not have such a concept. Be that as it
may, my main point still stands, to wit that if there is any
connection at all between epistemic justification and knowledge
on the internalist account it is not close enough to explain how
justification and truth yield knowledge.

16. The happy phrase "Occam's eraser" is due to Paul Ziff in his book *Semantic Analysis* (New York: Cornell University Press, 1960). His intent was to encourage philosophers not to multiply senses of a word beyond necessity. In contrast, "Occam's razor" is to be used in order not to multiply theoretical entities beyond necessity.

Charles H. Lambros

Clarke on "Reliability and Two Kinds of Epistemic Justification"

I will begin with a summary of three main points that appear in Clarke's paper.

First, the distinction between two kinds of epistemic justification. A belief X is said to be *objectively justified* (in the epistemic sense) when it is formed on the basis of a reliable cognitive process R (and when there is no other reliable process available to the believer, which, had it also been used, would have resulted in the disbelief of X). A belief X is *subjectively justified* (in the epistemic sense) when it is formed by a believer S by some process R, when S has "every reason," or "good reason" to believe R is reliable (or when any "representative" cognitive agent would have believed X in exactly the same circumstances). The distinction, as emphasized by Clarke, rests on the different roles played by R in the definitions: that between *being* reliable—i.e., being a belief-forming process that generally produces true beliefs—and there being *good reasons* to believe R to be reliable.

Second: Both "senses" of justification have philosophically sound foundations; and accordingly, both make valuable contributions to the understanding, or analysis, of justification. Objective justification is needed in the analysis of knowledge. Subjective justification is needed to make an important distinction that cannot be made by the objectivist—i.e., the distinction between

171

those objectively nonjustifiable beliefs that are nevertheless reasonably formed, and those objectively nonjustifiable beliefs that
are, in addition, unreasonably formed.

Third: The issue about which sense of justification is the correct one is to be resolved—or should we say dissolved—by making
room for both. Each is to have its distinct and nonconflicting
usage: the objective sense when attainment of knowledge is the
issue, the subjective when only attainment of reasonable belief is
the issue.

I take this last to be Clarke's main point. First, let us note
that there is a certain plausibility to Clarke's suggestion. The call,
I take it, is a call for peaceful coexistence. How might a program
of peaceful coexistence be carried out in practice? There are clear
examples, I think, when one rather than the other sense of justification is already determined by context to be the appropriate
one. In mathematics, for example, the appropriate "belief-forming
process," if they may be called that, are generally of such a high
degree of rigor that outright knowledge claims are made on their
basis. Questioning assertions in a mathematical context, and between experts, are typically a call for objective justification—a
proof. (Perhaps mathematical knowledge is even a paradigm example of objective justification, although recall that René Descartes invoked the [original] evil demon argument even at that
level.) On the other hand, "Will it rain tomorrow?"—given the
generally admitted lack of reliable belief-forming processes in that
discipline—perhaps is best construed as an inquiry about reasonable belief.

Examples could also be given where the appropriate sense of
justification is ambiguous—not determined by context. "Is Fer-
mat's last theorem true?" when asked of one layman by another,
may be a call for a proof—objective justification—in which case
the answer is "We don't know." Or, more modestly, it may be a
call for evidence sufficient to sway the intellect; in which case,
the answer is "Yes, you see . . . (and so on.)" In order to carry out
the program of peaceful coexistence, we need only recommend
that the layman of whom the question is asked proceed by responding: "In which sense of justification do you mean? If you
mean in the sense that . . . (and so on)." It appears, then, at least
from these examples, that Clarke's reconciliation view has plausibility. Not only might we invoke such a distinction, it appears
already to be in common practice.

I suspect, however, that Clarke's conciliatory view will quiet neither the reliabilist nor the subjectivist. Clarke does appreciate the strength of the philosophical arguments behind each petition. But these arguments, like a good many philosophical arguments, serve two purposes: positively, to provide the foundation for their own point of view; and negatively, to show the outright error of opposing views. Clarke appreciates the positive purpose, but not the negative—or at least, not sufficiently so. Let me explain.

First, the objectivist: His fundamental point is that there is *only* one thing that can justify a belief in the epistemic sense, that which contributes to the likelihood of the belief being *true*. How does the argument go? The point—the intention—of forming a belief is to take a stand on the truth. Indeed, what it *means* to form a belief is to take something *as* true. So, the intention in forming a belief is to get at the truth. But the *right* way of doing this is one that is likely to fulfill the intention. (In this sense, there is a *right* way of robbing a bank, or committing murder.) So, the right way of forming a belief is a way that is likely to get me to the truth. And a justified belief is one formed in the right way.

The point to be emphasized in all this is that the reliabilist is not merely arguing (in the positive sense) that there is *a* sense of justification that is objective, but also (negatively) that any different sense is wrong, or inadequate. It is difficult to see how he could agree that there is a second epistemically relevant sense distinct from his own, with an area of epistemic application distinct from his own.

According to this view, "justified" in the subjective sense may have psychological relevance, but not epistemological relevance. Suppose objectivist *O* and subjectivist *S* both to have formed the same mistaken belief, but one justified for both in their respective senses. Upon learning that the belief was false, *O*'s justification lies in his having used a generally reliable truth-producing process. But what can *S* say for himself? "Well, I was wrong, but I did just what any other reasonable agent would have done" or "Well, I was wrong, but it could have been worse—I might have been guessing." But such accounts lamentably sound like excuses, providing psychological comfort perhaps.

Is the issue thus resolved in the objectivist's favor? Not quite so easily, I think. When the subjectivist is on the attack, his arguments appear to be just as persuasive. The evil demon argument is central here: it contends that we are never in possession of objective "truth"—*a fortiori* it is idle, or philosophically useless, to speak of cognitive processes that generally lead to true results. It is always possible that there is an evil demon so clever and powerful that reality is always hidden from us. Or we may actually be on the laboratory table of an evil computer scientist, with wires from the computer attached to our brains, and the computer programmed to provide us with such and such experiences, and so on. Being justified in our belief forming processes, then, can only mean that we have *good reasons* to take such processes as ones generally leading to true beliefs—not that they actually are. That they are is something that in principle can never be known. (Perhaps it is more in the spirit of the subjectivist view to say, rather than "generally leading to true beliefs," that the process generally leads to a belief concerning which nothing subsequently happens that indicates it was false.)

I agree here with Clarke—and others—that there is a useful analogy to this point in the objective-subjective distinction sometimes drawn in ethics. The act-utilitarian, for example, distinguishes between an act that *in fact* will provide the greatest happiness for the greatest number of people (such acts constitute our objective duty); and an act that, according to our *best calculations,* will produce the greatest happiness for the greatest number of people (such acts constitute our subjective duty). Due to the fact that we cannot know the future, we can never know our objective duty. But we can know our subjective duty, and that, consequently, is what we must perform.

Now my point, again, is not merely that the subjectivist view has something interesting to offer—which it does—but that it contradicts—is *inconsistent* with—the reliabilist view. And such inconsistency militates against the possibility of a conciliatory resolution. Back to the ethical analogy: The point of the subjective act-utilitarian is not merely that he has an alternative sense of duty useful in those cases when objective duty is not known; it is that his sense is the right one for all cases. In fact, when objective duty and subjective duty are not the same, and one does his objective duty, he has done something *wrong* on this account!

As a final critical point, let me say that it appears that Clarke is a bit too ready to admit to the plausibility of this part of the subjectivist argument: that the subjectivist view is needed to be able to draw distinctions that the objectivist cannot make. I am referring to Cohen's example in which *A* and *B* are reasoners in an evil demon world. Neither is objectively justified, but there clearly is a difference in the worth of *A's* reasoning and that of *B*. And this can only be put in terms of subjective justifiability.

The objectivist reply here seems obvious: namely, that he also can make the distinction. The distinction, in the objectivist sense, is that there are various ways to go wrong, some of which are not as bad as others. What makes *A* the better reasoner (though still not objectively justified, is that if there *were* no evil demon behind his world after all, he would in fact be using (presumably) a reliable belief forming process—and the same cannot be said of *B*.

The resolution of the debate remains an intriguing question, for how can we admit to the soundness of two arguments that lead to inconsistent conclusions? In closing, allow me to indicate, in an admittedly very sketchy way, a possible path of solution. As should be clear from the above, I do not believe that conciliation of the two views—unmodified from the versions before us here today—is possible. Rather, what I propose is a union, a marriage if you will, of the two in *modified* form. The hope is that the best of both—the insights each offers—will be preserved in the union.

How is this to be done? By requiring both sides to be explicit about the concept of "truth" in their theorizing about justification. Thus, if the objectivist takes the evil demon argument seriously, as he should, he might see the desirability of adopting a pragmatic, or perhaps coherence, theory of truth. The result would be that in a stupid evil demon world—one in which our experience flowed coherently, and our "reasonable" expectations were never thwarted—truth in a coherence or pragmatic sense *would* be achievable. And in *that* sense of truth, we *could* speak of reliable belief-forming processes. And the subjectivist, in this world, might also be willing to modify *his* sense of justification such that having good reasons to hold a belief-forming process reliable is tantamount to its *being* reliable. With such compromises, it would not be so clear that the two are saying something so very different. The compromise on the part of the objectivist would be to give up his realist sense of 'true' and 'objective'. The compromise on the part of the subjectivist would be to no longer find use of the concept 'true' philosophically hopeless. But then, as in all good marriages, if I may extend the metaphor, compromises are necessary.

In a *non*stupid evil demon world—where our experiences did not flow coherently, and even the most reasonable of our expectations were thwarted—we should note that, of course, none of this would matter.

Paul Weirich

A Naturalistic Approach
to Rational Deliberation

Familiar rules for rational decision, such as the rule to maximize expected utility, apply to the set of options the decision-maker has under consideration. The rules say little about the character of this set of options. Perhaps they assume that the set of options considered should be the set of all options. This assumption is warranted if the rules are advanced for ideal cases where considering all options is feasible. But it is unwarranted if the rules are advanced for actual human decisions, since considering all options is beyond our abilities.

On the other hand, perhaps familiar decision rules assume that nothing need be said about the set of options under consideration. Perhaps they assume that this set constitutes a part of the decision problem, a "given," not itself subject to evaluation. This assumption is warranted if the rules are advanced just to evaluate a *choice* from among a set of options. But it is unwarranted if the rules are advanced to evaluate a *decision* completely. To make a completely rational decision one must consider a rational set of options as well as rationally choose among the op-

I am very grateful to the participants of the Naturalism and Rationality Conference, especially Marjorie Clay, the commentator, for helpful discussion of the paper. Also, I would like to thank my colleague Richard Feldman for many helpful suggestions.

tions considered. For instance, if a person chooses a career without considering some of the obvious, attractive careers open to him, his decision can hardly be completely rational even if he rationally chooses among the options he considers.

Consequently, those interested in completely evaluating actual decisions must formulate some standards of rationality for the consideration of options. Here I will propose some standards of this kind, and I will give one special attention. In particular, I will develop it in a naturalistic way. In other words, I will develop the standard so that whether a decision-maker conforms to it is an empirical matter open to scientific investigation. I take this approach not only because it is plausible, but also because it affords an opportunity to enrich our understanding of rationality by means of empirical as well as philosophical research.

By considering an option I mean only entertaining it. I do not mean mulling it over, evaluating it, or imagining one adopts it. The standards for these other parts of deliberation are different from those governing the mere consideration of options.

The standards I propose for the consideration of options are intended to be humanly attainable. They do not assume any idealizations, e.g., that decision-makers have no cognitive limitations. However, these standards accommodate most of the difficulties of human decision-making by means of evasive qualifications rather than direct confrontation. They directly address only the difficulties of considering options. These difficulties receive special treatment since they are the ones that make it unfeasible to consider all options and so give rise to the problem treated in this paper.

The standards I propose for the consideration of options are procedural rather than substantive. That is, instead of evaluating a set of options in terms of its membership, they evaluate the set in terms of the procedures that produced consideration of the set. Procedural standards of rationality are proposed elsewhere. For example, Herbert Simon[1] proposes some for behavior, and Jon Elster[2] proposes some for beliefs and basic desires. Procedural standards seem appropriate for the consideration of options since a decision-maker is unable to meet the salient substantive goal of considering all options, and since he has more control over the procedures governing the consideration of options than over the sets of options considered.

To begin, I distinguish two kinds of deliberation. Then, for each, I propose a procedural standard for the consideration of options.

SIMPLE AND COMPLEX DELIBERATION

Sometimes in the course of the deliberation preceding a decision, a person reflects about the set of options under consideration: Are they the best available? Has some attractive option been overlooked? Such reflection can lead to the discovery of options that are better than those currently being considered. For instance, imagine a person trying to make a six-egg omelet. Suppose he has already broken five eggs into a bowl. He has just one egg left and is about to add it when he notices a faint odor that makes him suspicious of the egg's wholesomeness.He wonders whether to proceed and risk spoiling the omelet, or be content with a five-egg omelet. If he reflects about his options, he might discover a better option than those he is considering, perhaps breaking the egg into a saucer for inspection before adding it to the bowl, or putting it aside. Or, imagine a person suffering from pectoral angina. Suppose he is considering whether to have a bypass operation. Reflection about his options may lead him to inquire about nonsurgical means of treating the angina. And as a result, he may learn that drugs can provide relief in many cases. When someone who is deliberating reflects about his options before deciding, I call his deliberation *complex* deliberation. I propose the obvious procedural standard for the consideration of options in complex deliberation, viz., that the set of options ultimately considered is rational if and only if it is the product of rational reflection about options.

There are, of course, cases where one does not reflect about options before deciding. First, there may be no opportunity for such reflection. In contrast to the cases discussed above, there may be no time to think up ingenious strategies or to solicit suggestions from others. Second, even if there is an opportunity to reflect about options, reflecting may not be worth the trouble if the decision is unimportant. I call deliberation in cases where there is ro reflection about options *simple* deliberation. In simple deliberation the rationality of considering a certain set of options has nothing to do with subsidiary deliberations about the suitability of the set of options one is considering. Some standard independent of the standard for complex deliberation is required.[3]

I assume that in a case of simple deliberation the set of options considered is rational only if, in view of the circumstances, it is rational for the decision-maker not to reflect about options: in other words, only if, in view of the circumstances, it is rational for his deliberation to be simple. Given this assumption, to obtain a standard covering the consideration of options in simple deliberation, I need only formulate a standard for those cases of simple deliberation that meet this condition. In the following sections, therefore, I will suppose that the cases of simple deliberation treated are ones in which it is rational for deliberation to be simple. After presenting a standard for them, I will develop it in a naturalistic way.

RESPONSIBILITY IN SIMPLE DELIBERATION

Some might object that there are no standards of rationality for the consideration of options in simple deliberation. The options considered there are not subject to review. So consideration of those options is acceptable whatever they happen to be. To apply standards of rationality to their consideration would be to hold the decision-maker responsible for something beyond the influence of his deliberations.

This objection misses an important feature of the set of options considered in a case of simple deliberation. Although that set is not subject to review in the course of deliberation, it generally has been influenced by earlier deliberations about the cultivation of habits of attention. Prior to some simple deliberation, a decision-maker often has had opportunities to improve the way in which his attention focuses on options in simple deliberation. In virtue of these opportunities, he is at least partly responsible for the character of the set of options he considers. If he failed to make good use of his opportunities to develop habits of attention, he may be to blame for considering inappropriate options. For instance, imagine a pilot who never trained seriously for emergencies, and did not develop habits of thought that would bring suitable options to mind in emergencies. Suppose now one of his engines fails, and he must quickly decide what to do without reflecting on the suitability of the set of options that come to mind. If the options that come to mind are inappropriate, he is to blame for that.

In general, life offers many opportunities for cultivating tendencies to consider appropriate sets of options spontaneously. One's use of these opportunities forms a basis for the evaluation of a set of options considered in simple deliberation. Roughly, to consider the set is rational if and only if such consideration is compatible with good use of opportunities for forming habits of attention. The set satisfies this criterion trivially if one has made good use of such opportunities. If one has not, the set satisfies the criterion just in case one might have considered the set even if one had made good use of such opportunities.[4] Accordingly, the set is irrational only if one's failing to make good use of such opportunities is relevant to the case at hand.

To refine this criterion, let us consider in more detail how one makes good use of opportunities to form habits of attention. Some terminology will be helpful. I will call the mental processes that govern the spontaneous considerations of options *attention-focusing processes*. As taken here, an attention-focusing process is a kind of sequence of events culminating in the consideration of a set of options. Such a process may have many instances of operation. Paying attention and daydreaming are processes similar to the ones I have in mind, but too crude. Accurate characterization of attention-focusing processes would require research in psychology.

The attention-focusing processes that come into play by nature are very good. This was made vivid to me last spring when I was trimming some trees. Placing my ladder against the lowest limb of a tree I intended to trim, I began sawing off limbs higher up. My attention wandered from the tedious work. Eventually, without thinking, I began sawing the limb supporting the ladder. As I came close to cutting through, my attention was drawn to the imminent fall of the limb, and from this to the urgency of moving the ladder. My good fortune was not the result of any habit of attention, but rather a natural tendency to notice salient features of one's environment. Evolution rather than training saved the day.

In spite of one's good natural endowment, much can be done

to improve the quality of the attention-focusing processes that come into play in simple deliberation. As indicated above, training can impart habits of considering appropriate options. Much job training, in fact, aims specifically at the acquisition of habits of considering appropriate options in situations that arise on the job. But there are many means, besides training, of making oneself attend to suitable options. For example, drinking coffee before driving may make one alert to important traffic options.

Making good use of opportunities for improving the quality of one's attention-focusing processes is a complicated matter. First, the quality of an attention-focusing process may vary from one instance of operation to the next. A process good on one occasion may not be good on another. To illustrate, paying attention, although generally better than daydreaming, may occasionally inhibit consideration of an optimum option that daydreaming would have thrown into relief. Hence there is some uncertainty about the quality of attention-focusing processes in future situations, and as a result, some uncertainty about the ones worth cultivating. Second, there are conflicts between the improvement of habits of attention and other worthy goals. For example, if one foresees a need for speed in attending to options, a good but slow attention-focusing process may be unattractive. Also, the effort required to cultivate a good attention-focusing process may be irksome.

Since opportunities for improving the quality of one's attention-focusing processes are so numerous and challenging it is virtually impossible to use all of them well. We will therefore say that one has made good use of them if and only if one has responded rationally to most of the important opportunities, and has taken suitable steps to compensate for errors.

With the foregoing in mind, let us say that considering a certain set of options in simple deliberation is rational if and only if consideration of the set is the product of an attention-focusing process compatible with good use of opportunities for improving the quality of one's attention-focusing processes.[5]

STEPS TOWARD A NATURALISTIC STANDARD

Before continuing the development of our standard for the consideration of options in simple deliberation, let us pause to consider what our objective should be. So far our standard resembles a certain naturalistic standard for belief, according to which a belief is rational if and only if it is the product of a reliable belief-forming process. It would be desirable, if possible, to exploit this resemblance in order to obtain a naturalistic standard for the consideration of options. This would establish a fruitful connection between normative matters concerning deliberation and empirical matters concerning attention-focusing processes, just as the naturalistic standard for belief establishes a fruitful connection between normative matters concerning belief and empirical matters concerning belief-forming processes.

Here I will not present in full a naturalistic interpretation of our standard for the consideration of options in simple deliberation. I will identify and supply the main ingredient of such an interpretation. But the other ingredients will simply be assumed.

Plainly, in order to make our standard naturalistic, we need a naturalistic analysis of making good use of opportunities for improving the quality of one's attention-focusing processes. As explained above, to make good use of these opportunities is to respond rationally to most of the important ones and take suitable steps to compensate for errors. I will assume that we can construe the importance of these opportunities and the suitability of compensatory steps in a naturalistic way. Given this, a naturalistic analysis of the good use of these opportunities requires in addition only a naturalistic analysis of the rationality of responses to them. So let us consider what is needed for a naturalistic analysis of the rationality of responses to one's opportunities for improving the quality of one's attention-focusing processes.

For the first such opportunity, this analysis requires (1) a naturalistic analysis of rational *choice* among options and (2) a naturalistic analysis of the quality of attention-focusing processes. The rationality of the set of options considered in any simple deliberation that arises in this first opportunity is assured since there have been no prior opportunities to improve the quality of one's attention-focusing processes. And the rationality of the set of options considered in any complex deliberation that arises can be analyzed by applying the analysis of rational choice to reflection about that set of options. For any opportunity following the first, the analysis of rational use of one's opportunities would require the same two subsidiary analyses and a derivative analysis of rational use of prior opportunities. Thus the basic components of the analysis of rational use of one's opportunities are the two subsidiary analyses mentioned above. The subsidiary analysis of rational choice seems possible given naturalistic accounts of rational belief and rational desire, and the soundness of the rule to maximize expected utility. Let us suppose it can be accomplished. The subsidiary analysis of the quality of an attention-focusing process requires some novelty. Let us see if we can formulate a plausible proposal.

In a decision problem, the quality of an attention-focusing process is not the same as the utility of the process. The quality of the process is an assessment of the process with respect to its cognitive role, which is to supply the mechanism for choice with suitable options. On the other hand, the utility of the process is an assessment of the process with respect to all of its consequences, whatever they may be. In unusual situations a process of high quality may have bad consequences and so have low utility.

Our model naturalistic standard for belief also takes the quality of a belief-forming process as an assessment of the process with respect to its cognitive role, namely, the production of true belief. According to the standard, the quality of a belief-forming process has to do with its probability of success in producing true beliefs, i.e., its reliability. Following this lead, we will propose that the quality of an attention-focusing process has to do with its probability of success in supplying suitable options.

In our standard for simple deliberation, the quality of an attention-focusing process is its quality in an instance of operation. So, before defining the quality of an attention-focusing process in terms of its probability of success, let us first specify that the probability of interest is a single-case probability rather than a statistical probability. More specifically, it is the process's propensity for success in a given instance of operation rather than a relative frequency of success.[6]

Next, let us define success for an attention-focusing process in a particular case of simple deliberation. An attractive proposal is that the attention-focusing process succeeds if and only if it causes one to consider an option of maximum expected utility.[7] But we must modify this proposal in order to take account of difficulties when considering options. These difficulties give rise to the problem that this paper addresses, and so ought to be recognized by our definition of success. Other cognitive limitations need not be acknowledged by the definition. They can be acknowledged as excuses for failing to cultivate the attention-focusing processes that are successful according to the definition.

Let us suppose that the difficulties of considering options can be quantified to give us the "costs" of considering options. These costs are pervasive and occasionally substantial. Considering any option involves at least some effort, and options of maximum expected utility are sometimes so complex that considering them requires tremendous effort. Also, although the cost of considering an option is the same no matter what attention-focusing process produces the option, the cost depends upon the circumstances. If there is a demand for speed, the cost of considering an option that takes much time to consider is greater than otherwise.[8] Let us say that in a decision problem one option is more *fit for consideration* than another if and only if its expected utility, minus the cost of considering it, is greater than the other's expected utility, minus the cost of considering it. Putting this in terms of an obvious scheme of abbreviation, $F(o) > F(o')$ iff $EU(o) - CC(o) > EU(o') - CC(o')$. Then let us say that success for an attention-focusing process is causing the consideration of an option of maximum fitness.

Finally, the quality of an attention-focusing process is not simply a matter of its probability of success. A decision-maker's options are generally fit for consideration in various degrees. And if options of maximum fitness are overlooked, it is desirable that an option of second greatest fitness be considered, or, failing that, an option of third greatest fitness, and so on. The quality of an attention-focusing process depends, therefore, not just on the probability of unqualified success, but also on the probabilities of approximations of success. Furthermore, the importance of the probability of success or an approximation depends upon the degree of fitness of the options with which it is associated. So let us say that the quality of an attention-focusing process in a decision problem is the sum of the probabilities of success and of approximations weighted by the degrees of fitness of the corresponding options.

More precisely, let F_1 be the degree of fitness of options of maximum degree of fitness, let F_2 be the degree of fitness of options of second greatest degree of fitness, and so on. And let $H(F_i)$ signify that F_i is the highest degree of fitness in the set of options considered as a result of the process. Thus $H(F_1)$, $H(F_2)$, ... are mutually exclusive possibilities. Also, since attention-focusing processes produce finite, nonempty sets of options, they are exhaustive possibilities. Our proposal, then, is that the quality of an attention-focusing process in a decision problem is $P(H[F_1])$ $F_1 + P(H[F_2])\, F_2 + \ldots$.

Since the quality of an attention-focusing process need not be precisely assessed by a rational decision-maker, it cannot be objected that its definition, which involves a ranking of all options for fitness, makes it too hard to calculate. Also, there is no objection to be drawn from disputes about the countable additivity of probabilities. Although there may be an infinite number of possible degrees of fitness, for any attention-focusing process only a finite number will have a chance of being realized.[9]

Given the foregoing naturalistic analysis of the quality of an attention-focusing process and our other assumptions, our standard for the consideration of options in simple deliberation has a naturalistic interpretation.

CONCLUDING REMARKS

I have demonstrated the need for standards of rationality for the consideration of options in deliberation. And I have proposed such standards for both simple and complex deliberation. As it turns out, the most plausible standard for simple deliberation lends itself to naturalistic development. For this purpose, one needs a naturalistic analysis of the quality of attention-focusing processes. And I made a proposal along these lines.

Given our naturalistic standard for simple deliberation, many empirical matters bear on the rationality of the consideration of options in simple deliberation: for example, empirical matters such as the evolution of attention-focusing processes, their probabilities of success, and the means of improving the quality of attention-focusing processes in simple deliberation. Empirical research may, for instance, discover situations where attention-focusing processes that are usually good fail. And we may be able to use such information to avoid the troublesome situations, or to foster reliance on other processes in these situations. In general, the naturalistic standard for simple deliberation constitutes an invitation for collaboration between students of rationality and students of cognition.

NOTES

1. Herbert Simon, "From Substantive to Procedural Reality," in *Philosophy and Economic Theory,* edited by Frank Hahn and Martin Hollis, (Oxford: Oxford University Press, 1979).

2. Jon Elster, *Sour Grapes* (Cambridge: Cambridge University Press, 1983), p. 15f.

3. A standard for the consideration of options in simple deliberation is necessary for a complete treatment of the consideration of options in deliberation. Moreover, it is necessary for further elaboration of the standard for the consideration of options in complex deliberation. To see this, notice that some of the subsidiary deliberations undertaken in the course of a complex deliberation must produce decisions without subsidiary deliberations about options, on pain of infinite regress. So some of the subsidiary deliberations undertaken in the course of a complex deliberation must be simple. As a result, an evaluation of a complex deliberation involves an evaluation of some simple deliberations and the consideration of options in them.

4. In this context, what might have been considered, given good use of one's opportunities, depends upon the laws of psychology, one's history, and so on. Kenneth Ferguson has an instructive general account of counterfactual possibility in "'Might' Counterfactuals in a System with CEM," 1985 meeting of the Western Division of the American Philosophical Association.

5. Even though a decision about the development of attention-focusing processes may involve simple deliberation, there is no danger of our standard being viciously circular. Although what is rational in such a decision does depend upon decisions about the development of attention-focusing processes, the decisions it depends upon are all prior decisions.

6. The probability that the consideration of options will succeed, taken as a propensity, varies with time. For example, as the period for consideration ends, the probability approaches either 0

or 1. Therefore, the probability that an attention-focusing process will succeed depends upon the time at which the process is taken to start. I count on psychology for the proper specification of the commencement of an attention-focusing process. More precisely, I count on the branch of *applied* psychology whose purpose includes the characterization of the mental processes to be used in formulating standards of rationality for simple deliberation.

7. In this preliminary work I ignore cases where there is no option of maximum utility.

8. For a discussion of similar features of decision costs, see my "A Decision Maker's Options," *Philosophical Studies* 44 (1983): 175–186.

9. Suppose that in a particular decision problem an attention-focusing process, *afp*1, produces with certainty an option of maximum fitness and no other options, and that another attention-focusing process, *afp*2, produces with certainty an option of maximum fitness and some other options as well. According to the definition of quality, the quality of *afp*1 equals the quality of *afp*2. But is not *afp*2 worse because of the costs of considering the extra options? My response appeals to the distinction made earlier between the quality and utility of an attention-focusing process. *Afp*1 does have greater utility than *afp*2 in virtue of its lower consideration costs, other things being equal. But it does not have greater quality since it does not fulfill the cognitive role of an attention-focusing process any better than *afp*2. The two processes supply the mechanism of choice with sets of options that are equally good, that is, with sets whose top options have the same degree of fitness.

Marjorie Clay

Weirich On "A Naturalistic Approach to Rational Deliberation"

I will expose my own philosophical biases at the outset: I do not believe that empirical issues can be resolved until the relevant conceptual work is done. More precisely, I believe that 'whether' or 'when' questions cannot be answered until we have asked the 'what' question. In this case, despite Weirich's reliance on mathematics to quantify his naturalistic standard, and his several rather vague appeals to psychology for data to support it, his discussion fails to give an adequate answer to the question he raises: whether standards for rational decision-making can be given a naturalistic interpretation. It fails because it attempts to answer the empirical question—*"When* do we consider a question to be rational?"*—without having first addressed the conceptual question—*"What* are we going to count as 'rational'?"

This paper is in response to both versions of Professor Weirich's paper: the one delivered at the conference, and the one submitted for publication. While I am pleased to see that Weirich has addressed some of the specific problems I noted at the conference, our philosophical differences have impelled me to discuss this version of the paper in more general terms than I did previously. However, near the end of my remarks I include a specific criticism of the revised version. I am very grateful to my colleague JoAnne Growney, Professor of Mathematics at Bloomsburg University, for her help in formulating that criticism.

SOME GENERAL COMMENTS

Since Weirich appeals to epistemology for a model of "what our objective should be" (first paragraph of his section titled "Steps Toward a Naturalistic Standard"), I will also use epistemology to explain why I consider his approach to be flawed.

Weirich divides deliberation into two kinds, simple and complex, and then develops a principle of rationality, or a standard, for "the consideration of options in simple deliberation." "Naturalizing" this standard means exploiting its resemblance to a similar issue in epistemology. If a belief-forming process is judged in terms of its success—i.e., in terms of its reliability in producing true beliefs—so might we judge our decision-making procedure in terms of *its* probability of success.

What exactly does this analogy suggest about decision-making? I take it that the point of the analogy is to suggest, from a naturalistic point of view, that criteria for good decisions are derived from what good decision-makers have done, but I am not at all clear about what the alternative would be. Nor am I sure what response a naturalized decision-maker would make to someone arguing for a nonnaturalistic criterion of judgment: would he (or she) claim that the nonnaturalized standard can be reduced ultimately to a naturalized account?

If we "exploit the resemblance" between the belief-forming process and the decision-making process, and look to epistemology for some idea of what is at stake in this dispute, we will find that one of the issues there is what an epistemology ought to do (or be), and another is where justification ends. According to the nonnaturalistic account, justification can come from outside of science (the set of true beliefs), from "reason," or "first philosophy," and so epistemology is concerned with a normative evaluation of those beliefs. The naturalized epistemologists deny both points: justification can only occur from within science, they say, since there is "no body of truths which are prior to and firmer than those which science has to offer," and so epistemology becomes an explanation of the acquisition of these beliefs, and not the justification of them.[1]

I mention these points because what is actually being debated here is a pair of linked concepts, justification and epistemology, and it is clear that a stalemate has been reached: nonnaturalized epistemologists deny that naturalized epistemology *is* epistemology; naturalized epistemologists deny that the justification that nonnaturalized epistemologists seek is even attainable (certainty, *a priority,* analyticity, and so forth). It may be that consensus about these concepts cannot be reached, that they are, to use W. B. Gallie's phrase, "essentially contested concepts."[2] But it is also clear that no resolution of the conflict between naturalized and nonnaturalized epistemology will be found until the disputants agree on what the issue is. I would make a similar statement about the issue Weirich addresses. If the analogy between belief formation and decision-making is a useful one, and the debate in epistemology turns out to be a dispute over the meaning of a central concept, it would follow that Weirich's question (whether a naturalized standard for rational decision-making can be developed) will also require conceptual clarity before it can be answered. Unfortunately, by assuming that he can use 'rational' as if its meaning were unequivocal and context-neutral, Weirich has begged what I take to be the important question here.

Perhaps it can be argued that Weirich does give an analysis of the concept of rationality, and so my criticism has missed the point of his paper: namely, we *can* understand what 'rational' is by looking at the natural history of rational decision-makers. My response to that objection is twofold: yes, it may be possible to develop an understanding of 'rational' by looking at the natural history of decision-makers; no, I do not believe that that is what Weirich has done.

In my view, a natural history of decision-making would have to acknowledge the importance of *context* in deciding whether a deliberation is rational. It would focus on the factors that affect how the situation is perceived, factors that may have psychological, moral, and prudential dimensions.[3] Perhaps the decision-maker will seek to define a problem by imaginatively inventing new options, rather than accepting a slate of options as "given" by the apparent constraints of the problem. Or he (she) suddenly realizes that options once thought to be discrete are in fact interconnected in such a way that a choice now will implicate a whole set of future choices. Without a context that allows us to answer questions such as "Who is doing the judging?" "What criteria are being used?" and the like, I do not see how we can say, as for example Weirich does, "If a person chooses a career without considering some of the obvious, attractive careers open to him, his decision can hardly be rational even if he rationally chooses from among the options he considers." Is our hypothetical decision-maker deciding simply on the basis of his or her own preferences and probability judgments? If so, perhaps he or she does not feel blameworthy or responsible for what *we* consider to be an impoverished set of options. Are we saying that it is irrational to settle for less than some optimal number of choices? Whose view of the situation do we accept? An ideal observer, the actual decision-maker at the time of the decision, the actual decision-maker at a later time?

The issue here is whether 'rational' is a concept with sharp boundaries—boundaries capable of precise mathematical formulation, as Weirich seems to believe—or whether it is a concept that is defined by the contexts in which it is used. I am inclined to agree with the keynote speaker of this conference, Max Black, who has suggested that we declare "a moratorium on these contentious and ill-defined epithets ['rational' and 'irrational'] and to speak of reasonable, sensible, and *intelligent* choices."[4] To do so sends our inquiry back into human life, where we can make judgments about decisions by focusing our attention on all of the multiple variables that determine the value of that choice. We may not uncover a sharply defined essence of rationality by consulting the rich, exceedingly complex, and dynamically interconnected system of belief that guides and corrects us in everyday life. But we will find reasons to support the judgments we make about those choices, and that is not, after all, such a bad outcome.

A SPECIFIC CRITICISM

In my comments on the original version of this paper, I questioned Weirich's probabilistic definition of the quality of an attention-focusing process. In his attempt to answer my challenge, Weirich has only added to the confusion. In a paragraph late in this paper, he says "the quality of an attention-focusing process in a decision problem is the sum of the probabilities of success and of approximations weighted by the degrees of fitness of the corresponding options" (henceforth referred to as "A"). In the next paragraph, he offers an equation that seems to have a different meaning: ". . . the quality of an attention-focusing process in a decision problem is $P(H\,[F_1])\,F_1 + P(H\,[F_2])F_2 + \ldots$." (henceforth referrred to as "B").

As I read his equation B, Weirich is saying that the quality of an attention-focusing process in a decision problem is the sum of the probabilities that options are the most fit weighted by the degrees of fitness of the options.[5] But this meaning is not what I take A to mean: namely, the sum of the probabilities of *success* weighted by the degrees of fitness of the corresponding options. An example may help illustrate the difference. Suppose I am trying to decide who to hire to trim my trees: Tom, Dick, or Harry. Let us suppose also that the probability that Tom will be good at this job is .5, that Dick will be good is .5, that Harry will be good is .9. These probabilities are the probabilities of the success of an option, or, to use the terms of our earlier distinction, these are the probabilities represented by A. However, it may also be that the probability that Tom is the best option is .3, that Dick is the best option is .1, that Harry is the best option is .6. As Weirich rightly notes, these latter possibilities are mutually exclusive—if Harry is the best option, neither Tom nor Dick will be best—and so the sum of the probabilities cannot exceed 1.0. But it seems clear that these two definitions of quality are fundamentally different: the probability of the success of an attention-focusing process, A, is not the same as the probability that the option is the best option, B. To slide from one to the other only confuses a discussion that, as I suggested before, is already seriously flawed.

NOTES

1. Harvey Siegel, "Empirical Psychology, Naturalized Epistemology, and First Philosophy," *Philosophy of Science* 51 (1984):667-676.
2. W. B. Gallie, "Essentially Contested Concepts," in Max Black, ed., *The Importance of Language,* (Englewood Cliffs, N.J.: Prentice-Hall, Inc., 1962), pp. 121-146.
3. Max Black describes the importance of freedom to decide how to perceive one's situation even in the case of chess, where decisions seem to be severely limited by the standard formulation

of chess notation: "The player may be wondering whether or not to make a move which will be canonically recorded as 'Bishop takes Pawn.' But his choice will be materially influenced by whether he conceives of that move as a 'sacrifice' (a deliberate loss in strength for the sake of future advantage), or as a 'psychological surprise' (a move objectively weak, intended to waste the opponent's precious time) . . . . Once having introduced psychological considerations, why ignore prudential and even moral ones?" (p. 42). Max Black, "Making Intelligent Choices: How Useful Is Decision Theory?" in *American Academy of Arts and Sciences,* pp. 30–49.

    4. Ibid., p. 48.

    5. I am not convinced that this equation, though mathematically correct, is a sensible definition of the quality of an attention-focusing process. Would we, for example, measure the quality of a shopping trip by multiplying the price of an item times the probability that we will use it?

Brice R. Wachterhauser

Contingency and Consciousness in Husserl's Phenomenology

> "The origin of thought must be sought in being, not being in thought."
> —Schelling

WHY DOES SOMETHING EXIST RATHER THAN NOTHING?

Regardless of what we think about the meaningfulness of such a question, we cannot deny, I think, that it stems from a real puzzlement concerning the ultimate reasons for the existence of the world. Not only can we ask why anything at all exists but we can also wonder why just *this* world, with its particular laws and quirks, exists and not another. Such questions, of course, receive no answers; reason remains dumb before the brute contingency of the world. For this reason, among others, many have justifiably thought that questions about existence as such are irrelevant for the task we want explanations to perform or that they are not focused sharply enough to have any real content. One cannot doubt, however, that such questions have been and are heuristic-

I would like to thank Professors Shaun Gallagher of Canisius College and Kah-Kyung Cho of the State University of New York at Buffalo for their helpful comments on an initial draft of this paper.

ally important. The simple recognition that all facts are ultimately contingent and that, likewise, knowledge of such facts has, as it were, built-in limits to its transparency, has sent countless philosophers on the search for necessary truth. Edmund Husserl's philosophy can be described as the attempt to understand just this relation between 'fact' and 'reason' or 'contingency' and 'transcendental necessity'. Wherever we look in his writings, from the *Fifth Investigation* with its distinction between 'sensations' and 'objectifying interpretations', to the *Ideen I* with its distinction between 'sensile ξλή' and 'intentional μορφή', from his classic distinction between *'Tatsache'* and *'Wesen'* to his last attempts to find the traces of transcendental subjectivity in the almost impenetrable contingency of the 'life-world', this problem constitutes the fundamental problem and unifying theme of Husserl's phenomenology. Husserl wanted to find a realm of being and truth that was not just fact; a realm of being and truth that presented itself as rationally necessary and certain. Husserl writes:

> Individual existence of every sort is, quite universally speaking, 'contingent'. It is thus; in respect of its essence it could be otherwise. . . . When we said that any matter of fact, 'in respect of its own essence', could be otherwise, we were already saying that *it belongs to the sense of anything contingent to have an essence and therefore an Eidos which can be apprehended purely. . . .*[1]

Husserl's project was precisely the clarification, delineation, and description of this supposed relation between the tangled growth of 'mere' contingent facts and their transcendental roots in the realm of necessary truth. For Husserl this realm of 'necessary truth' was not primarily linguistic in nature. Husserl's transcendentalism cannot be understood primarily as an attempt to articulate conditions of meaningful speech. Instead, it is ontological in nature; he is looking for a realm of necessary being that he claims is the corollary of all contingent realities.

> The essence (Eidos) is a new sort of object. Just as the datum of individual or experiencing intuition is an individual object, so the datum of eidetic intuition is a pure essence.[2]

Husserl hoped not only to convince his readers that such a realm of being existed but also to explain the relation between so-called necessary being and contingent being. Contingent being, for Husserl, was equated with the world of fact. For example, facts about our biology, history, and psychology are relevant to understanding the state of our species at any particular point in time. But when we turn our attention to questions of rationality, particularly to questions about the meaning of what it means to be rational, Husserl claimed that we enter a realm of necessary being, a realm where considerations concerning contingent facts are irrelevant. Husserl claimed that this realm of necessary being corresponds to certain universal structures of our experience as rational beings, which in no way depend on the contingencies of biology, history, or psychology. For example, Husserl might look for the 'essence' or 'eidos' of perception in certain repeatable structural features in our experience of visible objects. His boldest claim was that these structural features in no way depend on contingent factors like our biology, legal history, or psychology. Instead, they represent necessary features of any rational being's experience of perception, and hence are immune from essential change.

Husserl thought that this project was not only clearly conceivable but also completable in principle. He thought he found the Archimedean point from which the philosophical world could be moved into a course of development toward a truly presuppositionless philosophy; a philosophy untainted by contingent points of departure in history, biology, or psychology, or any of the empirical sciences whose concern is 'mere' facts. Husserl's point of leverage was the discovery of what he thought was a noncontingent realm of consciousness (which he called transcendental consciousness) whose necessary features would provide the necessary conditions for any meaning whatsoever. Husserl insisted that the empirical sciences did not realize that both their methods and results presupposed categories or structures of meaning grounded in transcendental consciousness. What this discovery amounted to was the realization that those sciences that investigated contingent facts, causally conditioned in innumerable ways, could not account for their own activity, as science, in terms of similar causal facts. From the *Logical Investigations* onward, Husserl always insisted that all the 'empirical' accounts of reason that assumed that reason, with its ability to give order and meaning to experience, was in some sense dependent on the facts that just happen to make up the world, were not only incomplete and one-sided but inconsistent and absurd as well. It was Husserl's claim that science could not consistently 'complete' itself or account for itself because it was compelled, on the one hand, to make universal and necessary truth claims, and, on the other hand, to insist that these same universal and necessary truths depend on 'contingent' factors of our biology, history, psychology, and so forth. Hence all such naturalistic philosophies are "absurd" and "inconsistent" because the only explanation they can give of the genesis of their own truth-claims is incompatible with the self-evident, universal, and necessary characteristics of these truth-claims. Husserl hoped to show that only by arguing that rational consciousness "emerges" out of nature in such a way that it becomes "causally discontinuous" and "self-regulating" can we account for our own activity as rational beings.

Husserl, to the best of my knowledge, never abandoned this fundamental attitude. He argued throughout his career that only an idealistic epistemology, which started from the assumption that the world of meaningful facts was dependent in some strong sense on the activity of a transcendental ego could succeed in defending an indispensable vision of ourselves as free and rational beings.

To be sure, Husserl understood this idealism differently at different points in his career. In his *Ideen I,* for example, Husserl claims a logical priority of consciousness over the world; the positive existence of the world is neither denied nor seen as a product of consciousness, but consciousness itself is logically prior to the world in the sense that consciousness is a necessary, but not sufficient, condition for the existence of the world as intelligible or meaningful.

> Our phenomenological idealism does not deny the positive existence of the real world and of nature . . . . Its sole task and service is to clarify the meaning of this world, the precise sense in which everyone accepts it . . . as really existing . . . . The real world indeed exists but in respect of essence is relative to transcendental subjectivity, and in such a way that it can have its meaning as existing reality only as the intentional meaning product of transcendental subjectivity.[3]

In the *Cartesian Meditations,* however, Husserl has a tendency to collapse this logical priority into a metaphysical priority.

He sees "the world to be inseparable from transcendental subjectivity, which constitutes actuality of being and sense."[4] Again
in the same work he writes, ". . . anything worldly necessarily
acquires all sense determining it, *along with its existential status,*
exclusively from my experiencing. . . ."[5] Similar claims are made
in the *Paris Lectures:* "For me the world is nothing other than
what I am aware of and what appears valid in such *cogitationes.*
The whole meaning and *reality* of the world rests *exclusively* on
such *cogitationes.*"[6] In both these examples, however, a common
claim can be discerned, namely, that there is a substratum of
transcendental rationality on which the most seemingly impenetrable contingency rests.

Even in the *Crisis of the European Sciences,* where Husserl
announces that transcendental subjectivity must be understood
as emerging out of the historical contingencies of the 'life-world',
he did not abandon the transcendental project. The *Crisis* can be
understood as the attempt to show, through a history of consciousness, how consciousness gradually ruptures its ties with
the contingent conditions of its genesis and becomes both causally discontinuous and self-regulating.[7] Although this is a much
more sophisticated attempt to defend transcendentalism than,
say, the dim adumbrations of a transcendental phenomenology
in the *Logical Investigations* or the subjective idealism that Husserl toyed with and quickly abandoned after the period of the
Cartesian Meditations, he never abandons the transcendental
project as such. The *Crisis,* Husserl's last nonposthumously published work, is filled with arguments against 'Objectivism', 'Naturalism', and all brands of 'contingent' accounts of rational consciousness. Even in the *Crisis* Husserl unequivocally asserts the
causal discontinuity and autonomy of the transcendental ego:

> The body is what it is as this determined body, as a substrate of
> 'causal' properties which is, in its own essence, spatiotemporally
> localized. Thus if one takes away causality the body loses its ontic
> meaning as body; its identifiability and distinguishability as a physi-
> cal individual. The ego, however, is 'this one' and has individuality
> in and through itself; it does not have individuality through caus-
> ality. . . . [I]ts (the ego's) distinguishability and identifiability in
> space for everyone, with all its psychophysically conditioned factors
> that enter in here make not the slightest contribution to its being as
> *ens per se.* For the ego, space and time are not principles of indivi-
> duation; it knows no natural causality.[8]

This implies, according to Husserl, that I cannot understand the phenomena that phenomenology studies as the effects of objective causes; I can only understand them *on their own terms,* as phenomena, which are defined in their being and their functions by factors wholly immanent to transcendental consciousnss itself.

> During the time in which I am a transcendental or pure phenomenologist, I am exclusively within transcendental self-consciousness, and I am my own subject matter exclusively as transcendental ego in terms of everything intentionally implied therein. Here there is no objectivity as such at all; here there are objectivity, things, world, and world-science (including, then, all positive sciences and philosophies), only as my—the transcendental ego's—phenomena.[9]

By these theses, Husserl places himself squarely in the tradition of German Idealism, which sees the world as 'conditioned' and the mind as 'unconditioned'. Consequently, he attempts to understand the world through the mind rather than trying to understand the mind through the world.[10] So convinced was Husserl throughout his career of the fundamental correctness of his approach that, even as late as 1933, he unequivocally endorsed Eugen Fink's bold description of his project as an attempt to understand "the origin of the world" through transcendental subjectivity.[11] Although we must say that Husserl's understanding of this project underwent many modifications in terms of his understanding of the best way to formulate and defend his transcendental idealism, he never abandons it; he never abandons the theses of the causal discontinuity of transcendental consciousness and its 'emergent' ability to be a self-regulating master of its own contents and cognitive development.

Unfortunately, I think Husserl's project failed because he failed to come to terms with the very contingency of consciousness itself. I will try to explain what I mean by this failure in the rest of this paper. In what sense is consciousness undeniably contingent? In at least two senses: (a) the 'fact' of consciousness and (b) the experience of consciousness of itself. Let us begin with the 'fact' of consciousness.

Husserl never addresses at length or in depth the seemingly

given and impenetrable fact that we just happen to have the type of consciousness we do. This is, admittedly, a tall order, but for anyone who claims to discuss the necessary conditions of any consciousness whatsoever, it must be met. He mentions once in passing what he calls "the irrationality of the transcendental factum,"[12] i.e., the fact that we just happen to have the type of consciousness that we do and hence also the type of experience we do, but he dismisses this as a legitimate problem for a transcendental phenomenology whose aim is the study of the structures of any consciousness whatsoever rather an empirical psychology whose aim is the study of the facts about some 'species-specific psyche'.[13] I think this is a fundamental mistake. The very possibility of Husserl's phenomenology rests on the assumption that the mere contingent facts about our consciousness can be distinguished clearly from a realm or mode or 'necessary being'. This necessary being or the transcendental structures of consciousness as such could not be otherwise: they supposedly pertain to *any consciousness whatsoever* and enable us to isolate and study truly universal conditions of meaning, which would hold for any conscious being, even God.[14] But Husserl has failed to show that any such distinction can be defended. Either we can isolate something like a transcendental core in every consciousness, which, furthermore, shows itself with self-evidence that it is necessary to any consciousness whatsoever, or we admit that we are dealing with a 'species-specific psyche' whose abilities to have a meaningful world are relative to the contingent features of the language, history, psychology, and biology of that species.

Against such 'contingent' accounts of consciousness Husserl proposed a transcendental account that was founded on the thesis that all consciousness—divine, human, or subhuman—must be 'intentional consciousness'. In terms of Husserl's classic description of intentionality, consciousness is always 'consciousness of . . .'; I think something, I feel something, I will something, I perceive something, and so on. In each case consciousness shows itself as having a specific form, or what Husserl calls an 'eidetic structure'. Consciousness is always an awareness of. . . , a directedness toward. . . , a feeling that. . . , and so forth. But can we know that this structure of our consciousness is a truly apodictic and transcendental condition of any consciousness whatsoever, even if that consciousness is divine, bovine, or canine? I doubt it. To begin with, Husserl's thesis of intentionality depends, it seems, on certain linguistic capacities. The ability to articulate it and hence to become aware of it depends on a language with subjects, predicates, and prepositions. Moreover, it presupposes a linguistic ability to objectify certain states and processes. This ability presupposes a level of neural development that enables us to distinguish between subject and object, between our awareness and that of which we are aware. It's not at all obvious that all conscious beings have this intentional consciousness. Does a frog, for example, distinguish between its need for food and the fly as a means to satisfy this need? Frogs react, I am told, only to moving flies. Stationary flies elicit no neural response whatsoever even when the frog is ravenous. This is not to suggest that the frog is somehow unconscious. This suggests, instead, that its biologically conditioned consciousness draws no necessary distinction between itself as subject and the things in the world as objects. Only when the contingent pressures of its biology make itself felt, does the frog's 'consciousness' become something like an intentional consciousness. In short, it is unclear that frog consciousness is always intentional. Moreover, Husserl seems to ignore all the evidence for subconscious states, i.e., states where something is going on in consciousness that consciousness itself is not aware of. Subconsciousness is not intentional but it is a mode of consciousness.

In light of these considerations it seems to me that we cannot be sure that there is a self-evident distinction between contingent and necessary realms of consciousness. I think that Husserl's claim that this distinction can be made is a bold and brilliant attempt, but ultimately a failure. Husserl failed to come to terms with the "irrationality of the transcendental factum"; he fails to demonstrate that the way we just happen to experience the world is anything more than a species-specific fact, about which we can generalize but never rise above. Husserl fails to show that the limits that condition our rational consciousness are indeed the limits of any rational consciousness whatsoever. Indeed, it seems to me that skepticism about the transcendental project is always possible because we can never be sure that the limits of our own ability to isolate seemingly permanent features of our consciousness coincide with the conditions of rational consciousness as such. The influences of our biology, language, psychology, and history all seem to bear out the thesis that there may always be more going on "behind the back" of consciousness than consciousness itself is aware of.[15] Hence we can never be sure that the structures of our consciousness that we take to be necessary to any consciousness whatsoever are not capable of substantive change and evolution due to the thoroughly contingent factors on which they may depend.

An example of what this could mean may help. Husserl claimed to have discovered transcendental conditions for such things as visual perception, which pertained not only to humans but to God and any beings whatsoever that are capable of perception. All perception occurs, and must occur, according to Husserl, *Abschattungsweise,* or perspectively.[16] We perceive an object from a limited point of view that never enables us to take in the whole object. But perception always also involves the indubitable conviction that there are other perspectives to be seen, that there is a backside of a chair, for example. In light of this transcendental structure of consciousness, all perceiving consciousnesses 'constitute' the chair as the 'same' and as a whole despite different perspectives on it. The chair is synthesized in consciousness and understood, although never perceived directly, as being a 'whole' object with different dimensions and hidden sides. It is constituted as the 'same' chair despite the fact that it shows itself differently at different times through different acts of perception. Now Husserl's transcendental claims about all visual perception having such a structure seems nothing more than a gratuitous thesis that he can never make good on. Given what we can know about our perception, Husserl may be given credit for showing us something about three-dimensional human perception, but given what we do not know about God, frogs, and bats, it remains an open question whether all perception must be of a 'perspective' that is 'synthesized' into an 'object'. Indeed, some species see only two dimensions and some have very limited abilities to perceive even distinct outlines. In all such cases, our ability to perceive 'objects', 'perspectives', and 'hidden sides' depends, on our nervous systems capacity to react, among other things, to different light frequencies. It is the perceived difference in light frequencies that, in conjunction with the other contingent features of our consciousness, enables us to differentiate surfaces, lines, shapes, contours, and the like, and hence to have a world of 'objects'. The point is that even the ability to apprehend a visual object depends on the contingent facts of biology and physics and cannot be adequately understood in terms of the supposed transcendental conditions of consciousness as such.

This brings me to my claim that the experience that consciousness has of itself is also contingent or conditioned. Consider Husserl's claims:

> [O]nly transcendental subjectivity has ontologically the meaning of Absolute Being, that it only is nonrelative, that is *relative only to itself.*[17]

and

> [C]onsciousness ... is absolute and not dependent in its turn on sense bestowed on it from any other source.[18]

These claims are absolutely fundamental to Husserl's work. I think, however, they are clearly false. Consciousness simply does not experience itself either as "relative only to itself" or "not dependent in its turn on sense bestowed from any other source." Quite the contrary, we experience ourselves as conditioned, dependent, and nonabsolute even when we admit that the existence of consciousness is logically prior to a meaningful world. This can be seen quite clearly when we reflect on the influence of social-historical circumstances on our intellectual activities. For example, when we take a paper out of our file, almost invariably we discover traces of historical interest affecting our most dispassionate work. Although it seemed to us at the time we wrote it to be a disinterested, objective account of some position or phenomenon, we immediately become aware that our insights are not the pure insights of an ahistorical ego, but the concerned, involved opinion of a limited and conditioned human being. In short, as consciousness comes to know itself, not in the white heat of a moment of insight, but over against the gray-on-gray traces of our past, we come to see that there is always more going on behind the back of consciousness than consciousness itself is aware of. Moreover, there is little reason to believe that consciousness will ever asymptotically approach the objectification and rational justifications of such concern. Consciousness is never in a position to make thematic all the conditions of its existence. The physical, the psychological, the historical, and the social factors that make us what we are will never be objectifiable in any exhaustive way. This is so because they happen to us much faster than we can ever become aware of them. They have the capacity to have a constantly changing effect that exceeds our awareness of them; they can affect us continually on a level that we can neither always control nor observe. One might say that consciousness presents itself as internally incongruous in that its involvement in the world always outstrips its understanding of that world. Despite the fact that we seem immediately aware and certain of the contents of our own consciousness and the phenomenal reality they present to us, the apparent self-evidence of this awareness is continually undercut by the fact that the world seems in league against consciousness in that it is constantly showing us points of implication in the world, which we had neither intended nor anticipated. Contingency itself seems to guarantee that we are always more involved than we are aware. If this is so, we can never be sure that the contents of our consciousness are not relative to contingent facts of which we are simply not aware. If we cannot be sure of this, how can we ever begin to look for transcendental conditions for any consciousness whatsoever? Any claim to have discovered a truly transcendental condition of consciousness is inexorably uncertain and unconfirmable because of the finitude of consciousness itself.

By way of conclusion, if I were to say in general where I think Husserl went wrong, I would argue that he mistakenly assumed that we cannot give a coherent account of such immanent features of rational activity as the application of normative standards of reason like clarity, simplicity, consistency, and the like, while assuming that these standards are determined by causal factors like biology, history, and psychology. I think this assumption confuses an account of the immanent features of reason's *normative use* with a causal account of its origin. For example, in explaining why a scientist preferred one theory over another on grounds of, say, simplicity and elegance, we can argue both that "reason demanded it" and give a causal account that might explain such a preference in terms of this scientist's previous training, her cultural heritage (which might include an account of something like 'Occam's Razor'), and in terms of the biology of our species, which has found simple and more elegant theories more useful in terms of dealing with its environment. I think this suggests that any adequate 'science of rational consciousness' must not only trace meaning in the world back to the ego, as Husserl never tired of suggesting, but it must also trace the activity of the ego itself back to the world again. The circle must be completed. I think we must proceed along the lines of something like Jean-Paul Sartre's 'dialectical comprehension', which emphasizes different levels of explanations and their 'continuous cross-reference' and 'reciprocal involvement'. As both subjects and objects we are "implicated both fore and aft in our knowing."[19] We cannot begin to understand who we are without thinking of ourselves as both a self-conscious subject with a limited but real autonomy, and an object in the world whose life is determined by the myriad of facts that make everything what it is. We cannot, furthermore, assign either logical or metaphysical priority to either pole of our dialectical being. Instead, we must move back and forth between the subjective and objective spheres of our existence. Only such a method, once developed, could make phenomenology credible by bringing it into closer contact and dialogue with the empirical sciences of man.

NOTES

1. Edmund Husserl, *Ideas Pertaining to a Pure Phenomenology and to a Phenomenological Philosophy.* First Book, F. Kersten, translator, (The Hague: Martinus Nijhoff, 1983), p. 7. References to *Ideas* are to the Kersten translation unless otherwise indicated.

2. *Ideas,* p. 9.

3. Found in the "Author's Preface to the English Edition" of the Boyce-Gibson translation of the *Ideas* (New York: Collier, 1975), p. 14. This Preface does not appear in the Kersten translation.

4. Edmund Husserl, *Cartesian Meditations,* D. Cairns, translator, (The Hague: Martinus Nijhoff, 1973), p. 62.

5. Ibid, p. 26 (emphasis added).

6. Edmund Husserl, *Paris Lectures,* P. Koestenbaum, trans-

lator, (The Hague: Martinus Nijhoff, 1964). Quoted in R. Solomon, *Phenomenology and Existentialism* (New York: Harper & Row, 1972), pp. 46, 47 (emphasis added).

7. In this respect, Husserl's project might be compared with Hegel's *Phenomenology of Spirit*. There is not only the theme of historical development but the theme of dialectical development toward on immanent *telos* through an inexorable logic of pure consciousness.

8. Edmund Husserl, *The Crisis of European Sciences and Transcendental Phenomenology,* David Carr, translator, (Evanston: Northwestern University Press, 1970), p. 218.

9. Ibid, p. 258. See also Husserl's *Erste Philosophie* II, Rudolf Boehm, ed. (The Hague: Martinus Nijhoff, 1956), sections 48 and 69. Hereafter cited as *Erste Philosophie.*

10. Martin Heidegger, *What Is A Thing?* (Chicago: Regnery, 1967), p. 48.

11. Eugen Fink, "Die phänomenologische Philosophie Edmund Husserls in der gegenwärtigen Kritik," *Kantstudien,* 38 (1933):338, "Die Grundfrage der Phänomenologie lässt sich formulieren als die Frage nach dem Ursprung der Welt." In the forward to this same article, which was written by Husserl himself, the father of phenomenology unequivocally endorses Fink's interpretation of his philosophy, "Auf Wünsch der verehrten Redaktion der 'Kant-Studien' habe ich diese Abhandlung genau durchgegangen, und ich freue mich, nun sagen zu können, dass in derselben kein Satz ist, den ich mir nicht vollkommen zueigne, den ich nicht ausdrucklich als meine eigene Überzeugung anerkennen könnte." A clearer, more emphatic self-authorization of an interpretation of a living author's thought can hardly be imagined.

12. *Erste Philosophie I,* p. 365.

13. See *Ideas,* pp. xix, xx.

14. This aspect of Husserl's transcendentalism seems clearly Kantian, particularly Kant of the second critique, where Kant claimed to discover necessary conditions of practical reason that were binding *sub specie aeternitatis* for all rational beings, even God.

15. This point is obviously indebted to Hans-Georg Gadamer's claim that "we are always more being than consciousness."

16. See *Ideas,* pp. 86-89.

17. "Author's Preface to the English Edition," *Ideas,* Boyce-Gibson translation, p. 14 (emphasis added).

18. *Ideas,* Boyce-Gibson translation, p. 153. Boyce-Gibson's translation is retained here for its clarity.

19. See Michael Ermarth's excellent essay "Hermeneutics and Historicity" in his *Wilhelm Dilthey: The Critique of Historical Reason* (Chicago: University of Chicago Press, 1978), pp. 341-358.

Shaun Gallagher

Contingency and the
Motives for Phenomenology
A Response to Wachterhauser

Husserlian scholars would most likely take issue with a number of statements made by Professor Wachterhauser in his paper on contingency and consciousness. His characterization of intentionality, his claims concerning Husserl's denial of the natural sciences, and his understanding of Husserlian transcendentalism are all open to question. More generally, in response to Wachterhauser's critique, the spirit of which is expressed in his opening citation from Schelling, the Husserlians might suggest that the meaning of 'being' can only be found where 'being' is thought— i.e., in consciousness.

The Husserlians may be correct in the details of textual interpretation and with respect to Husserl's intentions, but Wachterhauser may be closer to the mark concerning Husserl's accomplishments. To lose oneself in the details of a Husserlian defense may be to miss the point of Wachterhauser's critique. Wachterhauser is correct in his claims (1) that Husserl's project, and any similar project, can never be completed; (2) that consciousness is contingent, both as fact and in its experience; and (3) that the contingency of consciousness is both a limit and condition of human thought. Given all of this, however, would it also be correct to assert that Husserl failed to "come to terms" with the contingency of consciousness and that his project was therefore a failure? In the spirit of dialogue rather than defense, I will focus my comments on three issues raised by Wachterhauser's paper.

The first issue concerns the claim that Husserl failed to "come to terms" with the contingency of conscious experience. Wachterhauser implies that Husserl failed to recognize that "the experience that consciousness has of itself is also contingent or conditioned." Indeed, he cites several pieces of Husserl's text to back his claim and provides the example of rereading our old papers to show that "as consciousness comes to know itself, not in the white heat of a moment of insight, but over against the gray-on-gray traces of our past, we come to see that there is always more going on behind the back of consciousness than consciousness itself is aware of." But certainly, even if one could accept Wachterhauser's interpretation of these texts, there are other texts that show that Husserl was well aware of the radical contingency involved in consciousness experiencing itself, even in the "white heat" of phenomenological illumination. For example, Husserl writes:

> We must, therefore, distinguish the pre-phenomenal being of the lived experiences, [i.e.,] their being prior to the relative glance of attention directed toward them, and their being as phenomena. Through the attending directed glance of attention and conprehension, the lived experience acquires a new mode of being. It comes to be "differentiated," "thrown into relief," and this differentiating is nothing other than the comprehending and the differentiation nothing other than being comprehended, being the object of the directed glance of attention.[1]

And again, with respect to phenomenological reflection directed toward a particular expiring stream of thought, Husserl indicates that the thought "becomes the glanced at and immanently percieved *Erlebnis,* fluctuating and fading away thus and thus in the glance of reflection. The freedom of the expiring of the thought suffers thereby, it is now conscious [to the reflector] in a modified way."[2]

If the contingency of the fact of consciousness constitutes a motive for the epoche, these texts, concerning the contingent modifications of the reflective experience of consciousness, indicate a motive for Husserl's eidetic reduction. The eidetic reduction can itself be viewed as Husserl's way of coming to terms with the contingency of conscious experience without denying this contingency. Indeed, his need of an eidetic reduction is itself evidence of his recognition of the contingency of conscious experience. Within this contingency Husserl sought a necessary realm. But even in seeking out eidetic necessity Husserl was required to deal with such contingencies as the fluctuating flow of consciousness, the perspectival adumbrations of perceived objects, and even the contingency of his eidetic method of imaginative variation, in reference to which he indicated the paradox that necessary truth is gained through the contingency of fiction.[3]

But there seems to be a more fundamental paradox involved here: all of these contngencies are absolutely necessary. This brings me to the second issue. I suggest that one of Husserl's most important discoveries concerns the necessity of contingency. Here I propose a distinction between phenomenological contingency/necessity, and metaphysical contingency/necessity; I also suggest that whereas Husserl was concerned with the former, Wachterhauser is most concerned with the latter.

Wachterhauser assumes the traditional metaphysical distinction between contingency and necessity.[4] To anyone who holds strictly to this distinction it must sound paradoxical to claim that Husserl was seeking the necessary within the contingent, or that he found the necessity of contingency. How can one say that necessity falls within contigency or contingency within necessity if these two terms must be kept metaphysically distinct? If, for example, consciousness is a contingent being, there can be no necessity within it; just as the metaphysician would hold that if God is a necessary being, there can be no contingency within God. If consciousness is contingent, it cannot harbor a transcendental necessity. Does not the entire contingent history of metaphysics attest to this necessary distinction?

But Husserl's phenomenology transcends this distinction. Husserl uncovers the necessity of contingency. When Husserl calls consciousness 'non-relative' and 'absolute', he does not make a metaphysical claim about consciousness. He does not mean, for instance, that the metaphysically real world depends on consciousness for its being, or that consciousness does not depend for its being on nature. Rather, he means that, *experientially,* consciousness is without why; it is, in Heidegger's terms, thrown into the world without ground (*Abgrund*), and is a complete mystery to itself with respect to its metaphysical origins. Husserl's claim to transcendental necessity is not a claim to metaphysical necessity. The absolute, phenomenological necessity of the quasi-temporal flow of consciousness is the fundamental metaphysical contingency—i.e., there is no reason within consciousness that would account for its own existence. In precise but paradoxical terms, the transcendental phenomenological necessity of consciousness attests to the metaphysical contingency of consciousness. Consciousness is necessarily contingent.

Even if Husserl did not clearly see the significance of this contingency, his project clearly reveals it. Moreover, the fact that his project must of necessity remain incomplete, as even Husserl indicates—"an infinite task"[5]—reaffirms and enlightens the continency of human existence. It is precisely in this sense that existentialism (as well as hermeneutics) learns from Husserl about the contingency and finitude of consciousness.

My final point concerns precisely what more we can learn from Husserl. Wachterhauser suggests that beyond Husserl we must attempt to construct a "science of rational consciousness" that would bring phenomenology into dialogue with the empirical sciences of man. Certainly the work of Maurice Merleau-Ponty would attest to the fruitfulness of this path. It is important that along with Merleau-Ponty we keep in mind that "beyond" Husserl does not necessarily mean "against" Husserl and that there are a number of lessons that we can learn from Husserl's project. I will close my comments by mentioning one lesson that seems relevant to Wachterhauser's suggestion.

Husserl criticized a naturalism that would deny to man the possibility of transcendence. From Husserl's viewpoint, as well as from the existentialist viewpoint, a naturalism that denies transcendence amounts to crisis and despair.[6] For the existentialist the facticity of consciousness does not preclude transcendence; it accounts for the fact that transcendence is not absolute. The contingency of consciousness provides the motives for and meaning of Husserl's project, at the same time that it denies its complete accomplishment. Husserl's task is infinite precisely because man is finite. The lack of completion reflects, not a failure on Husserl's part, but human contingency. That the individual is what he is, the reasonable product of tradition, language, historical, and biological constraints, is not a matter of absurd chance. The "truth of naturalism," to borrow Merleau-Ponty's phrase,[7] does not show nature to be irrational. Nature itself is rational. Here we need not resort to gods, or even to Hegel. The rationality that we live, that we discover within the natural attitude and in philosophical naturalism, is the subject matter of Husserl's phenomenology. He calls upon this rationality to speak for itself.

NOTES

1. Edmund Husserl, *The Phenomenology of Internal Time-Consciousness,* ed. Martin Heidegger, trans. James S. Churchill, (Bloomington: Indiana University Press, 1964), pp. 178-179.

2. Edmund Husserl, *Ideen zu einer reinen Phänomenologie und phänomenologischen Philosophie* I Buch, Husserliana III, ed. Karl Schuhmann (The Hague: Martinus Nijhoff, 1976), original ed. p. 146; also see p. 151.

3. *Ideen* I, p. 132; also see pp. 139ff.

4. With respect to this distinction, some guidance may be gained from Jean Patočka, "The Husserlian Doctrine of Eidetic Intuition and its Recent Critics," in *Husserl: Expositions and Appraisals,* eds. Frederick Elliston and Peter McCormick (Notre Dame: University of Notre Dame Press, 1977), pp. 150-159.

5. Edmund Husserl, *The Crisis of European Sciences and Transcendental Phenomenology,* trans. David Carr (Evanston, Ill.: Northwestern University Press, 1973), p. 279.

6. See, e.g., Kierkegaard, *The Sickness unto Death,* trans. Walter Lowrie (Garden City, N.Y.: Doubleday, Anchor Books, 1953), p. 179: "Every human existence which is not conscious of itself as spirit . . . every such existence is after all despair."

7. Maurice Merleau-Ponty, *The Structure of Behavior,* trans. A. L. Fisher (Boston, Mass.: Beacon Press, 1963).

Part Three

Special Problems

Allan Gibbard

Rationality and Human Evolution

What does it mean for something to be "rational"? To call a thing "rational" is to endorse it in some sense, and that in turn suggests a scheme for eliciting the meaning of *rational*. Instead of seeking to define a property, "rationality," by giving the conditions under which a thing would have that property or lack it, start with the use of the term. Fix on the dictum "To call a thing rational is to endorse it" and search for a sense of the term *endorse* for which the dictum holds true.

The word *rational* has a learned flavor, but the concept I am tracking is familiar enough. It is the one we use when we talk a-bout "what it makes sense" to do or to believe, or when we speak of actions as "reasonable" or "unreasonable," or when we search for the "best thing to do" in a way that does not presuppose that we are searching for the morally best thing to do. There does seem to be a common notion involved in all these turns of phrase; one test is that to affirm one of an action while denying another would be to invite puzzlement, not to invoke a distinction we could expect the audience to grasp antecedently. When we use the more learned term *rational*, it is often this notion we are trying to apply.

What I say in this paper will thus be sketchy and incomplete, but I hope it will suggest directions for thought. I begin by laying out some characteristics of rationality as it appears in ordinary thought, suitably refined. These are characteristics we might want an analysis of the term *rational* to capture. Cryptically put, my analysis is that *to call something rational is to express one's acceptance of norms that permit it.* That leaves much to be explained: among other things, what it is for a person to accept a norm. In the last part of the paper, I speculate on the psychological nature of the acceptance of norms. I sketch how the psychic mechanisms involved might be explained naturalistically; they can be understood, I suggest, as devices for interpersonal coordination. Normative discussion coordinates emotions and actions, and in the life of a social animal, such coordination can be vital.

The analysis I broach is noncognitivistic, in the narrow sense that on the analysis, to call a thing "rational" is not straightforwardly to attribute a property to it, but to do something else. I have argued elsewhere that leading cognitivistic accounts of what 'rational' means fail; the same kinds of arguments as G. E. Moore used to discredit 'naturalistic' definitions of moral terms apply to 'rational' as well.[1] I shall not repeat these arguments here, but I should say at the outset that what I say here presupposes that attempts to treat rationality as a straightforward property fail. They miss a crucial element of endorsement that the term connotes.

My analysis is not meant to capture a substantive view on the nature of rationality; rather it is meant to capture the common element in dispute when people disagree on the nature of rationality. It is supposed to tell us what it is to debate what is rational and to wonder what is rational. If I am right, deciding what sorts of things are rational is in effect deciding what norms to accept for a given domain of appraisal.

WHAT IS APPRAISED AS RATIONAL OR IRRATIONAL

In everyday life we appraise a wide variety of human attributes as "rational" or "irrational." Not only can a person act rationally or irrationally, but he can believe rationally or irrationally, and he can be angry or grateful or envious rationally or irrationally. It is irrational, for example, to be angry at the messenger who brings bad tidings, but rational to be angry at the miscreant who deliberately wrongs one. Or at least this, I take it, is what we tend to think in the normal course of life. If the word *rational* seems overly learned here, I suggest close substitutes with a more homely flavor: "It does not make sense" to be angry at the person who brings bad news that he had no part in making. You "should not be grateful" to someone who benefited you only inadvertently in seeking his own gain.

It is this family of appraisals that I seek to interpret. Do they make genuine sense, and if so, how are they to be understood? If the term *rational* can be applied intelligibly to as wide a range of human attributes as we seem to think, does it have the same meaning in all these contexts?

It might be thought that for something to be rational is for it to be desirable or advantageous. Such a crude pragmatism, though, would leave ordinary thought about rationality mysterious: It fits actions, perhaps, but not beliefs and attitudes. Take the stock example of the man who has some evidence that his wife is unfaithful. Whether it is still *rational* for him to believe her to be faithful depends on his evidence, and on his evidence alone. Whether it is *desirable* for him to believe her to be faithful, and whether his believing her to be faithful is *good for him,* depend as well on how his beliefs would affect his feelings toward her. The rationality of a belief and its desirability, then, are different, if ordinary thought is to be trusted. Likewise, it might be disadvantageous for one of Cleopatra's courtiers to be angry at her, even if she ordered an execution unjustly, and it thus "made sense" to be angry at her. For the courtier might want to ingratiate himself with her, and he might rightly fear that anger would cloud his countenance and spoil his charm. In that case, he would have every reason to want not to be angry, and still, we seem to think, it would make sense for him to be angry. It made no sense for Cleopatra to be angry at the slave who brought news of Antony's defeat, however therapeutic or palliative her anger might have been. For anger to make sense is not for it to be advantageous.

In all this we must distinguish saying that it makes sense for a person *to be* angry from saying that it makes sense *that* the person *is* angry. If I have had a bad day and now face a new disappointment, it "makes sense that I am angry"—we can expect me to be angry in the circumstances, for reasons we understand—even if it does not "make sense for me to be angry" because the

new disappointment is no one's fault. Likewise, it makes sense
that Cleopatra was angry at the messenger, but it made no sense
for her to be angry at him. Misdirected anger in the circumstances
was to be expected, but the bad news was not the messenger's
fault.

Are these ordinary distinctions truly intelligible? Can we
really distinguish anger making sense from anger being desirable? If we understood the word *rational,* we could put the distinction as follows. In the case of the courtier and the queen, even
though it is rational for him to be angry with her for ordering an
execution unjustly, it may also be rational for him to want to
ingratiate himself with her, for his own good or for that of her
subjects. If anger would prevent that, then it may be rational for
him to *want* not to be angry with her. Thus, in such a case, it is
rational *to be angry,* but also rational *to want not to be angry.*
This pattern applies not only to emotion but also to belief. Take
the stock case of a deceived husband: his evidence may make it
rational for him *to believe* that his wife is unfaithful, but the way
the belief would affect his feelings toward her may make it
rational for him *to want to believe* that she is faithful. Rationally
feeling or *believing* something is distinct from rationally *wanting*
to feel or believe it.

Talk of emotions as "rational" or "irrational" will strike many
readers as dubious. True, we may say the kinds of things I have
been claiming we say: that it "makes sense to be angry" in certain
cases and "it makes no sense to be angry" in others. It may still
be asked, though, whether these judgments can bear scrutiny. It
may well seem that we can appraise as rational or irrational only
what is under a person's voluntary control. Emotions fail this
test, since they are not under a person's direct voluntary control.
True, they can be nurtured or repressed, but a person cannot
simply be angry at will, or grateful at will. Nor can a person
refrain from any of these things simply at will. What can be
appraised as rational or irrational is not an emotion itself, it may
be said, but taking measures to nurture or repress it.

Now I accept, of course, that emotions cannot be had or cast
off at will. What I deny is the dictum that "only the voluntary
can be appraised as rational or irrational." Beliefs seem prime
examples of what we can appraise as rational or irrational, but
beliefs, like emotions, cannot be had or cast off at will. We may

be able to "make believe" at will, but that is not the same as really believing at will.

None of this is to say that when we call an act, belief, or an emotion "rational" we are saying something intelligible; that remains to be seen. I am saying that we talk and think as if such appraisals are intelligible. It may be worthwhile, then, to see if we can interpret them as intelligible.

AN ANALYSIS OF 'RATIONAL'

What does it mean to call something "rational"? One way of tackling such a question is to psychologize it. What, we may ask, is the psychological state of *regarding* something as rational, of *taking* it to be rational, of *believing* it rational? The answer I want to give is noncognitivistic. To call an action, belief, or attitude "rational," if I am on the right track, is not to express a proposition; it is to do someting else. What that "something else" is I shall try to explain psychologistically by saying what it is to *think* something rational.

Put cryptically, the hypothesis I shall develop is this: that to *think something rational* is to accept norms that permit it. This rough analysis needs much elucidation and refinement, and I will not be able to say here nearly all I think should be said. I do hope to give you some intimation of what I hope can be done along the lines I am suggesting.

Take my first use of the word *norm*. By a "norm" here, I mean a possible rule of prescription, either general or specific. The prescription need not actually be made by anyone, or accepted by anyone, to count as a "norm" as I am using the term; I am thus using the term as a short way of saying "possible norm." The main thing to be explained, then, is not what a "norm" is, but what "accepting a norm" is—or more precisely, what it is for something to be permitted or required by "the norms" a person "accepts." I mean these latter notions to be psychological: They are meant to figure in an explanatory theory of human experience and action.

Consider next some schematic illustrations. Delilah, let us suppose, is pondering whether various of Samson's acts, beliefs, and emotions are rational. What is it, on the proposal, for her to conclude that one of Samson's acts, beliefs, or emotions indeed is rational? It is for her to accept norms that, as applied to Samson's situation as she thinks it to be, permit that act, belief, or emotion. Thus when Samson destroys the Philistine temple, Delilah considers the act rational if and only if she accepts norms that permit—for Samson's situation as she takes it to be—destroying the temple. She might, for instance, accept the norm, "When in the hands of one's enemies with no hope of escape, kill as many of them as possible, even if you must kill yourself in the process." Then, if she believes that Samson is in the hands of his enemies with no hope of escape, and that destroying the temple will kill as many of his enemies as possible, she considers his action rational. Earlier, Samson believed Delilah to be loyal. Delilah, then, thinks this belief to have been rational if and only if she accepts norms for belief that, for Samson's situation at the time as she now conceives it, permit one to believe one's woman to be loyal. Samson hates the Philistines, and Delilah considers his hatred rational if and only if she accepts norms that, for his situation, permit such hatred.

Nothing I have said here, I stress, speaks to whether Samson's actions, beliefs, and emotions really *were* rational. My hypothesis is not that a person's action, belief, or emotion really *is* rational if someone—be it I, the person in question, or a commentator—accepts norms that prescribe it for that person's circumstances. It is not directly a hypothesis about what it *is* for something to be rational at all. It is a hypothesis about what it is to *think* or *believe* something rational, to *regard* it as rational, to *consider* it rational. An observer *believes* an action, belief, or emotion A of mine to be rational, so the hypothesis goes, if and only if he accepts norms that permit A for my circumstances. It follows that if we want to decide what really *is* rational, we shall have to decide what norms to accept ourselves—for that is what it is to form an opinion as to the rationality of something.

To believe something rational, I have said, is to accept norms that permit it. In this cryptic form, the proposal says very little, and even what little it says will need to be refined and modified in various ways. Many of its problems I shall not be able to address here. I will, though, try to say a little about two sets of problems: first, what a norm is and what it is to accept one, and second, what distinguishes norms of rationality from other kinds of norms, such as norms of morality, norms of etiquette, and aesthetic norms.

A moral norm forbidding an action, I want to propose, is a norm of rationality governing guilt and resentment. We might likewise speculate that all norms are primarily norms of rationality, and the various different kinds of norms governing, say, a given action—moral norms, aesthetic norms, norms of propriety—are each norms for the rationality of some one kind of attitude that an individual can have toward an action. Just as moral norms are norms for the rationality of guilt and resentment, the aesthetic norms that apply to an action might be norms for the rationality of kinds of aesthetic appreciation of actions, and norms of propriety might be norms for the rationality of shock at an action. Norms of moral praiseworthiness, we can say, are norms for the rationality of an emotion of moral approbation. To call an action praiseworthy, on this proposal, is to say that it would make sense to feel moral approbation of the agent for having performed it. To say that, in turn, is to express one's acceptance of norms that permit that feeling, given the facts of the situation as one takes them to be.

ACCEPTING A NORM AND BEING IN ITS GRIP

To think something rational, I have been proposing, is to accept norms that permit that thing. This is cryptic and incomplete in many ways, and I shall be able to take up just one central respect in which it is incomplete. The analysis, as I have stated it, gives the meaning of 'rational' in terms of another notion that has so far been left unexplained—in terms of a person "accepting norms." This places great demands on the notion of accepting a norm.

The most straightforward way to elucidate the "acceptance of norms" would be further analysis: we might look for an analysis of what it means to say things like "Mary accepts the following norm: . . . . " I doubt, though, that such an analysis is possible. Instead of trying for an analysis, I shall engage in incipient psychological theorizing. "Accepting a norm," I want to suggest, is a significant kind of psychological state that we are far from entirely understanding. What we can hope to do is not define this state precisely, but to point to it.

Start by considering a case of "weakness of will." Suppose I "can't get myself to stop" eating nuts at a party. What is happening? One common-sense description is this: I think it "makes sense" to stop eating the nuts—indeed, that it does not "make sense" to go on eating them—but I nevertheless go on. In this case, it seems, I accept a norm that prescribes eating no more nuts, but go on eating them even so.

In this common-sense account, it is assumed that the acceptance of a norm is motivating, at least to a degree: believing I ought to stop tends to make me stop. On this occasion, though, the motivation that stems from my accepting a norm is "overpowered" by motivation of another kind: my craving or appetite for nuts. The craving is not itself a matter of my accepting norms; indeed, such cravings are sometimes referred to as "animal": we think that they are motivations of a kind we share with beasts.

This is a picture of two motivational systems in conflict. One system is of a kind we think peculiar to human beings; it works through a person's acceptance of norms. We might call this kind of motivation *normative* motivation, and the putative psychological faculty involved the *normative control system*. The other putative system we might call the *animal control system,* since it, we think, is the part of our motivational system that we share with the beasts. Let us treat this picture as a vague psychological hypothesis.

"Weakness of will" involves conflict, and so far in my discussion the conflict has been one between an appetite and the norms that a person accepts. Many apparent cases of "weakness of will," though, are not of this kind. Often, what we experience is not a conflict between the norms we accept and a bodily appetite, but a conflict between our "better judgment" and powerful social motivations. We are paralyzed by embarrassment, or by a desire to ingratiate, or by some other motivation that is peculiarly social. Examples abound: I may be unable to get myself to walk out of a lecture, even though it is important for me to be somewhere else. I may find myself unable to say something that will be painful to my listener, even though I think it needs to be said. My discussion of "normative control" seems not to have addressed cases like these.

An especially powerful demonstration of the kind of conflict I have in mind lies in Stanley Milgram's series of experiments on compliance. Subjects of his experiments were told to administer electric shocks—shocks that were increasingly painful, and eventually lethal—to another subject (who in fact was not being shocked, but was acting as a confederate of the experimenter). Roughly two-thirds of the subjects eventually did all they were ordered to do, although they were upset and protested vigorously.[2]

Now when we read about these experiments, we are appalled by what the subjects did. Their actions violate norms that we accept. The near uniformity with which the subjects substantially acquiesced, however, should suggest the following to each of us: "Had I been a subject in one of these experiments before I first read or heard of them, I, too, would have cooperated with the experimenter—perhaps fully, and almost certainly more than I would like to acknowledge. I would have felt immensely disturbed about the situation in which I found myself, and I would have protested vigorously and regarded the experimenter as a madman. Nevertheless, I probably would have complied."

A typical subject in one of these experiments clearly experiences conflict of some sort; that is shown by his protests and his extreme agitation. The conflict, though, is not between a norm he accepts and a bodily appetite. It seems rather to be a conflict between one norm and another. The subject accepts the norm against intentional harm in terms of which we ourselves, as we read about the experiment, condemn his behavior. Nevertheless, he obeys an experimenter who tells him to violate that norm, and he does so, it would appear, because he is strongly motivated to be polite and cooperative—because to refuse, having originally agreed to participate in the experiment, would be uncooperative and insulting to the experimenter. The conflict, we might therefore say, is between opposing norms: a norm of nonharm on the one hand, and norms of politeness and cooperativeness on the other.

What is the role of norms here? The conflict is between one set of norms and another, true enough, but that suggests a symmetry that is specious. The two sets of norms play different psychological roles. The norm of noninfliction of harm prevails in the judgments of detached observers, whereas the norms of cooperativeness and politeness control the agent in the heat of social encounter. Ordinary language has devices that come close to labelling this contrast. We, as judges, *accept* a norm against infliction of harm, and *accept* that this norm, in the situation of Milgram's subjects, overrides those norms of politeness and co-operativeness that we also accept. The subjects, on the other hand, do not genuinely *accept* that in their situation, norms of politeness and cooperativeness override all other norms. Rather, we might say, they are *in the grip* of these norms. In common language, then, the contrast is between *accepting* a norm (or more precisely, *accepting* that one set of norms outweighs another in a given situation) with *being in the grip* of a norm.

Now presumably, whatever happens when I am "in the grip" of a norm that I do not "accept" happens also, much of the time, when I do accept a norm. Take again our ordinary norms of politeness and cooperativeness. In my usual dealings with people, I not only accept these norms as having some weight; I accept them as having enough weight to override any conflicting norms that apply to my situation. I normally give people directions when asked, even if I am in a slight hurry, and this I do, not out of weakness of will, but because I accept that it makes sense to help people who need it when the cost is small. In these cases, we would not say that I am "in the grip" of the norms of politeness and cooperativeness that guide my conduct, since I accept them as reasonably controlling in the situation. It may well be, though, that these norms would control my behavior even if I did not accept them, or did not accept them as having greatest weight in my situation. In this respect, my psychological state is like the state of being in the grip of a norm.

We need, then, some term for what is common to situations in which I am "in the grip" of a norm and situations of the more usual kind: situations in which I accept a norm as rightly controlling on balance, but would be in its grip if I did not. I propose the colorless, rather technical term *internalizing* a norm.

I have pointed to three sources of motivation that can be teased out of common-sense accounts of weakness of will: appetites, the internalization of norms, and the acceptance of norms. If there are distinctions of this kind to be drawn, how are they tied to ascriptions of rationality? I proposed that rationality has something to do with norms: to call something rational is to express one's acceptance of norms that, on balance, permit it. Once "accepting" a norm has been distinguished from "internalizing" it, we need to ask which of the two belongs in the analysis of 'rational'. Now in the examples, the answer seems clear: It is "accepting" norms that matters here, not "internalizing" them. What, after all, does a subject in one of Milgram's compliance experiments think it rational to do? If his plight is genuinely one of "weakness of will," that is presumably because he thinks that it makes no sense to cooperate, but finds himself cooperating nevertheless. In other words, he does what he thinks irrational. What he actually does, in this case, is a matter of the norms that have him "in their grip"—norms of politeness and cooperativeness that he has internalized. What he thinks it is "rational" to do, on the other hand, is what is required by norms against inflicting pain and danger—and these are the norms he "accepts" as having most weight in his situation. Thinking something rational or irrational thus seems to be a matter not of internalizing norms, but of accepting them.

THE NATURE OF ACCEPTANCE

How might we explain the acceptance of norms as a psychological phenomenon? I shall only be able to give the briefest sketch of some lines for investigation that strike me as promising.

In the first place, I have distinguished "accepting" a norm from "internalizing" a norm, and so let me say briefly how I think we should understand the latter. The capacity to internalize norms, I suggest, is one we share with other mammals, and especially those who live in groups. Two dogs meeting on neutral ground will engage in elaborate "rituals," and this anthropomorphic language suggests that something akin to human norm internalization may be in play. As in the human case, these animal interactions follow certain regular patterns that seem, in a way, to have a rationale. They presumably constitute adaptations; that is to say, they are the result of natural selection favoring these patterns. Internalizing a norm, I suggest, involves tendencies toward action and emotion, tendencies that are coordinated with the tendencies of others in ways that constitute matched biological adaptations, or are the results of matched adaptations. We share the capacity to internalize norms with other animals, although the greater complexity of human social life may well mean that our capacities to internalize norms are more refined than those of any other animal.[3]

If that is what it is to "internalize" a norm, what is it to "accept" one? To understand acceptance, I suggest that we look to language. Think of what language has to do with motivation, apart from simply making us aware of the states of affairs we confront. Although the most obvious function of language is to convey information, much of it is more than merely informative. Language is used to exhort, to criticize, and to summon up emotions. Language influences actions and emotions not only by conveying information that prompts those actions or emotions, but in many other ways as well.

A central way in which language affects human motivation is by enabling people to share a picture of an absent situation. Reactions can then be shared—not only reactions to the immediate situation but to past, future, and hypothetical situations as well. Various kinds of reactions can be expressed in various ways: Emotional responses can be shared simply by evincing them. Hypothetical decisions—decisions on what to do in the place of someone who is in the situation being discussed—can be expressed in language. Emotionally laden words can be used to label actions and characters. Explicit precepts can be formulated. Discussion, then, allows for shared evaluation.

A capacity for shared evaluation would be biologically fitness-enhancing in a species with a complex social life. Those who can work out together reactions to an absent situation—what to do and what to feel—are ready for similar situations. They are better prepared than they would otherwise be to do what is advantageous in a new situation, and they can rely on complex schemes of interpersonal coordination. On general evolutionary grounds, then, we might expect shared evaluation to figure centrally in a complex social life.

Working out, in community, what to do, what to think, and how to feel in absent situations, if it has these biological functions, must presumably influence what we do, think, and feel when faced with like situations. It is in such control of action, belief, and emotion, I suggest, that we can find a place for phenomena that constitute acceptance of norms, as opposed merely to internalizing them. When we work out at a distance, in community, what to do or think or feel in a situation we are discussing, we come to accept norms for the situation. This is the tentative hypothesis I want to propose; I shall be calling the discussion involved *normative discussion*.

We evaluate in community, but part of what goes on is individual. Groups do, to be sure, reach normative consensus in many situations, but sometimes they do not. Even when consensus is reached, it may well emerge from individuals taking positions and then, to some degree, persuading each other. Acceptance of norms is tied not only to a consensus that emerges from normative discussion, but to individuals' taking positions in normative discussion. This taking of normative positions I shall call *normative avowal.* By "avowal" here, I mean to include a wide range of kinds of expression that we might count as taking a position in normative discussion—in the discussion of absent states of affairs. The simplest kind might be the evincing of an emotion toward an absent situation. Other kinds of avowal are linguistically more explicit: we may express a hypothetical decision in words or label an action in emotively charged words. To understand acceptance of norms, we need to look to such avowals—the kind of avowal from which consensus emerges and which may persist even without approach to consensus.

What is the connection of avowal to acceptance? As a first approximation, we might say that to accept a norm is to be prepared to avow it in normative discussion, at least when the discussion is reasonably unconstrained, so that the avowal would be spontaneous rather than calculated. Acceptance, though, involves more than this; it involves a response to demands for consistency. Normative discussion consists of taking positions; even a conversational groan stakes out a position. Consensus may then be reached by a mechanism that is incipiently Socratic. Discussants hold each other to consistency in their positions, and thus force each other to shift positions by exposing inconsistency. A person, then, must take positions in order to engage in responsible normative discussion, and in doing so, he exposes himself to pressures toward consistency. To accept a norm, we might say, is to be disposed to avow it in unconstrained normative discussion, as a result of the workings of demands for consistency in the positions one takes in such discussion.

To prepare oneself to meet demands for consistency requires a strong imaginative life. A person will engage in imaginative rehearsal for actual normative discussion; he practices by holding himself to consistency. I do not mean to suggest that the pressure for consistency will be as strong as it is in good philosophical discussion, but there will be some demand for consistency, and it may exert a significant pressure. From this imaginative rehearsal, a kind of imaginative persona may emerge, an "I" who develops a consistent position to take in normative discussion. It is then, perhaps, that we can speak most clearly of what the person accepts; he then has a worked-out normative position to take in unconstrained contexts.

Why expose oneself to these demands for consistency? We do it naturally, but what selection pressures might have shaped us to do so? The answer should be clear from what I have said. The demands for consistency are reciprocal, and the system of mutual demands is part of a coordinating device. It is partly because of these mutual demands that there is any hope of reaching consensus in normative discussion. A person who refuses these demands must therefore be a poor candidate for cooperation of any kind—and in human life, cooperation is vital. It is fitness-enhancing, then, to stand ready to engage in normative discussion, and so to accept the demands for consistency it involves.

On the picture I have sketched, the difference between accepting a norm and internalizing it is this: Accepting a norm is something that we do primarily in the context of normative discussion, both actual and imaginary. We take positions, and thereby expose ourselves to demands for consistency. Normative discussion of a situation influences action and emotion in like situations. It is then that we speak of norms as "governing" action and emotion, and it is through this governance that normative discussion serves to coordinate. The state of accepting a norm, then, is a syndrome of tendencies toward action and avowal—a syndrome produced by the language-infused system of coordination peculiar to human beings. The system works through discussion of absent situations, and it allows for the delicate adjustments of coordination that human social life requires. Internalizing a norm is also a matter of coordinating propensities, but of a different kind: these propensities work independently of normative discussion.

NORMATIVE THEORY AND HUMAN PSYCHOLOGY

A chief reason for my concern with human psychology in this paper is that, in a sense, the analysis of 'rational' that I have given reduces the meaning of normative terms to matters of psychology. The point is not that to call something "rational" is to make a strictly scientific claim, but that, on the analysis, we are to understand the term *rational* by understanding what it is for a person to think something "rational"—by understanding what it is to have a "normative opinion." The state of having such-and-such a normative opinion is, I am claiming, a signficant kind of human psychological state, to be understood, eventually, by the methods of empirical science.

How, then, are we to understand rationality as part of nature? The key must be that human beings live socially: we are, in effect, designed for social life. This much is a truism, but it should also be puzzling. The initial puzzle is in what sense we are designed at all. Charles Darwin and his successors offered this answer: we result not from design in the literal sense, but from a remarkable surrogate for design, namely, genetic variation and natural selection. The deeper puzzle, then, is what we could expect human beings to be like on the basis of Darwinian considerations. If we grapple with this latter puzzle, new and fruitful ways of thinking about ourselves may surface. The picture that emerges will, I think, be familiar in many ways—after all, we know much about our species in a way entirely independent of evolutionary thinking—but there may be patterns that we had not fully seen before.

More specifically, I have been suggesting that the key to human moral nature lies in *coordination* broadly conceived. The need for complex coordination, I am claiming, stands behind much of the way language works in our thoughts, feelings, and social life. It figures centrally in our emotional dispositions, especially for those emotions with a strong bearing on morality: outrage, guilt, shame, moral admiration, and moral inspiration. Matters of coordination, on the picture I am sketching, stand squarely behind the psychology of norms, and hence behind what is involved in thinking something rational or irrational. Primitive human life is intensely social; in the conditions under which we evolved, anyone's prospects for survival and reproduction depended crucially on the beneficial human bonds he could cultivate. Human cooperation has always rested on a refined network of kinds of human rapport, supported by emotion and thought. A person sustains and develops this network, draws advantages from it, and on occasion keeps his distance from certain aspects of it, only in virtue of a refined configuration of emotional and cognitive dispositions. It is this picture of human biology, that, I think, holds some promise of including figures that, blotchy though they may be, are recognizably human.

In pursuing these hints, we must avoid the presumption that biological pictures of humanity must be simplistic. It is easy to suppose that any picture of humanity that emerges from biological thinking must depict us as crude, beastly creatures, stripped of what renders us most delightfully and inspiringly human. That it is easy to paint such a picture I fully admit, and much of behavioral human biology falls into this trap. That, however, cannot be adequate biology. We are evolved animals, and so biological evolution must account for our potentialities; if a theory misses some of them, it is in that regard a defective biological theory. Inevitably, of course, any theory we can invent will be too crude for its subject matter, but we should try to do as well as we can. The challenge we face now, in evolutionary thinking about humanity, is to work for more richly successful theories—theories that combine biological rigor with a humanistic eye for the complexities of the human psyche, along with the anthropologist's sense of the scope of cultural variation and the typical patterns of human life, and analytical tools drawn from the social sciences. We can realistically aspire only to pictures of human nature that are vastly oversimplified, but we can try to do increasingly better as we think further.

In our evolutionary explanations, it is crucial to distinguish human goals from the Darwinian surrogate of purpose in the "design" of human beings. Darwin's achievement was to show how the appearance of purpose and intricate design in living things, which suggested marvelous divine workmanship, could be explained without supposing purposeful design. The Darwinian evolutionary surrogate for divine purpose is now seen to be inclusive fitness maximization. It has not, as far as I know, been anyone's purpose; but the biological world looks as if someone quite resourceful had designed each kind of living thing with that purpose. Let me then call inclusive fitness maximization our evolutionary *telos*. It explains our having the propensities in virtue of which we have the goals that we do, but the goals we have are distinct from our *telos*.

Our evolutionary *telos* has no straightforward bearing on

what it makes sense to want and to act to accomplish. Specifically, that something would fulfill our *telos* is neither a reason for wanting it to come about nor a reason for wanting it not to. A like conclusion would hold if I knew that I was created by a purposeful deity: his purpose need not be my goal. If, fantastically, I knew that I had been created by a perverse deity so that he could laugh at my discomfitures, that would give me no reason to seek discomfitures, though it would, perhaps, give me some reason to expect them. Likewise, if I know that my evolutionary *telos* is inclusive fitness maximization, that gives me no straightforward reason for wanting many descendants, nephews, and nieces, or for caring for my kin in preference to my friends—nor, of course, will it give me any straightforward reason to the contrary. Any link between evolutionary considerations and what it makes sense to want will be subtle and indirect.

NOTES

1. See my "A Non-Cognitivistic Analysis of Rationality in Action," *Social Theory and Practice* 9 (1984), especially pp. 200–206.

2. Stanley Milgram, *Obedience to Authority* (New York: Harper and Row, 1974). A fascinating discussion of these experiments and their implications is to be found in John Sabini and Maury Silver, *Moralities of Everyday Life,* (Oxford: Oxford University Press, 1982), especially chs. 3–5, 9–11.

3. The classic discussion of coordination in the broad sense I have in mind, is Thomas Schelling's *The Strategy of Conflict,* (Cambridge, Mass.: Harvard University Press, 1960), ch. 2. It is, of course, a theme that runs through the political theories of Thomas Hobbes and David Hume. Matched adaptations are treated in John Maynard Smith's theory of "evolutionarily stable strategies"; see "The Evolution of Behavior," *Scientific American* 239 (1978):136–45, and *Evolution and the Theory of Games* (Cambridge, England: Cambridge University Press, 1982).

Zeno G. Swijtink

Gibbard on "Rationality and Human Evolution"

Professor Gibbard has set the stage for a new kind of criticism that one may direct at some current theories of rationality, for instance, those based on satisficing or maximizing a utility level. For, although he has not given us a substantive theory of rationality (a system of norms that we should accept and propagate), the account he does give us (of what it is to say, to debate, to wonder, etc., what is rational) is incompatible with these substantive theories, for the very simple reason that the criteria these theories formulate are not possible norms: they are not the type of things that can be internalized or accepted.

This will be the main point I shall argue for in my commentary. To show this, I have to lead his paper in a direction different from the one in which he takes it. He would like to see his philosophical analysis connected with human psychology. I believe that one should primarily look at sociology and social psychology, since *norms* come together with *sanctions*. One of the social scientists I will refer to later actually *defines,* in a behavioristic vein, a norm as a *pattern of sanctions.* One may well think that this definition leaves out something, especially if one wants to focus on what Gibbard calls the "acceptance of norms as it is exhibited in normative discussion," but it certainly points at an important way of individuating norms.

I will first make a couple of remarks that are somewhat critical of Gibbard's interesting paper. These will, I hope, naturally lead to the new kind of criticism, implied by his ideas, of some current theories of rationality.

I am puzzled by what Gibbard says about the distinction between norms of rationality and moral norms governing a certain kind of action. He proposes to look at both of them as norms of rationality concerning an attitude: a moral norm is a norm of rationality of feelings of guilt and resentment. This seems to imply that someone who consistently goes against the moral injunctions of his society, but always has the appropriate feelings of guilt and resentment, exhibits a high level of moral rationality. Since this conclusion is absurd, I must not understand. Maybe what is meant is this: to say that a certain action is morally blameworthy is to express norms of rationality for feelings of guilt and resentment and to claim that the facts are such that the agent, having done the action, is permitted to have those feelings. This rings odd. For one thing, it was the action that was not permitted. Who cares about the feelings? Secondly, and anticipating my discussion of sanctions, feelings of guilt and resentment are related to sanctions, but are not themselves sanctions. They function, as it were, as self-inflicted sanctions; they are unpleasant and an agent will try to avoid having them. But feelings are not public and, therefore, cannot function as sanctions. The question is this: why focus on pseudosanctions instead of the sanctions themselves?

A central point in Gibbard's account is the relativization to circumstances: I have to look at your circumstances when I consider whether what you did was rational. Elsewhere he has used the felicitous expression "I have to put myself in your shoes."[1] I have to consider what my norms prescribe for someone with your beliefs about the external circumstances you are in, and your abilities, tastes, ideals, moral convictions, preferences, and so on. The difficulty I see here is this: if all these features are part of the shoes I have to stand in, where does that leave room for my norms? How can my norms take into account the norms you accept? Or should I separate your tastes, ideals, moral convictions, preferences, and the like, from the norms of rationality you accept? But how? Problems of this kind, I guess, have led people to adopt an internal coherency account of rationality.

Let me illustrate this problem with an example Professor Gibbard has discussed elsewhere:

> Suppose Sly Peter the gambler has the ideal of being a successful cheater, come what may. Suppose he knows that if he tries to cheat, he will succeed but will later be shot for it, but that he wants to cheat even so. Even realizing that he wants to cheat, I may regard it as inadvisable for him to do so: that is, I may actually prefer to play it safe if I am in his exact situation, even though it is part of my being in his situation that I there have an overriding ideal of being a successful cheater. For it is also part of my being in his situation that if I cheat I will be shot, and I may actually care more about not being shot if I am in his situation than about satisfing the ideals the hypothetical "I" holds in this situation—ideals I do not actually hold.[2]

In deciding what to do if he were in Sly Peter's situation Gibbard has to dissolve Peter's autonomy as a practical reasoner who makes all-things-considered judgments, and to import some of his own norms and values. What, then, remains of the relativization to someone's circumstances?[3]

I now turn to the acceptance of norms. "To accept a norm," Gibbard has said, "is to be disposed to avow it in unconstrained normative discussion, as a result of the workings of demands for consistency in the positions one takes in such discussion."[4] What do these normative discussions give us? "When we work out at a distance, in community, what to do or think or feel in a situation we are discussing, we come to accept norms for a situation."[5] A. J. Ayer, an earlier proponent of a cognitivistic account of moral judgments, gave a different role to normative discussion. Moral disagreement, he said, is often over matters of fact. We argue with an opponent

> in the hope that we have only to get our opponent to agree with us about the nature of the empirical facts for him to adopt the same moral attitude towards them as we do. And as the people with whom we argue have generally received the same moral education as ourselves, and live in the same social order, our expectation is usually justified. But if our opponent happens to have undergone a different process of "moral coditioning" from ourselves, so that, even when he acknowledges all the facts, he still disagrees with us about the moral value of the action under discussion, then we abandon the attempt to convince him by argument.[6]

"In short," Ayer concludes, "we find that argument is possible on moral questions only if some system of values is presupposed." In this conclusion Ayer is basically correct, I believe. But this does not mean that moral discussion is only about matters of fact. One reason Gibbard thinks a moral discussion about norms is possible is the constraint he sees in "the demands for consistency in the positions one takes in normative discussions." But although I agree that there are such demands, they do not account for the role discussion plays in the emergence of new norms. Ironically, both Ayer's and Gibbard's mistake follows from the shared assumption that norms are "rules or prescriptions, either general or specific."

I will mention two characteristics of norms that seem relevant for our present discussion. The first relates to the inconsistency of norms and the possibility of a discussion about what "to do or think or feel in a situation." The second may explain why normative consensus cannot just arise from discussion.

Norms are not general rules. For instance, a moral principle like 'Lying is wrong' cannot coherently be treated as a universally quantified conditional, but should be construed to mean something like, 'That an act is a lie *prima facie* makes it wrong'. Moral principles are not universalized conditionals, but *prima facie* ones. Given this, inconsistency of norms held by one and the same person will be rare. To detail this requires a logic of the notion *prima facie,* which I cannot go into here. Let me just say that if practical moral deliberation resolves an issue only on the lowest level (the particular case) straightforward inconsistency of norms will hardly arise.

But even when one agrees with Ayer that moral argument is possible only if some system of norms is presupposed, debaters may converge upon the same resolution of a moral dilemma when accepted *prima facie* rules give conflicting judgments for a so far undiscussed case. The discussion would be central to the convergence, but the latter cannot be explained as the conclusion of an argument with factual and normative premises. Similarly, negotiation may be essential for an agreement, without the agreement being the consequence of previously shared principles.

On the other hand, such convergence upon the same resolution of a moral dilemma does in itself not yet constitute a new norm. For sharing a norm is not just assenting to the same *prima*

facie conditional. In his book *Internalization of Norms: A Sociological Theory of Moral Commitment* John F. Scott defines a
norm as a *pattern of sanctions.*[7] Sanctions are essential both for
the internalizaiton or learning of norms and for remaining committed to them. Scott's work allows me to indicate the promised
implication of Professor Gibbard's analysis: a new type of test
one may apply to a theory of rationality and morality. The implication is based on the well-known inference from *ought* to *can,* or
rather from *cannot* to *ought not.* Scott develops a Skinnerian
learning theory with operant conditioning to account for the internalization of norms and for the maintenance of the commitment an agent has to norms. If correct, his theory has important
philosphical implications: if the learning and maintainance of
norms depend on operant conditioning via sanctions, via rewards
and punishments, both adherence to norms and violation of
norms have to be *public* events, at least in principle. Otherwise
no conditioning can take place. This means that a prescription of
rationality, such as 'maximize subjective expected utility', cannot
be a possible norm: violation of such a rule is not a sufficiently
public event for there to be a system of sanctions that can sustain
it as a norm that a community of agents is committed to. One
may object that the maximization rule can at least be a meta-rule,
a criterion by which norms can be judged, as in rule utilitarianism. But this objection presupposes that subjective utility or
preference constitutes an independent realm, and underestimates
the radicalism of the sociological turn. The personal preferences
underlying subjective utility are themselves very much shaped by
the norms of the community the agent participates in. Gibbard
may, indeed, have set out upon a striking departure from the
received thinking in this country.

NOTES

1. See his "A Noncognitivistic Analysis of Rationality in Action," *Social Theory and Practice* 9 (1983):199–221, on page 207.
2. Ibid., pp. 208–209. I disregard here a distinction between
"being advisable" and "being rational" that Professor Gibbard

has introduced, for the problem I point at is independent of it.

3. The intricacies of the counterfactual assumption "If I were her, . . ." also enter in interpersonal comparisons of utility. See Paul Weirich, "Interpersonal Utility in Principles of Social Choice," *Erkenntnis* 21 (1984):295–317.

4. See this volume p. 229.

5. Ibid., p. 228.

6. A. J. Ayer, *Language, Truth and Logic,* 2d ed. (London: Gollancz, 1946), p. 111.

7. J. F. Scott, *Internalization of Norms: A Sociological Theory of Moral Commitment* (Englewood Cliffs, N.J.: Prentice-Hall, 1971).

Steven J. Brams and D. Marc Kilgour

Optimal Deterrence

1. INTRODUCTION

The policy of deterrence, at least to avert nuclear war between the superpowers, has been a controversial one. The main controversy arises from the threat of each side to visit destruction on the other in response to an initial attack. This threat would seem irrational if carrying it out would lead to a nuclear holocaust—the worst outcome for both sides. Instead, it would seem better for the side attacked to suffer some destruction rather than to retaliate in kind and, in the process of devastating the other side, seal its own doom in an all-out nuclear exchange.

Yet, the superpowers persist in their adherence to *deterrence,* by which we mean a policy of threatening to retaliate to an attack by the other side in order to deter such an attack in the first place. To be sure, nuclear doctrine for implementing deterrence has evolved over the years, with such appellations as "massive

Steven J. Brams gratefully acknowledges the financial support of the Ford Foundation under Grant No. 845-0354 and the National Science Foundation under Grant No. SES84-08505. D. Marc Kilgour gratefully acknowledges the financial support of the Natural Sciences and Engineering Research Council of Canada under Grant No. A8974. His research for this paper was done while a visiting associate professor in the Department of Systems Design at the University of Waterloo, Ontario, during 1984-1985. From *Social Philosophy and Policy* vol. 3, no. 1 (Autumn 1985):118-135. Copyright © 1985 Basil Blackwell Publishers, Ltd. Reprinted with permission.

241

242 Part Three: Special Problems

retaliation," "flexible response," "mutual assured destruction" (MAD), and "counterforce" giving some flavor of the changes in United States strategic thinking.

All such doctrines, however, entail some kind of response to a Soviet nuclear attack. They are operationalized in terms of pre-selected targets to be hit, depending on the perceived nature and magnitude of the attack. Thus, whether U.S. strategic policy at any time stresses a retaliatory attack on cities and industrial centers (countervalue) or on weapons systems and armed forces (counterforce), the certainty of a response of some kind to an attack is not the issue. The issue is, rather, what kind of threatened response, or *second strike,* in the parlance of deterrence theory, is most efficacious in deterring an initial attack, or *first strike.*

This is the issue we address in this paper, though not in the usual way. Instead of trying to evaluate the relative merits of concrete nuclear retaliatory doctrines, we shall define these doctrines somewhat more abstractly in terms of "probabilistic threats." More specifically, by letting threats vary along a single continuous dimension from certain retaliation to no retaliation, we can compare different levels of threats in terms of the expected payoffs that they yield in a game. Additionally, by introducing probabilities of a first strike (or preemption) by both sides, we can analyze the relationship between preemption and retaliation probabilities and game outcomes.

Because the expected payoffs of probabilistic preemption and retaliation have certain equivalents, in that a player would be indifferent between choosing a lottery (over nonpreemption/preemption or nonretaliation/retaliation) and a sure thing (a reduced level of preemption or retaliation), they can be interpreted in terms of *levels* of preemption and retaliation short of full-fledged first and second strikes. The first question we seek to answer is what levels render certain outcomes stable, in a sense to be specified later.

In the game we use to model deterrence, which is derived from the game of Chicken but is not Chicken itself, we identify four stable outcomes, or equilibria, three of which correspond to those in Chicken. The new equilibrium, which emerges when we incorporate the possibility of (probabilistic) preemption and retaliation into Chicken, we call the "deterrence equilibrium." It corresponds to the cooperative outcome in Chicken (never preempt), which by itself is unstable; in the new (deterrence) game, this outcome is rendered stable by the threat of retaliation above a calculable threshold, which makes preemption irrational.

But a threshold alone does not specify what level of threat (above this threshold) is optimal. Accordingly, we suggest a theoretical calculation of "robust threats" that makes retaliatory threats as invulnerable as possible to misperceptions or miscalculations by the players. We also indicate how precommitments to carry out these threats are in fact made credible, at least on a probabilistic basis, by the superpowers.

We think the deterrence equilibrium—and the robust threats that support it—is superior to any other equilibrium in the game we postulate as a model of deterrence. To be sure, this equilibrium is imperfect in the sense that it is irrational to carry out one's threats; however, because it renders preemption irrational, even when one thinks one's opponent might preempt, it is hard to see why retaliation would ever be necessary, at least in theory. This theoretical rationale for a particular kind of deterrence, *coupling a no-first-use policy with robust threats, appears to us the best one can do in a world that seems to make superpower confrontations unavoidable.*

The challenge facing the policy-maker is to prevent such confrontations from escalating into nuclear war. As deleterious as threats are to the development of trust and good will, we conclude that they are inescapable for deterrence to be effective. It is far less clear whether the threats the superpowers hurl at each other today, and their concomitant actions to indicate that the threats are not empty, are at an optimal level.

2. DETERRENCE AND THE GAME OF CHICKEN

There is a large literature on deterrence, but little of it is explicitly game-theoretic. That which is, or is pertinent to game-theoretic formulations, is discussed by Brams from both a theoretical and empirical perspective, so we shall not review it here.[1] Suffice it to say that we believe game theory not only provides a framework uniquely suited to capturing the interdependent strategic calculations of players but also that it can be adapted to modeling the threats necessary to deter an opponent from taking untoward action against oneself.

To incorporate threats into the structure of a game, we shall assume that players can precommit themselves to carrying out their threats with a given probability. Exactly how they do so will be considered later, but for now we shall assume precommitments are allowed by the rules of the game.

Because a game is defined by the rules that describe it, there is no problem in permitting precommitments as long as they are not inconsistent with other rules. In fact, as we shall show, the major issue precommitments raise is the rationality of holding to them in the play of a game. We shall discuss this issue after deriving the equilibria of the so-called Deterrence Game and analyzing their properties.

The Deterrence Game is based on the two-person game of Chicken, which we shall define and analyze. In Chicken, each player can choose between two strategies: cooperate (C) and not cooperate (C̄), which in the context of deterrence may be thought of as "not attack" and "attack," respectively. These strategies lead to four possible outcomes, which the players are assumed to rank from best (4) to worst (1). These rankings are shown as ordered pairs in the outcome matrix of Figure 1, with the first number indicating the rank assigned by the row player and the second number indicating the rank assigned by the column player. Chicken is defined by the following outcome rankings of the strategy combinations of the two players:

1. Both players cooperate (CC)—next-best outcome for both players: (3,3).
2. One player cooperates and the other does not (CC̄ and C̄C)—best outcome for the player who does not cooperate and next-worst outcome for the player who does: (2,4) and (4,2).
3. Both players do not cooperate (C̄C̄)—worst outcome for both players: (1,1).

Outcomes (2,4) and (4,2) in Figure 1 are circled to indicate that they are *Nash equilibria:* neither player (Row or Column) would have an incentive to depart from these outcomes because he would do worse if he did. For example, from (2,4) Row would do worse if he moved to (1,1), and Column would do worse if he moved to (3,3). By contrast, from (3,3) Row would do better if he moved to (4,2), and Column would do better if he moved to (2,4).

Figure 1.

OUTCOME MATRIX OF CHICKEN

Column

		Cooperate (C)	Do not cooperate (C̄)
	Cooperate (C)	(3,3) Compromise	(2,4) Column "wins," Row "loses"
Row	Do not cooperate (C̄)	(4,2) Row "wins," Column "loses"	(1,1) Disaster

KEY: (x,y) = (rank of Row, rank of Column)
    4 = best; 3 = next best; 2 = next worst; 1 = worst
    Circled outcomes are Nash equilibria

There is a third Nash equilibrium in Chicken, but it is not in *pure strategies,* or specific strategies that players would choose with certainty. Rather, it is in *mixed strategies,* which are defined by a probability distribution over a player's pure strategies. Because the calculation of equilibria involving mixed strategies requires that payoffs be given in cardinal utilities—not just ordinal ranks—we will postpone discussion of these strategies and the third equilibrium until the development of the Deterrence Game in Section 3.

The shorthand verbal descriptions given for each outcome in Figure 1 suggest the vexing problem that the players confront in choosing between C and C̄: by choosing C̄, each can "win," but risks disaster; by choosing C, each can benefit from compromise, but can also "lose." Each of the Nash equilibria shown in Figure 1 favors one player over the other, and the stability of these equilibria, as such, says nothing about which of the two—if either—will be chosen.

Other concepts of equilibrium distinguish (3,3) as the unique stable outcome, but the rules of play that render compromise stable presume that the players (1) act nonmyopically or farsightedly and (2) cannot threaten each other.[2] If threats are possible in repeated play of Chicken under still different rules, the stability of (3,3) is undermined.[3]

The effect that threats may have in Chicken is not hard to grasp. If one player (say, Row) threatens the other player (Column) with the choice of $\bar{C}$, and this threat is regarded as credible, Column's best response is C, leading to (4,2).

Clearly, the player with the credible threat—if there is one—can force the other player to back down in order to avoid (1,1). Although Row would "win" in this case by getting his best outcome, Column would not "lose" in the usual sense by getting his worst outcome, but instead his next-worst. This is because Chicken is not a *constant-sum* game, in which what one player wins the other player loses. That is why we have put "win" and "lose" in quotation marks here and in Figure 1. In nonconstant-sum games like Chicken, the sum of the players' payoffs at each outcome (if measured cardinally by utilities rather than ordinally by ranks) is not constant but variable. This means that *both* players may do better at some outcomes [e.g., (3,3)] than others [e.g., (1,1)]. Outcomes, such as (1,1) in Chicken, which are inferior for *both* players to some other outcomes in a game, are called *Pareto-inferior;* those outcomes that are not Pareto-inferior are *Pareto-superior,* as are the other three outcomes in Chicken.

We have shown that Chicken is vulnerable to the use of threats, by which we mean precommitment (before the play of the game) to the choice of a strategy by one player in order to force the other player to choose a strategy, and hence an outcome (defined by a pair of strategy choices), favorable to the threatener. For a threat to be *effective* (i.e., force the threatened player to choose the strategy the threatener prefers), it must be *credible:* the threatened player must believe that the threatener will in fact carry out his threat.

Thus, for example, if Column did not believe that Row would actually choose $\bar{C}$ in Chicken (e.g., because he himself also threatened to choose $\bar{C}$), Column presumably would choose $\bar{C}$ in the belief that Row would back down and choose C, leading to Column's best outcome of (2,4). Of course, if Column's belief were mistaken, the outcome for both players would be disastrous. In the Deterrence Game, we shall explore how mutual threats in Chicken may induce compromise rather than push the players toward the precipice.

Chicken is not the only game vulnerable to threats. There are seventy-eight distinct strict ordinal 2 x 2 games in which two players, each with two strategies, can strictly rank the four outcomes from best to worst. In forty-six of them, one or both players has "threat power" of either a "compellent" or "deterrent" kind.[4] Chicken, however, is the only one of the seventy-eight games that satisfies the following four conditions:

1. *Symmetry:* the players rank the outcomes along the main diagonal (CC and $\bar{C}\bar{C}$) the same; their rankings of the off-diagonal outcomes (C$\bar{C}$ and $\bar{C}$C) are mirror images of each other.

2. *Cooperation is preferable to noncooperation:* both players prefer CC to $\bar{C}\bar{C}$.

3. *Unilateral noncooperation helps the noncooperator and hurts the cooperator:* Row prefers $\bar{C}$C to CC to C$\bar{C}$, and Column prefers C$\bar{C}$ to CC to $\bar{C}$C.

4. *Retaliation for noncooperation is irrational:* if one player does not cooperate (i.e., the initial outcome is $\bar{C}$C or C$\bar{C}$), retaliation by the other player (to $\bar{C}\bar{C}$) is worse for the retaliator (as well as the player whom he retaliates against).

It is evident that all except condition 1, which we assume in order to pose the same strategic dilemma for each player,[5] conspire to make Chicken a harrowing game to play. Cooperation is at the same time desirable (condition 2) and undesirable (condition 3). But the crux of the dilemma is that if one player is intransigent (i.e., noncooperative), the other player has good reason not to be intransigent (condition 4). If condition 4 does not obtain, but instead $\bar{C}\bar{C}$ is better than $\bar{C}$C and C$\bar{C}$ for the cooperative player, then the resulting game is a Prisoners' Dilemma, which presents the players with a very different kind of strategic problem.

We believe, however, that the heart of the problem with deterrence, especially of the nuclear kind, is the apparent irrationality of retaliating against a first strike by an opponent.[6] What sort of threats (if any) are credible and will deter a first strike, so as not to put one in the unenviable position of having to decide whether to retaliate and court mutual annihilation? When is a policy of deterrence involving mutual threats of retaliation stable? How can players make their precommitments to retaliate compelling? We shall explore these and other questions in our analysis of the Deterrence Game, which permits the players to choose both levels of preemption and levels of retaliation.

3. THE DETERRENCE GAME (WITH PREEMPTION AND RETALIATION PROBABILITIES)

The Deterrence Game is defined by the following rules:

1. The final outcome will be one of the four outcomes of Chicken. The payoffs are the same as those of Chicken, except that cardinal utilities replace ordinal rankings. Thus, r_4 and c_4 signify the highest payoffs for Row and Column, respectively, r_1 and c_1 the lowest, and so on.

2. The players do not choose initially between C and $\overline{C}$, as in Chicken, but instead choose (unspecified) actions that have associated with them a nonpreemption probability (s for Row and t for Column) and a complementary preemption probability (1-s for Row and 1-t for Column). With these probabilities, the actions will be interpreted as cooperative (C) and noncooperative ($\overline{C}$) strategy choices, respectively.

3. If *both* players' initial choices are perceived as the same, the game ends at that position (i.e., CC or $\overline{CC}$). If one player's choice is perceived as C and the other's as $\overline{C}$, the former player then chooses *subsequent* actions with an associated nonretaliation probability (p for Column and q for Row) and a complementary retaliation probability (1-p for Column and 1-q for Row). With the retaliation probability, the conflict is escalated to the final outcome $\overline{CC}$; otherwise it remains (at $C\overline{C}$ or $\overline{C}C$).

4. The players choose their preemption probabilities and retaliation probabilities before play begins. Play commences
when each player simultaneously chooses initial actions
that may be interpreted as either C or $\overline{C}$, with associated
preemption probabilities. One player may then choose subsequent actions, according to rule 3, with the associated retaliation probability specified at the beginning of play.

Figure 2.

PAYOFF MATRIX OF DETERRENCE GAME

Column

		t	1-t
Row	s	(r_3,c_3)	$q(r_2,c_4) + (1-q)(r_1,c_1)$ $= (qr_2,q)$
	1-s	$p(r_4,c_2) + (1-p)(r_1,c_1)$ $= (p,pc_2)$	$(r_1,c_1) = (0,0)$

KEY: (r_i,c_j) = (payoff to Row, payoff to Column)
r_4,c_4 = best; r_3,c_3 = next best; r_2,c_2 = next worst; r_1,c_1 = worst
s,t = probabilities of nonpreemption; p,q = probabilities of nonretaliation
Normalization: $0 = r_1 < r_2 < r_3 < r_4 = 1$; $0 = c_1 < c_2 < c_3 < c_4 = 1$

The Deterrence Game is represented in Figure 2. Note that
besides the fact that the initial strategy choices of the two players
are probabilities (with assumed underlying actions), rather than
actions (C and $\overline{C}$) themselves, this payoff matrix differs from the
Figure 1 outcome matrix in having expected payoffs rather than
(certain) payoffs in its off-diagonal entries. This is because we
assume that if one player is perceived to preempt, the other player's (probabilistic) retaliation will be virtually instantaneous, so it
is proper to include in the off-diagonal entries a combination of
payoffs—reflecting both possible retaliation and possible nonretaliation—by means of an expected value.

We assume, of course that $0 \leq s, t, p, q \leq 1$ because they represent probabilities. To simplify subsequent calculations, we normalize the payoffs of the players so that the best and worst payoffs are 1 and 0, respectively. Hence,

$$0 = r_1 < r_2 < r_3 < r_4 = 1$$
$$0 = c_1 < c_2 < c_3 < c_4 = 1$$

Because we assume the preemption and retaliation probabilities are chosen independently by the players, the expected payoffs for Row and Column are simply the sums of the four payoffs (expected payoffs) in the Figure 2 matrix, each multiplied by the probability of its occurrence:

$$E_R(s,q; t,p) = str_3 + (1-s)tp + s(1-t)qr_2;$$
$$E_C(t,p; s,q) = stc_3 + s(1-t)q + (1-s)tpc_2.$$

In the Appendix we show that there are effectively four Nash equilibria in the Deterrence Game, and that they can be grouped into three classes:

I. *Deterrence Equilibrium:* $s = 1$, $q \leq c_3$; $t = 1$, $p \leq r_3$. This equilibrium is one in which the players never preempt ($s = t = 1$), but Row retaliates with probability $1-p > r_3$ and Column retaliates with probability $1-q > c_3$. Essentially, these inequalities ensure that a player's expected payoff as the sole preemptor—p for Row and q for Column, as shown in the off-diagonal entries in Figure 2—is not greater than what is obtained from the cooperative outcome of the underlying Chicken game, with payoffs (r_3, c_3).

II. *Preemption Equilibria:* (1) $s = 1$, $q = 1$; $t = 0$, p arbitrary; (2) $s = 0$, q arbitrary; $t = 1$, $p = 1$. The first equilibrium is certain preemption by Column and no retaliation by Row; because Row is deterred by Column's initiative, Column's retaliation probability is arbitrary since it never comes into play. The second equilibrium is analogous, with the roles of Column and Row switched. At these equilibria, the outcomes of the Deterrence Game are the outcomes of the underlying Chicken game associated with wins for Column and Row (discussed above), with payoffs $(r_2, 1)$ and $(1, c_2)$, respectively.

III. *Naive Equilibrium:*

$$s = \frac{c_2}{1 - c_3 + c_2}, \quad q = 1; \quad t = \frac{r_2}{1 - r_3 + r_2}, \quad p = 1$$

At this equilibrium, each player preempts with some nonzero probability (which depends on the other player's payoffs and is always less than one) but never retaliates. Each of these preemption probabilities in fact (see Appendix) makes the opponent indifferent as to his level of preemption; in other words, a player's payoff depends only on his opponent's, and not his own, level of preemption. Because retaliation would only degrade these expected payoffs, it is suboptimal. As shown in the Appendix, however, the Naive Equilibrium is Pareto-inferior to the Deterrence Equilibrium, which is the reason for our nomenclature. It corresponds to the mixed-strategy equilibrium of the underlying Chicken game (discussed but not given in Section 2), which is similarly deficient, as well as difficult to interpret as a one-shot choice of rational players in this game.

4. RATIONAL PLAY IN THE DETERRENCE GAME

Of the four Nash equilibria, only the Deterrence Equilibrium in class I depends on the possibility of retaliation—specifically, pre-committed threats to respond (at least probabilistically) to a provocation when it is viewed as equivalent to the choice of $\bar{C}$. Such threats distinguish the Deterrence Game from the underlying game of Chicken, in which retaliation against the choice of $\bar{C}$ is not permitted.

Note that the two Preemption Equilibria in class II, and the one Naive Equilibrium in class III, occur only when retaliatory threats are never used ($p = 1$ or $q = 1$ or both). They correspond precisely to the three Nash equilibria in Chicken and so introduce no new element into the analysis of deterrence beyond what was earlier provided by Chicken. However, when a threat structure is added to Chicken to give the Deterrence Game, a qualitatively different equilibrium (the Deterrence Equilibrium) emerges in the latter game that demonstrates how threats can work to the advantage of both players to stabilize the Pareto-superior cooperative outcome (r_3, c_3), which is unstable in Chicken without the possibility of retaliation.

Because the Deterrence Equilibrium depends fundamentally on threats, it is not surprising that it is neither perfect nor subgame-perfect in Reinhard Selten's sense.[7] Nevertheless, the Deterrence Equilibrium possesses a dynamic-stability property that should, once the equilibrium forms, contribute to its persistence in repeated play. That is to say, given that the players are at the Deterrence Equilibrium, if one player (say Column) for any reason suspects that the other player (Row) may contemplate preemption, thereby rendering $s < 1$, Row can do no better than continue to choose $t = 1$. In other words, even should Row think he might be preempted, he should still continue to refuse to preempt, in order to keep his expected payoff at its maximum. This obviates the problem that Thomas Schelling called "the reciprocal fear of surprise attack" that leads inexorably to preemption.[8]

We prove this dynamic-stability property of the Deterrence Equilibrium in the Appendix, which shows, in effect, that any perceived departures of s or t from 1 will not initiate an escalatory process whereby the players are motivated to move closer and closer toward certain preemption. The fact that the Deterrence Equilibrium is impervious to perturbations in s or t means that the players, instead of being induced to move up the escalation ladder, will have an incentive to move down should one player deviate from $s = t = 1$.[9]

The restoration of the Deterrence Equilibrium depends on probabilistic threats of retaliation that satisfy

$$0 < q < c_3, 0 < p < r_3. \qquad (1)$$

But note that if deterrence should fail for any reason, it is irrational to retaliate, even on a probabilistic basis, because retaliation leads to a worse outcome for the threatener, having to carry out his threat, as well as for the player who preempted and thereby provoked retaliation.

The apparent irrationality of retaliating in the Deterrence Game is, as we indicated earlier, precisely what makes the Deterrence Equilibrium imperfect. Despite its imperfectness, we believe there are at least two ways in which it may be strengthened, one theoretical and one practical.

In theory, all threats that satisfy inequalities (1), given that $s = t = 1$, define a Deterrence Equilibrium. But in the intervals defined by (1), which values of p and q should be used? One of us proposed, as most insensitive to misperceptions or miscalculations by the players, *robust threats,*

$$q = \frac{c_3 - c_2 r_3}{1 - c_2 r_2}, \qquad p = \frac{r_3 - r_2 c_3}{1 - c_2 r_2},$$

which are easily shown to satisfy (1).[10] Such threats, when carried out, are equally damaging to the preemptor, and equally costly to the retaliator, whichever strategy (preempt or not) either player perceives the other might choose at the start. This property makes each player's preemption decision independent of his reading of his opponent's choice—the damage or cost will be the same whatever he chooses—and should serve to enhance the stability of the Deterrence Equilibrium.

A by-product of robust threats is that they render nonpreemption (strategies s and t in the Figure 2 Deterrence Game) *strictly dominant*—better for each player whatever his opponent does—and hence unconditionally best. This, of course, is not true of the C strategies in Chicken, which are *undominated*—sometimes best (when the opponent chooses C̄) and sometimes not (when he chooses C).

In practice, the Deterrence Equilibrium depends on the credibility of threats satisfying (1). But how does a player persuade his opponent that he will retaliate if attacked, even though retaliation would be irrational at the time it is undertaken?

In the case of the superpowers, both the United States and the Soviet Union have institutionalized detailed procedures for responding to a nuclear attack that are designed to ensure—insofar as possible—that retaliation will occur, even if communcation, command, control, and intelligence (C^3I) capabilities are damaged by the attack.[11] However, although each side promises that a first strike will inevitably be met by a second strike, there is significant uncertainty about each side's likely response because of a number of operational factors, including problems related to identifying the attacker, identifying the magnitude of the attack, failures of weapons being used for the first time on a massive scale, problems of communication and control, lack of resolve, and the like. In light of these difficulties, both sides have, not surprisingly, resorted less to making probabilistic threats and more to employing their certain equivalents—usually controlled steps up the escalation ladder.

These . . . may be thought of as probabilistic threats insofar as they give an opponent a better idea of how close each side is moving toward full-scale retaliation—that is, they indicate more palpably the probability that the opponent will carry out a threat and what its expected damage will be. So far, fortunately, these probabilistic threats have been sufficient to persuade the two sides to back off, beyond a certain point, from continued escalation.[12]

We conclude that: (1) the deterministic threats proclaimed by the superpowers today are, in truth, probabilistic (as we have modeled them); and (2) they have in fact deterred nuclear war. Moreover, there seems little doubt that both sides have precommitted themselves to retaliating, even if the resulting doomsday machines have built-in uncertainties because of possible failures in C^3I—some of which may be irremediable—and other factors (e.g., lack of will to order a second strike).

5. CONCLUSIONS

Deterrence means threatening to retaliate against an attack in order to prevent it from occurring in the first place. It is widely held that only through continuing mutual deterrence has a nuclear confrontation of the superpowers been avoided. Yet the central problem with a policy of deterrence is that the threat of retaliation may not be credible if retaliation leads to a worse outcome—perhaps a nuclear holocaust—than a side would suffer from absorbing a limited first strike and not retaliating.

We analyzed the optimality of mutual deterrence by means of a Deterrence Game, in which each player chooses a probability (or level) of preemption, and of retaliation if preempted. The Nash equilibria, or stable outcomes, in this game duplicate those in the game of Chicken, on which it is based, except for a Deterrence

Equilibrium at which the players never preempt but are always prepared to retaliate with a probability above a calculable threshold. This equilibrium is Pareto-superior, dynamically stable, and—when supported by robust threats—as invulnerable as possible to misperceptions or miscalculations by the players.

How do these results accord with the strategic doctrine of MAD? First, MAD is not only an acronym for "mutual assured destruction" but also for "mutual assured deterrence." In its former incarnation, MAD is more of an epithet than a statement of policy, except insofar as it implies that to save the world each side must be willing to destroy it.

Second, our Deterrence Equilibrium suggests that this is only partially true: there is not, and need not be, "assured destruction," but only a probabilistic threat of it to induce "assured deterrence." If the threat of retaliation is sufficiently great, and perceived to be credible, neither side will find it advantageous to preempt.

Credibility depends on precommitments by both sides to implement a (probabilistic) threat. Such precommitments, backed up by the formidable second-strike capability of the superpowers' largely invulnerable submarine-launched missiles, certainly seem to characterize the nuclear retaliatory policies of the superpowers. As we indicated earlier, however, probabilistic threats of full-fledged retaliation may be interpreted as diminished responses to a provocation, but carried out with certainty. Such responses in repeated play of a game would, it seems, drive one up the escalation ladder. Fortunately, the nuclear rung has never been reached in any superpower confrontration, which seems at least partially explained by the dynamic stability of the Deterrence Equilibrium—after any perturbation in a player's preemption probability, that probability tends to be restored to zero. Thus, equilibrium is maintained by a powerful force.

This self-restoring quality of the Deterrence Equilibrium will be reinforced by robust threats, which are always above the threshold level necessary to deter but never commit a player to certain retaliation. Because these threats are both equally damaging and equally costly whatever one thinks the other might do, they would, we believe, enhance the stability of the Deterrence Equilibrium in a game of incomplete information.

The difficult question to answer is: what, operationally, constitutes a robust threat? We argued earlier that the present nuclear doctrines of the superpowers seem to preclude a certain response except, perhaps, to a massive nuclear attack wherein all signs are unambiguous. On the other hand, they would seem to imply probabilities above the (minimal) threshold values. But are these threats, and the actions to make them credible, as non-provocative as practicable?

If false signals should trigger an unprovoked attack, the consequences surely would be deadly. It therefore seems better to err on the side of not being responsive enough—having "only" a probabilistic threat, which our model indicates is quite sufficient if a doomsday machine largely beyond human control undergirds it—rather than making one's retaliation too automatic or too sensitive to provocation.

If it is hard to say exactly what constitutes a robust threat today, there is no ambiguity in our model about the undesirability of preemption. It is *never* optimal unless one can rest assured that the other side will never retaliate. Since this presumption seems hopelessly naive, there seems no good reason ever to contemplate preemption, given at least threshold threats of retaliation by both sides.

Yet this is not necessarily to commend "no first use" at levels below that of superpower confrontation. In response to conventional attacks, it is conceivable that holding out the possibility of introducing nuclear weapons into a conventional conflict may help to deter an attack in the first place. But then this benefit must be weighed against the increased risk of nuclear escalation should the attack actually occur and there is no self-imposed restraint on the first use of nuclear weapons.

This and other instances of potentially apocalyptic conflict that deterrence may prevent from erupting seem capable of game-theoretic modeling. At least in the case of the Deterrence Game, the effects of threats that underlie nuclear deterrence seem salutary. But when threats themselves become provocative and severely undermine trust, one must ask whether their deterrent value outweighs the costs of creating an inflammatory situation.

APPENDIX

In this appendix we shall conduct an exhaustive search for Nash equilibria in the Deterrence Game and analyze their properties. The rules of this game, along with payoff and strategy definitions, are given in Section 3. The game is depicted in Figure 2.

The expected payoffs of Row (R) and Column (C) are repeated below:

$$E_R(s,q; t,p) = str_3 + (1-s)tp + s(1-t)qr_2; \qquad (2)$$

$$E_C(t,p; s,q) = stc_3 + s(1-t)q + (1-s)tpc_2 \qquad (3)$$

Our search will be broken down according to the values of s and t at the equilibrium.

Case 1: $s = t = 1$.

From (2), if $t = 1$, then $\dfrac{\partial E_R}{\partial s} = r_3 - p$. Since $s = 1$ at equilibrium only if $\dfrac{\partial E_R}{\partial s} \geq 0$, $p \leq r_3$ is necessary. Analogous consideration of (3) shows that $q \leq c_3$ at any equilibrium with $s = 1$. Now suppose that $t = 1$ and $p \leq r_3$. From (2), R's expected payoff is

$$E_R(s, q; 1, p) = p + s(r_3-p),$$

so that R can never do better than to choose $s = 1$ and $q \leq c_3$. Similarly, $t = 1$, $p \leq r_3$ is C's best response to $s = 1$, $q \leq c_3$.

Therefore, the only equilibria consistent with Case 1 are

$$s = 1, q \leq c_3; t = 1, p \leq r_3. \qquad (4)$$

The family (4) is called the *Deterrence Equilibrium,* since every strategy combination in the family leads to the same outcome—the cooperative outcome of the underlying Chicken game, with payoffs (r_3,c_3). Properties of the Deterrence Equilibrium will be adduced below.

Case 2: $t = 0$.

From (2), if $t = 0$, then

$$E_R(s, q; 0, p) = sqr_2,$$

so that R can maximize his expected value only by choosing $s = q = 1$. If $s = q = 1$, then (3) shows that

$$E_C(t, p; 1, 1) = 1 - t(1 - c_3),$$

so that C's best choice is $t = 0$, and his payoff does not depend on p.

Therefore, the only equilibria consistent with Case 2 are

$$s = 1, q = 1; t = 0, p \text{ arbitrary},$$

which we call the *Preemption by C Equilibrium*. At this equilibrium, the outcome of the Deterrence Game is always the outcome of the underlying Chicken game associated with a "win" for C—the outcome with payoffs $(r_2, 1)$.

Case 3: $s = 0$.

This case is analogous to Case 2, and reduces to the *Preemption by R Equilibrium*:

$$s = 0, q \text{ arbitrary}; t = 1, p = 1.$$

The outcome corresponds, in Chicken, to a "win" for R, and has payoffs $(1, c_2)$.

Case 4: $0 < s < 1, t = 1$.

If $0 < s < 1$, (3) implies that $\dfrac{\partial E_C}{\partial p} = (1-s)tc_2 > 0$ provided $t > 0$. Thus, at any equilibrium with $0 < s < 1$ and $t = 1$, $p = 1$ also since E_C is increasing in p. Now if $t = 1$ and $p = 1$,

$$E_R(s, q; 1, 1) = 1 - s(1 - r_3)$$

by (2), so that R's expected payoff is maximized only when $s = 0$. This contradiction shows that there are no equilibria consistent with Case 4.

Case 5: $s = 1, 0 < t < 1$.

This case contains no equilibria, by an argument analogous to that for Case 4.

Case 6: $0 < s < 1, 0 < t < 1$.

Equation (2) shows that $\frac{\partial E_R}{\partial_q} = s(1-t)r_2$ so that, for an equilibrium with $0 < s < 1$ and $0 < t < 1$, $q = 1$ is a necessary condition since E_R is increasing in q. Analogously, so is $p = 1$. Now suppose that $0 < t < 1$ are fixed. To maximize

$$E_R (s,q; t,1) = t + s [tr_3 - t + (1-t)qr_2],$$

it is clear that R must choose either $s = 0$ or $s > 0$ and $q = 1$. We discard $s = 0$ since it is not consistent with Case 6. Now in order that some s satisfying $0 < s < 1$ maximize E_R, it must be that $\frac{\partial E_R}{\partial s} = 0$, i.e.,

$$tr_3 - t + (1-t)r_2 = 0.$$

This equation implies that

$$t = t^* = \frac{r_2}{1 - r_3 + r_2}.$$

Note that $0 < t^* < 1$. Analogously, for fixed s and q satisfying $0 < s < 1$ and $q = 1$, $p = 1$ and some t satisfying $0 < t < 1$ maximize E_C only if

$$s = s^* = \frac{c_2}{1 - c_3 + c_2},$$

where, again, $0 < s^* < 1$. Finally, one can verify directly that

$$s = s^*, q = 1; t = t^*, p = 1 \tag{5}$$

is an equilibrium. We refer to this equilibrium as the *Naive Equilibrium*.

It is easy to show that, at the Naive Equilibrium, the players' expected payoffs are

$$E_R^* = \frac{r_2}{1 - r_3 + r_2}, \qquad E_C^* = \frac{c_2}{1 - c_3 + c_2}$$

and that $r_2 < E_R^* < r_3$ and $c_2 < E_C^* < c_3$. Thus, the Deterrence Equilibrium (4), with payoffs (r_3, c_3), is Pareto-superior to the Naive Equilibrium (5).

The Deterrence Equilibrium possesses a dynamic-stability property which, once it forms, will (in repeated play) contribute to its persistence. To see this, assume that the Deterrence Equilibrium (4) has become established, and, further, that

$$0 < q < c_3, \, 0 < p < r_3 \qquad (6)$$

holds. Suppose that player C is concerned that there is some chance that R will preempt, i.e., that $s < 1$, and that C is therefore contemplating whether he should preempt with some positive probability. In other words, C is no longer sure that $s = 1$, and is reconsidering his choice of $t = 1$. But now differentiation of (3) yields

$$\frac{\partial E_C}{\partial t} = s(c_3 - q) + (1 - s)pc_2,$$

so that, if (6) holds, $\dfrac{\partial E_C}{\partial t} > 0$ for every value of s satisfying $0 \le s \le 1$. Therefore, C is motivated to choose $t = 1$, despite his doubts about the value of s, since E_C is increasing in t. A similar calculation shows that R is motivated to choose $s = 1$ regardless of his perception of the value of t, providing (6) holds. Thus, probabilistic threats of retaliation that are more than minimal ($q = c_3$, $p = r_3$) but less than certain ($p = 0$, $q = 0$) will tend to restore the Deterrence Equilibrium if it is perturbed.

NOTES

1. Steven J. Brams, *Superpower Games: Applying Game Theory to Superpower Conflict* (New Haven, Conn.: Yale University Press, 1985), chaps. 1 and 2.

2. Steven J. Brams and Donald Wittman, "Nonmyopic Equilibria in 2 x 2 Games," *Conflict Management and Peace Science* 6 (Fall 1981):39–62; D. Marc Kilgour, "Equilibria for Farsighted Players," *Theory and Decision* 16 (March 1984):135–157; see also Frank C. Zagare, "Limited-Move Equilibria in 2 x 2 Games," *Theory and Decision* 16 (January 1984):1–10.

3. Steven J. Brams and Marek P. Hessel, "Threat Power in Sequential Games," *International Studies Quarterly* 28 (March 1984):15–36.

4. Ibid. The original distinction between compellent and deterrent threats is due to Thomas C. Schelling, *Arms and Influence* (New Haven, Conn.: Yale University Press, 1966).

5. The validity of the symmetry condition in the context of Soviet-American conflict is supported by the following statement of an authority on Soviet defense policy: "The answers [to the problems posed by nuclear war and nuclear weapons] the Soviet leaders have arrived at are not very different from those given by Western governments. . . . The Soviet Union has not been able to escape from the threat of nuclear annihilation. Its leaders and its people share our predicament." David Holloway, *The Soviet Union and the Arms Race* (New Haven, Conn.: Yale University Press, 1983), p. 182.

6. For debate on this point, see Frank C. Zagare, "Toward a Reformulation of the Theory of Mutual Deterrence," *International Studies Quarterly* 29 (June 1985):155–169; Brams and Hessel, "Threat Power in Sequential Games"; and Brams, *Superpower Games,* chap. 1.

7. Reinhard Selten, "Reexamination of the Perfectness Concept for Equilibrium Points in Extensive Games," *International Journal of Game Theory* 4 (1975):25–55; see also Martin Shubik, *Game Theory in the Social Sciences: Concepts and Solutions* (Cambridge, Mass.: MIT Press, 1982), pp. 265-270.

8. Thomas C. Schelling, *The Strategy of Conflict* (Cambridge, Mass.: Harvard University Press, 1960), chap. 9.

9. In a more complete dynamic analysis, we show that there is a trajectory or path from either of the Preemption Equilibria to the Deterrence Equilibrium that the player who is preempted can trigger by threatening to move—with a probability above a particular threshold—to the mutually worst outcome. Although this player incurs a temporary cost in making this threat, the rational

262   Part Three: Special Problems

response of the preemptor is to move to the Deterrence Equilibrium, whose dynamic stability would then preclude a rational move away from it. See Steven J. Brams and D. Marc Kilgour, "The Path to Stable Deterrence," *Dynamic Models of International Relations,* Urs Luterbacher and Michael D. Ward, eds. (Boulder, Colo.: Lynne Rienner, 1985). pp. 11–25. A game analogous to the Deterrence Game, but based on Prisoners' Dilemma rather than Chicken, permits the players to move from the Pareto-inferior "Escalation Equilibrium" to the Pareto-superior "Deescalation Equilibrium." This move is costless to the player who initiates it. See Steven J. Brams and D. Marc Kilgour, "Rational Deescalation," *Evolution, Games, and Learning: Models for Adaptation in Machines and Nature, Physica 16D,* Burton Wendroff et al., eds. (Amsterdam: North Holland, 1986).

10. Brams, *Superpower Games,* chap. 1.

11. Paul Bracken, *The Command and Control of Nuclear Weapons* (New Haven, Conn.: Yale University Press, 1983). Gauthier claims that such precommitments are not necessary to deter aggression, but threats that are not credible are empty, and empty threats invite attack. His calculus of deterrence, we believe, is sensible only when his retaliator's threats will assuredly be implemented because of precommitments. See David Gauthier, "Deterrence, Maximization, and Rationality," *Ethics* 94 (April 1984):474–495.

12. Brams, *Superpower Games,* pp. 45–46.

Paul Diesing

Brams and Kilgour on "Optimal Deterrence"

Brams and Kilgour first summarize basic deterrence theory by means of a 2 x 2 Chicken matrix. There are two equilibrium cells, DC in which A (Row) wins, and CD in which B (Column) wins. In both cases, deterrence has failed for the loser and succeeded for the winner. A CC outcome would be one in which deterrence succeeded for both players, and DD one in which it failed for both.

The problem that Brams and Kilgour address is, how is a stable equilibrium CC outcome possible? How can both sides avoid the war outcome and the surrender outcome by successful deterrence? It seems that CC cannot be an equilibrium outcome, because retaliation against preemption (D) is irrational in a one-play game. Nuclear Chicken is a one-play game if the outcome is DD. The game is over. Retaliation is not irrational in a repeated-play game, since retaliation establishes the threat credibility that makes deterrence successful on later plays. As Nigel Howard observes, the metagame shows that a strategy of not retaliating loses in repeated play.[1]

The solution involves somehow putting many plays into a potential one-play game. Brams and Kilgour do this by setting up a deterrence game, which is an extensive form Chicken (game tree) with probabilistic strategies. Later (pp. 253-254 of this volume) they substitute escalation steps in an expanded matrix for the probabilistic strategies to give the model empirical relevance, since diplomats do not formulate probabilistic strategies.

In an extended game, there are several moves. Graduated retaliation is rational, since it does not immediately produce the DD payoff, and since it establishes threat credibility. Consequently, in later moves the opponent must include retaliation in his calculations.

Brams and Kilgour then ask whether a stable CC equilibrium exists, given credible threats to retaliate for escalation toward DD. They find that a stable CC equilibrium exists if a unilateral shift toward DD reduces expected payoff. (What else could it be?) That is, if the expected retaliation for a shift toward D reduces its expected payoff to less than the C payoff, then preemption is irrational.

What sort of retaliation would produce a negative net payoff for a shift toward D, a preemptive move? It would have to be a "robust" retaliation, one that is not weakened by preemption. That is, an invulnerable retaliatory force. A threat to retaliate with such a force is a "robust threat." They suggest that submarine-launched missiles would constitute such a threat.

In the last sentence, Brams and Kilgour introduce an essential qualification to their argument, the danger that any threat will produce an inflammatory situation. The danger here is that the threat will be perceived as unprovoked aggressiveness, the start of a bullying strategy that must be stopped before it gets bolder and more reckless. The opponent then is perceived as an evil empire to be eliminated by any possible means. The DD payoff becomes second best rather than worst (better dead than Red), the game is no longer Chicken, and deterrence is impossible.

This qualification points to a sometimes neglected aspect of a rational deterrent strategy. A rational strategy not only deters, but also maintains mutual trust and communication. Without effective communication one may easily misinterpret the opponent's moves, and cannot even be sure that one's own proposal has been understood or believed; so the whole situation can get very confused, as in Lebanon 1958 when both the United States and the Soviet Union were getting inflamed over imaginary dangers.

To avoid provocation, a rational threat must be limited and specific, as Alexander George, David Hall, and William Simons argue.[2] It must forbid a specific action against a clearly vital interest, without condemning the opponent totally or suggesting that all his goals and intentions are illegitimate.

NOTES

1. Nigel Howard, *Paradoxes of Rationality: Theory of Meta-games and Political Behavior* (Cambridge, Mass.: MIT Press, 1971), pp. 182-184.

2. Alexander George, David Hall, and William Simons, *The Limits of Coercive Diplomacy* (Boston: Little, Brown, 1971).

Zeno G. Swijtink

Brams and Kilgour on "Optimal Deterrence"

Since the early 1960s game theorists have developed and analyzed games that, they hope, will help us to understand better the East-West conflict, so that we can modify its constraints and make its possible consequences less horrendous.[1] Professors Brams and Kilgour's Deterrence Game is a modification of Chicken. It has a probabilistic superstructure and a sequential extension. In my comments I will make some remarks about the conceptual structure of the game and its solution, and about its fit with the "real world."

A conceptual point raised in the paper is the proper interpretation of randomization or mixed strategies in nonzero-sum games; and a technical point, somewhat related to it, is what properties the preference relation over outcomes should have if the model and the calculations made within it are guaranteed to be meaningful. As a minimal assumption, though certainly not the weakest possible, let us assume that the preference relation of each player can be represented by a real-valued utility function $u_a(x)$, such that outcome of o_1 is preferred by the player over outcome o_2 *iff* $u_a(o_2) < u_a(o_1)$.[2]

A two-person zero-sum game is a game of complete antagonism. One player's loss is the other player's gain. In terms of the utility functions representing the players preference, this means that their preference over outcomes can be represented by two functions u_a and u_b, such that $u_a(o) + u_b(o) = 0$ for all outcomes o.[3] The generally accepted requirement for the solution of a zero-sum game is for both players to play a maxmin strategy: to play that strategy whose worst possible outcome is best compared with the worst possible outcome of the other strategies open to the agent. Often, however, this will not give a unique pair of strategies for the two players, as in

$$P_2$$

		$j = 1$	2
P_1	$i = 1$	1	0
	2	0	1

This game matrix has no *saddle point,* no value obtained by a unique pair of maxmin strategies of both players. (The "safety level" of strategy 1 and of strategy 2 for P_1, the worst that could happen to P_1, is 0; the safety level of both P_2's strategies is -1.) However, as John von Neumann proved in 1928, if mixed as well as pure strategies are allowed, every matrix game has a saddle point. The solution concept of two-person zero-sum games becomes: play that (potentially mixed) strategy whose safety level gives a saddle point. For instance, in the matrix above, if both players play their two available pure strategies with probability $\frac{1}{2}$, P_1 will assure himself of a utility of $\frac{1}{2}$, while P_2 can hold his disutility to $\frac{1}{2}$, both in expected value. The calculation of the expected value of a mixed strategy presupposes, however, that the utility function satisfies an extra constraint: if two utility functions u'_a and u''_a represent the same preference ordering of the player a, they will be related by a linear transformation: there are real numbers $\alpha > 0$, and β such that $\alpha u'_a(o) + \beta = u''_a(o)$. I mention this because later I will point out that Brams and Kilgour have to make even stronger assumptions on the utility functions for their model and calculations to make sense.

If a two-person game is not zero-sum, its game matrix has to give two utility numbers for each combination of strategies of the two players. A necessary condition on a solution of such a game is that of a *Nash equilibrium.* A combination of two strategies is a

Nash equilibrium if each of the two strategies is the best answer to the other strategy. So in Chicken, C for Row and $\overline{C}$ for Column is a Nash equilibrium in pure strategies, as is $\overline{C}$ for Row and C for Column. Again there is a theorem: John Nash proved in 1950 that, if mixed as well as pure strategies are allowed, every finite n-person game has at least one Nash equilibrium point. What Brams and Kilgour call the *Naive Equilibrium* is basically the third equilibrium point made available to the players when independent mixed strategies are allowed. There do not seem to be, however, additional constraints on what counts as a solution of a nonzero-sum game that leads to uniqueness, as the concept of a saddle-point value in zero-sum games.

Another difference between the two types of games is in the justification of using mixed strategies.[4] In zero-sum games a mixed strategy protects one against any of the strategies the opponent may play. Because his gain is your loss, this seems cautious. But in a nonzero-sum game, an advantage to an opponent may not mean a personal disadvantage, and one may actually want the opponent to know what strategy one will play, as is for instance involved in announcing that one will preempt. Coordination and cooperation between players may, to a certain extent, be profitable to both players in nonzero-sum games. This has led to the study of correlated probabilistic strategies and their equilibrium properties. John C. Harsanyi and Reinhard Selten observed in 1972 that any point in the convex hull of the Nash equilibrium payoffs of a nonzero-sum game can be achieved by an appropriate correlated mixed strategy, and will also be in equilibrium.[5] Robert Aumann showed in 1974 that points outside the convex hull can also be reached in this manner. He actually gives a Chicken-type matrix and a pair of correlated strategies that are in Nash equilibrium and give an outcome Pareto-superior to the noncorrelated, mixed strategy equilibrium point.[6]

The relevance of all this is that Brams and Kilgour's "Deterrence Game" is an Aumann-type game with correlated strategies, or rather a family of such games, since Row and Column can choose r and q, and s and p, respectively. The game is equivalent to flipping two coins, one with probability s of heads, the second with probability t of heads; if coin 1 and coin 2 both come up heads, Row and Column cooperate; if both come up tails, Row and Column do not cooperate; if coin 1 comes up heads while coin

2 comes up tails, Row cooperates with probability q while Column does not cooperate; and, finally, if coin 1 comes up tails and coin 2 heads, Row does not cooperate while Column does with probability p. I find even this representation of the mathematical structure Brams and Kilgour have introduced more perspicious than their own. For they describe the probability s, for instance, as the probability with which an (unspecified) action of Row will be interpreted by Column as cooperative. This means that Row and Column are introduced both as players and as (stochastic) automata that react to stimuli in a lawful fashion. Such a modelling goes against sound game-theoretic methodology.[7] I will come back to their interpretation of the nonpreemption probabilities later.

Let me make two technical remarks. I have mentioned already that mixed strategies make sense only when the utility functions used to calculate expected utility are uniquely determined up to a linear transformation; that is, they are cardinal utilities. However, Brams and Kilgour, without telling us, must make stronger assumptions if their model and their calculations are to make sense. For instance, in their calculation of the *Deterrence Equilibrium*, they derive the upperbound $q \leq c_3 c_4$. (I disregard here their normalization, which is a mathematical convention to ease calculation but has no meaning in terms of utility.) But suppose now that I transform to another utility scale: the upperbound then becomes $(\alpha c_3 + \beta)(\alpha c_4 + \beta)$, which is an altogether different upperbound, unless $\beta = 0$. Thus the derivation presupposes that the utility function of a player has a meaningful zero-point, which is an extra constraint. Similarly, their notion of a *robust threat*, which identifies a unique q in the range left open by their calculation of the upperbound c_3, c_4, namely, $q = (c_3 - c_2 r_3)$ $(1 - c_2 r_2)$, presupposes interpersonal comparison of utility. (I have left in their normalization; without it the characterization of q becomes intractable. But it is necessary to consider it to see that q is indeed insensitive to a transformation of scale factors if Row and Column's utility functions are transformed by the same factor, and only then.) The interpretation of interpersonal comparisons of utility is, in my opinion, still an unsolved conceptual problem.

My second technical point is more a query than a critique. Probabilities make sense only if a kind of trial is indicated. Sometimes this involves a discrete model, as in the flip of a coin. In the deterrence game one may think of a continuous model: s is the probability of Row preempting (at least/exactly??) once *within a certain time interval,* twenty-four hours, a year, or whatever. I do not well understand how Brams and Kilgour's model can imply certain exact probability values as optimal without any considerations of the time intervals these probabilities are attached to. Or do the utility functions contain certain hidden assumptions about the intended time interval?

This last remark is also relevant to testing the Deterrence Game model and to its explanatory force. I can only make a few remarks. There seems to me a lack of testing methodology in the literature, a lack that is reflected in the paper by Brams and Kilgour. Most importantly, one should understand that testing a model should involve the consideration of alternative models, and the possible rejection of some of them. Rejection of models is easier; and if the models have some initial plausibility, rejection may lead to interesting questions, as Rapoport realized in his 1967 paper "Games which Stimulate Deterrence and Disarmament." His message does not seem to be well understood.[8]

Brams and Kilgour have suggested that their work addresses the so-called irrationality of deterrence: can it be rational to form an intention to retaliate (in order to deter) that will be irrational to carry out if and when deterrence fails? I fail to see why a probabilistic intension mitigates the apparent paradox, because after deterrence has failed even probabilistic retaliation is irrational.[9]

Brams and Kilgour have shown that their *Deterrence Equilibrium* has a dynamic-stability property in the sense that, even should, say, Row think he might be preempted, he should still continue to refuse to preempt, in order to keep his expected payoff at its maximum. One may well think that this disconfirms the model, since it leads to an important flaw in the game: it is commonly assumed that to preempt is to the advantage of the preemptor *in an irrevocable way.* Although the superpowers are symmetrically placed at the beginning of the game, the one who moves first has at least a chance of preempting a response. This dynamic element is completely lost in the Deterrence Game, because it concerns an asymmetry in consequences.

In closing let me return to Brams and Kilgour's interpretation of the nonpreemption probabilities. To remind you, the probability s in the model is the probability with which an unspecified action of Row will be interpreted by Column as cooperative. This rings odd: Row intends to retaliate with probability q if he interpreted Column as noncooperative, while Column interpreted Row as cooperative. In the "real world," of course, it is for Row immaterial how Column interprets what he does. For Row to retaliate he has to interpret Column as noncooperative, while he was himself trying to cooperate. These matters of perception seem to defy quantification, whether probabilistic or not. In any case, how could Row ever so fine-tune his behavior that Column will interpret it as cooperative with any precise probability, even of an interval type? Here I would concur with Nigel Howard that much of contemporary game theory is the quantitative method gone astray.[10]

NOTES

1. For instance, T. C. Schelling, *The Strategy of Conflict,* (Cambridge, Mass.: Harvard University Press, 1960), who already recognized the possibilities of conditional probabilistic threats. See his chapter 7, "Randomization of Promises and Threats," esp. page 186.

2. This implies that all outcomes are comparable, and that preference is irreflexive, asymmetric, and transitive.

3. This is not completely correct. Zero-sum really amounts to constant-sum, because there is no meaningful zero-point presupposed.

4. I rely here on M. Shubik, *Game Theory and the Social Sciences,* (Cambridge, Mass.: MIT Press, 1982), esp. pages 249–250.

5. See John C. Harsanyi and Reinhard Selten, "A Generalized Nash Solution for Two-Person Bargaining Games with Complete Information," *Management Science* 18 (1972): 80–106.

6. R. J. Aumann, "Subjectivity and Correlation in Randomized Strategies," *Journal of Mathematical Economics* 1 (1974): 67–96.

7. See Shubik, pp. 16–17.

8. A. Rapoport, "Games which Simulate Deterrence and Disarmanent," *Peace Research Review* vol. 1, no. 4. (1967).

9. See also D. MacLean (ed.), *The Security Gamble; Deterrence Dilemma in the Nuclear Age* (Towota, N.J.: Rowman & Allanheld, 1984), esp. the papers by Gauthier, Kavka, and Lewis.

10. N. Howard, *Paradoxes of Rationality: Theory of Meta-games and Political Behavior* (Cambridge, Mass.: MIT Press, 1971).

Index

Ability, and justification, Robert G. Meyers on, 150

Acceptance, Allan Gibbard on, 223-230; Alvin Goldman on, 81-98

Alexander, C. H. O'D., 40

Anatomical realism, Christopher Cherniak on, 101-103

Anatomy, and rationality, Christopher Cherniak on, 99-107

Anderson, J. A., 97, 106

Aristotle, on rationality, 29-30, 64

Attention-focusing processes, 181-187, 192-193

Aumann, Robert, 269, 272

Austin, J. L., 15, 31

Avowals, normative, Allan Gibbard on, 229

Axelrod, Robert, on cooperation, 16

Ayer, A. J., on moral judgments, 237-238, 240

Baier, Kurt, 75

Ballard, Dana, 84-85, 89, 91, 97, 99, 100, 106-107

Barber, Kenneth, v

Baron, Marcia, 132

Bayesian choice theory, 27, 39

Belief, and uncertainty, Alvin Goldman on, 80-98

Berg, Charles, on psychoanalysis, 50

Black, Max, on chess and rationality, 35-37; on choice, 51; on conceptual field, 34; on metaphor, 56, 192, 193-194; on paradigm cases, 31; on 'rational' and 'rationality', 11, 13-15, 25-40

Blanshard, Brand, definition of reasonable person, 12

Boehm, Rudolf, 207

Bonjour, Lawrence, 132; 153-154, 159, 167

Boyce-Gibson, 206-208

Bracken, Paul, 262

Brams, Steven J., Paul Diesing on, 263-265; on optimal deterrence, 241-265; on social dimension of rationality, 16, 21; Zeno G. Swijtink on, 267-273

Brandt, Richard, 168

Brown, Murray, v

Buchler, Justus, 97

Bunn, James H., on Antony Flew, 13, 53-57

Butler, Douglas, 135

Bybee, Joan, v

Cairns, D., 206

Capp, Andy, comic strip, 41, 43, 55

Carr, David, 207, 213

Causes, senses of, 43

Chanda, A., 107

Chess, Max Black on as model of rationality, 35-37

Chicken, game of, 242-248, 263-265

Cherniak, Christopher, on computational complexity, 123-124, 132; on Alvin Goldman, 18-19, 99-107; on memory limitations, 104-105; on rationality and anatomy, 99-107

Chisholm, Roderick M., 153-154

Cho, Kah-Kyung, v, 195

Choice, Antony Flew on, 41-51; David Hume on, 55-56; J. S. Mill on, 57

Churchill, James S., 213

Cicero, on rationality, 30

Clarke, Murray, on internal and external justification, 20; on reliabilism, 159-168, 171-176

Clay, Marjorie, on Paul Weirich's naturalized deliberation, 20, 177, 189-194

Cleopatra, 220-221

Cohen, Stuart, his externalist theory, 159-168, 175

Coherence, in epistemology, Hilary Kornblith on, 121-125

Computational complexity, Christopher Cherniak on, 124-125

Conceptual field, Max Black on, 34

Consciousness, Shaun Gallagher on, 209-213; Brice R. Wachterhauser on, 195-208

Cooperation, Robert Axelrod on, 16

Cornsweet, T., 107

Cummins, Robert, 132

Darwin, Charles, 231-232; on reason, 28

Davidson, Donald, on decision theory, 106, 139

Davis, Morton D., 40

Dearden, R. F., 27

deGrott, Adrian D., on chess, 36, 40

Deliberation, rational, 177-194

Delilah, 221-222

De Saussure, Ferdinand, on language as a structured system, 33

Descartes, René, his internal perspective, Hilary Kornblith on, 116-118, 143, 172

Description, and naturalism, 12-13

Determinism, Antony Flew on, 41-51; metaphor of imprisonment, 54-57

Deterrence Game, Steven J. Brams on, 16; Zeno G. Swijtink on, 17

Deterrence, optimal, Steven J. Brams and D. Marc Kilgour on, 241-262; Paul Diesing on, 263-265; Zeno G. Swijtink on, 267-273

Dicker, Georges, v

Diesing, Paul, on Steven J. Brams and D. Marc Kilgour, 16-17, 263-265

Dold, A., 107

Dretske, Fred, 138, 152-154

Eckmann, B., 107

Einhorn, Hillel, 133

Elliston, Frederick, 213

Elster, Jon, 178, 187

Epistemic responsibility, Murray Clarke on, 20; Hilary Kornblith on, 19, 125-131

Epistemology, justificationist, 143; naturalistic, 17-21, 213

Ermath, Michael, 208

Evidence, 12

Evolution, Allan Gibbard on, 217-233; Zeno G. Swijtink on, 235-240

Externalist theory of justification, 115-134, 159-168, 171-176

Feldman, Jerome, 84-85, 89, 91, 97, 99, 100, 106, 107

Feldman, Richard, 177

Ferguson, Kenneth, 187

Fink, Eugen, on Edmund Husserl, 200, 207

Fischer, Bobby, 35

Fisher, A. L., 213

Fleischauer, Marie, v

Flew, Antony, James H. Bunn on, 13, 53-57; on choice, 41-51; on naturalism, 12-13, 21; on rationality as social, 15

Fodor, Jerry, 132

Freed, Bruce, 159, 168

Freedom, Antony Flew on, 41-51

French, Peter, 167

Gadamer, Hans-Georg, 207

Gallagher, Shaun, 195; on Brice R. Wachterhauser, 21, 209-213

Gallie, W. B., 191, 193

Game theory, 16-17, 241-265

Gauthier, David, on deterrence, 262; on rationality, 62, 71

Geach, Peter, 33, 41-42, 44-45

George, Alexander, 264-265

Gert, Bernard, 75

Gettier, Edmund, 17
Gewirth, Alan, 75
Gibbard, Allan, on human
    evolution, 217-233; on nat-
    uralism, 13; on norms,
    221-233; on rationality,
    15-16, 217-233; Zeno G.
    Swijtink on, 235-240
Giere, Ronald, v
Goldman, Alvin, on accept-
    ance and subjective prob-
    abilities, 81-84; Christo-
    pher Cherniak on, 99-107;
    on justification and pru-
    dence, 92-97, 150, 152-154,
    159-168; on new connec-
    tionism, 18, 79-98; Erwin
    M. Segal on, 13, 19, 109-
    114
Gracia, Jorge J. E., v
Grip, of norms, 223-227
Growney, JoAnne, 189

Hacker, Peter, 59
Hahn, Frank, 187
Hall, David, 264-265
Hare, R. M., 75
Harsanyi, John C., 269, 272;
    on rationality, 62-71
Hegel, G. F. W., 207, 213
Heidegger, Martin, 207, 211
Heller, Mark, 115
Hessel, Marek P., 261
Hinton, G. E., 97, 99, 103,
    106
Hobbes, Thomas, 16, 233
Hogarth, Robin, 133
Hollis, Martin, 187
Holloway, David, 261
Howard, Nigel, 263, 265,

272-273
Hubel, David, 103, 107
Hume, David, on cause, 43;
    on choice, 55-56; on John
    Locke, 48-49; on natural
    belief, 45; his political
    theory, 233; on rational-
    ity, 30, 60, 71
Humean causation, 13
Husserl, Edmund, Eugen
    Fink on, 200; Shaun Gal-
    lagher on, 209-213; Brice
    R. Wachterhauser on, 20-
    21, 195-208

Imprisonment, metaphor in
    determinism, 54-57
Internalist theory of justifi-
    cation, 115-134, 159168,
    171-176

Jonson, Ben, 55
Justificationist epstemol-
    ogy, inferential, 151; Rob-
    ert G. Meyers on, 143-144,
    156

Kahneman, D., 98, 113-
    114, 129-130, 133
Kant, Immanuel, 207; on
    freedom, 13, 47
Kaplan, Mark, v
Katz, Jarold, v
Kearns, John T., on Rob-
    ert G. Meyers, 19-20, 155-
    157
Kemp-Smith, Norman,
    45, 51
Kersten, F., 206
Kierkegaard, Søren, 213
Kilgour, D. Marc, Paul Dies-

ing on, 263-265; on optimal deterrence, 241-265; on social dimension of rationality, 16-21; Zeno G. Swijtink on, 267-273

Knowledge, as justified, true belief, 17; of nonhumans, 141, 147, 156; perceptual versus inferential, 19

Knuth, D. 107

Koestenbaum, P., 206

Kornblith, Hilary, on coherence in epistemology, 121-125; on epistemic responsibility, 125-131, 159, 167; on internal and external perspectives, 115-134; Duncan MacIntosh on, 19, 135-139; his naturalized epistemology, 19, 115-133

Kotov, Alexander, 40

Kuhn, Thomas, 17

Kyburg, Henry, v

Lambros, Charles, on Murray Clarke, 20, 159, 171-176

Language, as a structured system for Ferdinand De Saussure, 33

Lawrence, D. H., 146

Lehrer, Keith, 93, 97

Leibniz, Gottfried, 144, 152

Lewis, C. I., 145, 152, 154

Locke, John, 28, 39-40, 47, 49, 54, 144, 152

Lucey, Kenneth, v

Luterbacher, Urs, 262

Mabbot, J. D., 27

McCormick, Peter, 213

McGeer, Victoria, 135

MacIntosh, Duncan, on Hilary Kornblith, 19, 115, 135-139

MacLean, D., 272

Macleod, Alistair M., Lansing Pollock on, 14, 73-75; on rationality as social, 15-16

MAD, 255

Maloney, Christopher, 115

Materialism, Robert G. Meyers on, 141-142

Memory, limitations, Christopher Cherniak on, 104-105

Merleau-Ponty, Maurice, 212-213

Metaphor, of imprisonment and determinism, 54-57

Meyer, Albert, 100-101, 107

Meyers, R., 107

Meyers, Robert G., John T. Kearns on, 19-20, 155-157; his naturalistic epistemology, 19, 141-154

Milgram, Stanley, his experiments, 224-225, 227, 233

Mill, J. S., 57

Miller, George, 105

Miner, H., 107

Mishler, William, v

Moore, G. E., his method, 26; on naturalistic definition, 218

Moral behavior, Lansing Pollock on, 73-75

Moral philosophy and epis-

temology, 116-138
Murphy, Patrick, v

Nash equilibrium, 244-245, 254, 268-269
Naturalism, 18, 21, 141-143, 182-186; and description, 12-13; and determinism, 12-13; Antony Flew's challenge to, 12-13, 41-51; and materialism, 13; naturalistic epistemology, 79-213; and normative, 12; two senses of, 12
New connectionism, Christopher Cherniak on, 18-19, 99-107; Alvin Goldman on, 18-19, 79-98; Erwin M. Segal on, 109-114
Nisbett, Richard, 128, 133
Norman, D. A., 97
Norms, Allan Gibbard on, 221-233; Zeno G. Swijtink, 235-240
Nozick, Robert, 152-154
Nyberg, David, v

Oakeshott, Michael, on rational conduct, 28
Occam's eraser, 166, 168
Optimal deterrence, Steven J. Brams and D. Marc Kilgour on, 241-265
'Ordinary language philosophy', as a term of abuse, 33

Pappas, George, 132, 154, 167
Paradigm cases, Max Black's

use of, 31
Parallelism, brains, Christopher Cherniak on, 99-100
Parfit, Derek, on rationality, 64, 71
Patočka, Jean, 213
Peirce, C. S., 90-91, 97, 144
Perspective, external and internal, Murray Clarke on, 159-168; Hilary Kornblith on, 115-134
Petrie, Hugh, v
Phenomenology, Shaun Gallagher on Husserl's, 209-213; Brice R. Wachterhauser on Husserl's, 195-208
Plato, definition of love, 25-26
Pollack, J. B., 110, 114
Pollock, John, 83, 132, 161, 168
Pollock, Lansing, on Alistair M. Macleod, 14, 59, 73-75
Popper, Sir Karl, on determinism, 44, 49, 54; on evolutionary epistemology, 17
Price, H. H., 51, 145, 152, 154
Prior, Arthur H., 39
Prisoner's Dilemma, Robert Axelrod on, 16
Probability, 16; Alvin Goldman on, 81-84
Prudence, Alvin Goldman on, 92-97
Psychoanalysis, and choice, 50
Putnam, Hilary, 147-148, 154

Quine, W. V., on epistemology naturalized, 17-18

Radner, Michael, v

Rapoport, A., 271-272

Rather, Dan, 117-118

Rationality, Aristotle on, 29-30; Max Black on, 13-15, 25-40; Brand Blanshard on, 12; Christopher Cherniak on, 99-107; Cicero on, 30; Charles Darwin on, 28; of deliberation, 177-194; Antony Flew on, 41-51; David Gauthier on, 62; Allan Gibbard on, 16, 217-233; John Harsanyi on, 62; David Hume on, 30, 60; John Locke on, 28; Alistair M. Macleod on, 14, 59-71; naturalizing, Hilary Kornblith on, 115-134; as normative, 12; Michael Oakeshott on, 28; Derek Parfit on, 64; Richard Robinson on, 29; Earl of Rochester on, 28; Bertrand Russell on, 27; Gilbert Ryle on, 28-29; scope of, 14; as social, 15-16; Stoic view of, 11; stringency of, 15; Zeno G. Swijtink on, 235-240; as word to be abandoned, 11

Rawls, John, 75

Realism, anatomical, Christopher Cherniak on, 101-103

Reductionism, Erwin M. Segal on, 109-114

Reliabilism, Murray Clarke on, 159-168, 171-176; John T. Kearns on, 19-20, 157; Robert G. Meyers on, 19, 141-154

Responsibility, epistemic, in simple deliberation, 180-182; Hilary Kornblith on, 125-131

Robinson, Richard, on rationality, 29

Robust threats, 243, 264

Rochester, Earl of, on rationality, 28

Rorty, Richard, on epistemology, 17

Ross, Lee, 128, 133

Rumelhart, D. E., 97

Russell, Bertrand, his definition of reason, 27, 28, 37

Ryle, Gilbert, on language philosophy, 45; on rationality, 28-29

Sabini, John, 233

Sample, Steven B., v

Samson, 221-222

Sanctions, Zeno G. Swijtink on, 235-240

Schelling, 195, 209

Schelling, Thomas, 233, 252, 261, 272

Schmitt, Frederick F., 153-154, 159, 167-168

Schuhmann, Karl, 213

Science, Wilfred Sellars on, 142-143, 152, 154

Scott, John F., on norms, 339-240

Searle, John, on dogs' be-

liefs, 156
Segal, Erwin M., on Alvin
    Goldman, 13, 19, 109-114
Self-interest, and rational-
    ity, Alistair M. Macleod
    on, 59-71; Lansing Pol-
    lock on, 73-75
Sellars, Wilfrid, on the giv-
    en, 17; on science, 142-
    143, 152, 154
Selten, Reinhard, 252, 261,
    269, 272
Shastri, Lokendra, 84, 97
Shatz, David, 115, 152-154
Sher, George, 115
Shubik, Martin, 261, 272
Siegel, Harvey, 193
Silver, Maury, 233
Simon, Herbert, 178, 187
Simons, William, 264-265
Slovic, P., 114, 133
Sly, Peter, 237
Social, rationality as, 15-16
Socrates, definition of love,
    25-26
Solomon, Robert, 207
Sosa, Ernest, 153-154
Sperry, Roger, 103, 107
Stevens, C., 107
Stockmeyer, Larry, 101, 107
Stoics, on rationality, 11
Stringency, of rationality,
    15
Swain, Marshall, 154
Swijtink, Zeno G., on Steven
    J. Brams and D. Marc
    Kilgour, 16-17, 267-273;
    on Allan Gibbard, 235-
    240; on rationality as so-
cial, 15; on sanctions,
    235-240

Trier, Jost, 34
Tversky, A., 98, 113-114,
    129-130, 133

Ullmann, S., 33
Uncertainty, and belief,
    Alvin Goldman on, 80-98

von Neumann, John, 268

Wachterhauser, Brice R.,
    Shaun Gallagher on, 21,
    209-213; on Edmund Hus-
    serl, 21, 195-208
Wagner, Judith, v
Waltz, D. L., 110, 114
Ward, Michael D., 262
Warwick, R., 107
Weakness of will, Allan
    Gibbard on, 224, 227
Weirich, Paul, 240; Marjorie
    Clay on, 20, 189-194; on
    naturalized deliberation,
    20, 177-188
Wiesel, Torsten, 103, 107
Wilcox, William, 115
Williams, P., 107
Wilson, James Q., 42-43
Winner-take-all mechan-
    isms, Alvin Goldman on,
    18, 80-98
Winters, Barbara, 132
Wittman, Donald, 261

Zagare, Frank C., 261
Ziff, Paul, 168

About the Editors

NEWTON GARVER, Ph.D., is professor of philosophy at the State Univeristy of New York at Buffalo, where he has taught since 1961. In addition to numerous lectures in Europe as well as the United States, he has also taught at the University of Minnesota, the University of Michigan, and Northwestern University. Dr. Garver's areas of interest include the philosophy of Wittgenstein and the ethics of violence and public policy. His articles have appeared in *Ethics, The Humanist, The Journal of Philosophy, Philosophical Investigations* and *Philosophy and Phenomenological Research.* He has also contributed to various anthologies in philosophy, as well as *The Encyclopedia of Philosophy* (edited by Paul Edwards, 1967).

PETER H. HARE, Ph.D., is Chairman and Professor in the Department of Philosophy at the State University of New York at Buffalo. In 1975 he coauthored (with Edward Madden) *Causing, Perceiving and Believing: An Examination of the Philosophy of C. J. Ducasse.* An active administrator and editor of *Transactions of the Charles S. Peirce Society: A Quarterly Journal in American Philosophy,* Dr. Hare's interests include contemporary metaphysics and epistemology, philosophy of religion, and medical ethics.

Notes on the Contributors

MAX BLACK, Ph.D., is Professor Emeritus at the Sage School of Philosophy at Cornell University, past president (1982-85) of the International Institute of Philosophy, and a leading authority on philosophical analysis and the philosophy of language. His most recent books include: *The Prevalence of Humbug, and Other Essays* (1983) and *Caveats and Critiques: Philosophical Essays in Language, Logic, and Art* (1971). In 1980 he delivered the prestigious Tarner Lectures at Cambridge University on the theme, "Models of Rationality." He has been an editor of *The Philosophical Review* since 1946, and serves as general editor of the Contemporary Philosophy series published by Cornell University Press.

STEVEN J. BRAMS, Ph.D., is professor in the Department of Politics at New York University. A leading proponent of the application of game-theory to the study of political science, he is the author of several books, most recently *Superpower Games: Applying Game Theory to Superpower Conflict* (1985) and *Rational Politics: Decisions, Games, and Strategy* (1985).

JAMES H. BUNN, Ph.D., is Vice-Provost for Undergraduate Education and professor of English at the State University of New York at Buffalo. He is the author of *The Dimensionality of Signs, Tools, and Models: An Introduction* (1981). His areas of interest include semiotics, eighteenth-century and romantic literature, and the history of ideas.

CHRISTOPHER CHERNIAK, Ph.D., is associate professor of philosophy at the University of Maryland, College Park, and the author of *Minimal Rationality* (1986). His work has appeared in *Mind, Synthese, Philosophy of Science,* and *The Journal of Philosophy.*

MURRAY C. CLARKE, Ph.D., is assistant professor of philosophy at the University of Ottawa, Ontario, Canada, and the author of "Doxastic Voluntarism and Forced Belief," *Philosophical Studies* 50 (1986):39-51. His areas of interest include epistemology, especially reliabilist accounts of justification and knowledge, as well as the history and philosophy of science.

MARJORIE CLAY, Ph.D., is associate professor of philosophy at Bloomsburg University, Bloomsburg, Pennsylvania. Her work has appeared in *The Humanist, Philosophical Investigations,* and *Proceedings of the Adam Smith Bicentennial Conference* (1976).

PAUL DIESING, Ph.D., is professor of political science at the State University of New York at Buffalo, and specializes in the philosophy of the social sciences. His most recent books include *Science and Ideology in the Policy Sciences* (1982) and *Conflict Among Nations: Bargaining, Decision Making, and System Structure in International Crises* (1977, with Glenn H. Snyder).

ANTONY G. N. FLEW, D. Litt., is Distinguished Research Fellow at the Social Philosophy and Policy Center, Bowling Green State University, Bowling Green, Ohio, and Emeritus Professor of Philosophy at the University of Reading, England. He is an internationally known author and lecturer whose recent work includes *David Hume: Philosopher of Social Science* (1986), *Thinking About Social Thinking* (1985), *A Rational Animal* (1978) and *Thinking Straight* (1977).

SHAUN GALLAGHER, Ph.D., is associate professor of philosophy at Canisius College, Buffalo, New York. A specialist in the fields of phenomenology, existentialism, hermeneutics, and political and economic philosophy, his most recent work is an article entitled "Lived Body and Environment," published in *Research in Phenomenology* (1986).

ALLAN GIBBARD, Ph.D., is professor of philosophy at the University of Michigan. His research interests include the study of ethics, social choice theory, and the foundations of modal logic. His articles have appeared in the *Australasian Journal of Philosophy, Econometrica,* and *Philosophical Studies.*

ALVIN I. GOLDMAN, Ph.D., is professor of philosophy at the University of Arizona, and author of *Epistemology and Cognition* (1986), *Morals and Values* (edited with J. Kim, 1978), and *A Theory of Human Action* (1970, 1977). His articles have appeared in *American Philosophical Quarterly, The Journal of Philosophy, The Philosophical Review,* and other scholarly journals.

JOHN T. KEARNS, Ph.D., is professor of philosophy at the State University of New York at Buffalo. He is author of *Using Language: The Structures of Speech Acts* (1984), and has had articles published in *The Journal of Philosophy, The Journal of Symbolic Logic, Notre Dame Journal of Formal Logic, Philosophy and Phenomenological Research,* as well as contributing to various edited collections.

D. MARC KILGOUR, Ph.D., is professor and Chairman of the Mathematics Department at Wilfrid Laurier University, Waterloo, Ontario, Canada. A specialist in the field of mathematical modeling, he is currently writing a book with Steven J. Brams on game theory as it applies to the superpower conflict. Dr. Kilgour's recent work has been published in *The Canadian Journal of Political Science, Public Choice,* and *Theory and Decision.*

HILARY KORNBLITH, Ph.D., is associate professor of philosophy at the University of Vermont. Specializing in epistemology, philosophy of language, and philosophy of mind, Dr. Kornblith is the editor of *Naturalizing Epistemology* (1985), and has had articles published in *The Australasian Journal of Philosophy, The Journal of Philosophy, The Monist,* and *Philosophical Review.*

CHARLES H. LAMBROS, Ph.D., is associate professor of philosophy at the State University of New York at Buffalo. His areas of interest include logic, set theory, and philosophy of language. Dr. Lambros's published work has appeared in *Methodology and Science, Mind, Notre Dame Journal of Formal Logic, Philo-*

sophical Studies, Philosophy and Phenomenological Research, and *Transactions of the Charles S. Peirce Society.*

DUNCAN MACINTOSH, Ph.D., is assistant professor of philosophy at Dalhousie Univeristy, Halifax, Nova Scotia, Canada, and specializes in the philosophy of science, philosophy of language, meta-ethics, and epistemology.

ALISTAIR MACLEOD, Ph.D., is Head of the Department of Philosophy at Queen's University, Ontario, and is author of *Paul Tillich: An Essay on the Role of Ontology in his Philosophical Theology* (1973). His articles have been published in *The Canadian Journal of Philosophy, Dialogue, Hume Studies,* and *The Journal of Philosophy.* Dr. Macleod has also contributed to several collections of essays in social and political philosophy.

ROBERT G. MEYERS, Ph.D., is Chairman of the Department of Philosophy at the State University of New York at Albany. Author of the forthcoming *The Likelihood of Knowledge,* his work has been published in such scholarly journals as *International Philosophical Quarterly, Journal of Philosophy, Locke Newsletter, Metaphilosophy, Philosophica, Philosphical Studies,* and *Transactions of the Charles S. Peirce Society.*

LANSING POLLOCK, Ph.D., is professor of philosophy at the State University of New York College at Buffalo, and the author of *The Freedom Principle* (1981). His articles have appeared in *Ethics, Mind, The Personalist,* and *Philosophical Studies.*

ERWIN M. SEGAL, Ph.D., is associate professor of psychology at the State University of New York at Buffalo, and author (with G. McCain) of *The Game of Science,* now in its fourth edition (1982). Dr. Segal has published widely on behavioral and cognitive sciences and the philosophy of language. His articles have appeared in such journals as *The American Psychologist, Cognitive Psychology,* and *The Journal of Experimental Psychology.*

ZENO G. SWIJTINK, Ph.D., is assistant professor of philosophy at the State University of New York at Buffalo, specializing in the philosophy and history of science. He has lectured and written extensively on aspects of probability theory and statistics. His work has appeared in *Studies in the History and Philosophy of Science, Philosophy of Science,* and *Studia Logica.*

BRICE R. WACHTERHAUSER, Ph.D., is assistant professor of philosophy at St. Joseph's University, and the editor of *Hermeneutics and Modern Philosophy* (1986). His research interests include nineteenth-century and contemporary Continental philosophy, especially hermeneutics.

PAUL WEIRICH, Ph.D., is assistant professor of philosophy at the University of Rochester. He is a Mellon Faculty Bridging Fellow, and is currently conducting interdisciplinary studies in political science and philosophy. Dr. Weirich's articles have appeared in the *Australasian Journal of Philosophy, Erkenntnis, The Journal of Philosophy, Pacific Philosophical Quarterly,* and *Theory and Decision.*